The Song of Rama

The Song of Rama

Visions of the Ramayana

By
Vanamali

as narrated by
SAGE VALMIKI

interpreted
and embellished by oral tradition.

BLUE DOVE PRESS
SAN DIEGO, CALIFORNIA • 2001

The mission of the Blue Dove Foundation is to deepen the spiritual life of all by making available works on the lives, messages, and examples of saints and sages of all religions and traditions as well as other spiritual titles that provide tools for inner growth.

We also offer the ancient original Sanskrit version of the *Ramayana,* by Valmiki and the *Ramacaritamanas* of Tulsidas. For a free catalog contact:

Blue Dove Press
4204 Sorrento Valley Blvd, Suite K
San Diego, CA 92121
Telephone: (858) 623-3330
Visit our website at: www.bluedove.org

FIRST EDITION

Special thanks to Jennifer Crawford for her dedicated and skilled work in the production of this edition.

Special thanks to Dr. Lance Nelson, Religious Studies Department, University of San Diego

Cover concept by Brian Moucka
Cover design: Sandra Shaw and Joyce Musial
Text design: Brian Moucka and Tracy Dezenzo
Copy editor: Mary Kowit

ISBN: 1-884997-24-4

Printed in Canada

Front cover art from popular Indian devotional painting, artist unknown
Back cover photograph courtesy of Bruce Burger

Eternal gratitude to Rahi Racharla, whose generosity and support made this edition possible.

Eternal gratitude to Swami Satchidananda, Anandashram, Kanhangad, Kerala, India, by whose grace the Blue Dove Foundation exists.

Library of Congress Cataloging-in-Publication data:
Vanamali, Devi
    Song of Rama : visions of the Ramayana / as narrated by Sage Valmiki in the Ramayana, interpreted and embellished by oral tradition by Vanamali.--1st ed.
    p. cm.
ISBN 1-884997-24-4
1. Valmiki. Ramayana. 2. Rama (Hindu deity) I. Title.

BL1139.2.V38 2001
294.5'922--dc21

                                                        2001035964

The Ramayana is indeed a Veda,
which was revealed to us by Sage Valmiki,
since the Supreme Being who is known
only through the Vedas, manifested Himself
as Rama, the son of Dasaratha

—*Sri Ramacaritamanasa*

ॐ DEDICATION

Dedicated to my revered father Rama,
who was a living embodiment of Sri Rama.

TABLE OF CONTENTS

Hari Aum Tat Sat

Sri Ramaya Namah!

Homage to Sri Rama.

PREFACE

BY HIS HOLINESS
SRI SWAMI KRISHNANANDAJI MAHARAJ
General Secretary, Divine Life Society, Rishikesh

The *Ramayana* of the sage Valmiki is a literary masterpiece in the Sanskrit language which excels in beauty, style and diction.

It is believed that the twenty-four letters of the Gayatri Mantra are hidden in the *Ramayana*. The Gayatri starts with the word "Tat" and the *Ramayana* also starts with the same word. Each word of the Gayatri is found in a consecutive sequence at the beginning of every thousand verses of the *Ramayana*.

The Holy *Ramayana* is believed to be the Veda itself: "*Vedah prachethiasath aseed sakshath Ramayanatmana.*" Valmiki wrote the Veda itself in this mighty epic. Spiritual seekers read it as a metaphor for all the problems of life, and it acts as a shield. It is a well-known practice among spiritual seekers to make a regular practice of reading the "Sundara Kanda" in order to imbibe into themselves the strength and prowess of Hanuman.

No one can really plumb the depths of the meaning of Valmiki's *Ramayana*. Usually the reading of the *Mahabharata* is done in the morning, of the *Ramayana* in the afternoon and of the *Srimad Bhagavatam* in the evening. The Sanskrit verse which describes this is as follows: "Good people engage themselves in dice play in the morning (meaning the *Mahabharata*), at noon they engage themselves in talks about women (meaning Sita in the *Ramayana*), and at night, in theft (meaning the *Srimad Bhagavatam*)."

There are many controversies in the *Ramayana*, such as the absence of Bharata during the coronation of Sri Rama, Rama's attacking Vali from behind a tree and accusing him with charges which don't seem feasible. Valmiki has produced in Rama an aspect of human nature which is impossible to understand. He brings together in the same person the might of God and the frailty of man. This kind of presentation of the ideal man is either totally ignored by devotees or subject to critical examination. Either way, the *Ramayana* is a great exercise in disciplining the mind in its attempt to bring God and man together in a single individual. Valmiki often refers to Rama as Narayana Himself. It is said that, in his last moments, Ravana saw Rama as the mighty Vishnu or the God of the universe.

The *Ramayana* should be studied diligently by everyone, for the dignity of the language in which it is written as well as for the depth of the message it conveys. It presents before the reader the inscrutable manner in which God works and the fickle nature of all human decisions. Valmiki brings God to earth and raises the earth to Heaven. Since this type of blending is inconceivable to the human way of perception, there are endless interpretations of the *Ramayana*, presented by pundits, storytellers and scholars. It is certain that an intensive study of Valmiki's *Ramayana* will fill the mind of everyone with inordinate strength and incalculable blessedness. Valmiki says that the glory of the *Ramayana* will prevail as long as the sun and the moon last. The astounding descriptions of the rule of Rama and his administrative capacity reflect the very conditions of a life in Heaven. Great is the *Ramayana*. Glory to the way of administration of Rama in every field of life in this world.

Mata Devi Vanamali has done a novel service to the religious community in expounding the involved meanings of the *Ramayana* text and making it attractive to the modern mind with beautiful English expressions. This book is a companion volume to her book on Lord Krishna called *The Play of God*.

Sri Ramachandra Bhagavan ki Jai!
The Divine Life Society, Shivananda Ashram,
Rishikesh,The Himalayas, India

FOREWORD

BY HIS HOLINESS
SRI SWAMI SATCHIDANANDAJI MAHARAJ
Anandashram. Kanhanghad

Sri Ramaya Namaha!

Homage to Sri Rama.

After once reading the earlier book, *The Play of God*, by Mata Devi Vanamali, we read it again and again, as it was so charming and inspiring that every reading gave added joy. So, when the author telephoned to say that she was bringing out her next book and that I should write a Foreword for the same, I was filled with joy; more so because the book was entitled *The Song of Rama* and I would be able to go through the manuscript in the near future.

I'm supremely happy that Devi Vanamali was inspired to write *The Song of Rama* also. Anyone who reads this wonderful book cannot help but be moved to tears. Though the book deals with the life of an *avatara*, who played the part of a perfect person, upholding dharma at any cost, the trials and tribulations He had to pass through during the entire period of His sojourn on this earth, except for a few years of His childhood and a few years of His wedded life, were severe and heartbreaking.

As the author mentions, the *Ramayana* is a love story. Sri Rama loved Sita Devi dearly; He had great love for His father, mothers, brothers and His subjects. But His love for dharma surpassed everything. He sacrificed everything, including His wife, father and brother for the sake of upholding dharma. Such incidents, which are many in the *Ramayana*, are brought out by the author, painting the characters concerned in such striking colors that they leave a deep impression on our mind and stir the emotions so much as to make us feel that the entire scene is enacted before us. We feel we are moving with Sri

Rama right from Ayodhya to all the places where the original scenes were enacted.

Many readers of the *Ramayana* are perplexed when they face some of the controversial issues, like why Sri Rama abandoned His wife whom He loved above all others. Before leaving Ayodhya for the forest, He had told His agitated wife, Sita Devi, folding her in His arms, kissing her tears away, "Not knowing the strength of your purpose, O Janaki, I tried to deter you, not because I wanted to leave you but only because it was my duty to point out to you the dangers of forest life. You know that I cannot bear to cause distress to you, my lovely princess. O beloved Sita, even heaven has no charms for me without your bewitching presence. I too would love to sport with you in the woods and glades of the forest and on the mountain tops, so make haste to gift away all your jewels and costly clothes and proceed to prepare yourself for a sojourn in the forest with me."

The same Rama in later years asked His brother Lakshmana to take Sita Devi, who was pregnant, to the forest and leave her there alone. What a sacrifice! What for? Only for upholding dharma. Then the killing of Vali and other events are all controversial points for those who give the epic only academic value, whereas devotees who love Sri Rama as the *avatara Purusha* will try to accept whatever the Lord has done as perfectly correct and no question bothers their mind. They know that our puny intellects cannot understand the ways of the Lord and therefore the best thing is to accept them, as He knows best. The author however has taken pains to beautifully explain such controversial subjects. Whatever Sri Rama did was for upholding dharma and therefore for the good of humanity.

The beauty of this book is that it is written by one who has great love and devotion for Sri Rama. It touches some subtle chords in the reader's heart and makes him or her ecstatic. The more we read it, the more devotion we develop. Those who have read *The Play of God* will surely be eager to posses this book. Thus may it reach every house, so that by reading it and listening to it and with the chanting of Sri Rama's glorious Name, pure love and devotion may overflow from the hearts of all to surcharge the entire atmosphere in the house with the fragrance of Sri Rama's eternal presence and make them live a life of righteousness.

Aum Sri Ram, Jai Ram, Jai Jai Ram!

AUTHOR'S
INTRODUCTION

Rama-
bhadraya
Namah!

Repetition of the name of Rama is equivalant to the chanting
of the thousand and one names of Vishnu.

Homage to
Rama the aus-
picious One.

T his is the story of the Lord's descent to earth as Rama, the seventh incarnation of Lord Vishnu, scion of the race of Raghu, pinnacle of human perfection. It is a story which has enthralled the minds of all who have read it, not only in India, the land of its origin, but in all the parts of the world. The story of Rama has spread everywhere, including places like Tibet, Turkey, Myanmar, South and Southeast Asia, particularly Indonesia, Malaysia and Thailand. In Bali and Thailand, as in India, Sri Rama is worshipped as God incarnate.

This flow of the *Ramayana* outside India has been in four directions. One stream went north, as proven by Tibetan and Turkish manuscripts. The fact that it had spread to China can be seen from the Chinese translation of the two Buddhist works— *Anamakam Jatakam* and *Dasarath Kathanakam*. The second flow was to Indonesia. Stone carvings in two of the ancient fourteenth-century Shiva temples in Jogjakarta and one in East Java at Pantaran depict scenes from the epic. Later, in both Indonesia and Malaysia, extensive literature on the *Ramayana* theme was composed. The third flow of the epic was to Indochina, Thailand and Myanmar. Inscriptions dated from the seventh century show that the Valmiki *Ramayana* was very popular in those regions. The story of Rama, which is widely read in Thailand, is known as "Rama Kiyn." The Burmese version is based on this and is known as "Rama Yagan." It is one of the most important poetic compositions of the country. The fourth stream of the Rama story is to be found in the writings of Western travelers and missionaries who visited India from the fifteenth century onwards. Manuscripts exist in many European languages such as English, French, Spanish and Dutch.

One may well marvel at the fact that this story, which is based on local episodes, has had such worldwide appeal and has continued to cast its spell through the ages. This is because the story is based on certain eternal verities, which appeal to the best in human nature. Indeed, these values have such a universal appeal that the character of Sri Rama has risen above the limits of sect, religion, race and country. Obviously, it is a tale capable of touching the human mind deeply.

The *Ramayana* is an ancient chronicle, but it has deep meaning even in modern times. We live in an age which is at a loss to know the meaning of human existence, and which doubts the existence of God Himself. We are perplexed as to how we can act with righteousness when the whole world seems to have gone mad, when the meaning of truth and love cannot be found and when hate and self-interest seem to be the only rules of conduct. Answers to these dilemmas can be found in the *Ramayana*, for human nature, as such, has hardly changed through the years. Situations may vary, but human nature remains the same and that is why we find that many *avataras* have come and gone, yet humanity remains the same. But the individual can and must change if society is to progress, and the characters found in this book are worthy of emulation.

Our lives may well take a turn for the better when we read of the heroic way in which Rama and Sita faced the trials and tribulations of their life. In fact, here lies the greatness of Rama. When we read the life of Krishna, we find that it is the story of God—a divine being who was the master of every situation and never the victim. That is why He is known as the *poornavatara*. In the case of Rama, however, there is a difference. In him, we see that God had taken on a human form, with all its frailties, in order to show us how our aspirations for a *dharmic* life can be fulfilled; how we can surmount our frailties and become divine, if we are prepared to completely subjugate our ego and live only for the good of the world and act in consonance with the duties and obligations of our particular position in society.

Valmiki's Rama is the portrait of a man who becomes divine by shaking off the limitations of mortality through strict adherence to truth and honor. If Rama, like Krishna, were above all human emotions, he would not have made such an impact on the Indian mind. Valmiki's Rama has all the qualities of the average man—the attachments, the desires, the anger and the love, the compassion and the enmity. The greatness of his character lies in the fact that he surmounted these obstacles and perfected himself so that he became a superhuman, one who put his duty above all personal considerations. This type of perfection is available to all of us, however weak we may be. Hence, the popularity of the *Ramayana*. Rama is a character to be held up as an example to all men, as Sita is to all women, and each one of us, when we read their story, can identify with them and then try to perfect our own character as they perfected theirs.

Another endearing feature of the *Ramayana* which makes it a classic, which has enthralled all those who have read it for centuries, is that it is, above all, a love story and love is a theme which never fails to touch a chord in even the most hardened of hearts. But the *Ramayana* is a love story with a difference. It deals with all facets of human love. It probes and analyzes all the different types of love of which a human being is capable, both *dharmic* and *adharmic*—the love of a father for his son, the love of the son for his father and mother, the love of a brother, the love of a husband, the love for a wife, for a friend and finally, even the love which is condemned by dharma—the passion for another man's wife. All these are depicted in the *Ramayana* in the highest and most exalted manner.

The author of the *Ramayana* is the sage Valmiki, considered to be the first of all poets, the *adi-kavi,* and the *Ramayana* itself is known as the *adi-kavya,* or the first poem to be ever composed in the world. It is also the first of the Indian epics, the second being the *Mahabharata* of Sage Vyasa.

An epic is generally a narration of events which have taken place long ago. The themes are heroic—the lives of great kings and warriors and inspiring events—by reading which the lives of ordinary people will be affected in a positive manner, enabling them to abide by those ancient rules of conduct which are described in the book. Miraculous deeds are everyday events and the gods join the humans in order to ensure that righteousness triumphs and truth prevails. The Greek epics—the *Iliad* and the *Odyssey*—are similar, but unlike the Greek epics which were recounted long after the events took place, the epics of India are unique, since the authors themselves were contemporaries of the main characters. They were not only living at the same time, but they had important roles in the drama which they chose to narrate, not as disinterested bystanders but as active participants.

When Valmiki composed his *Ramayana*, India was at the peak of its cultural and moral refinement, when people were acutely aware of the importance of living according to the dictates of dharma, or the highest moral values. Thus, they were able to appreciate all the qualities of a noble character, like Rama, who was prepared to sacrifice everything at the altar of dharma.

The life of Krishna, though filled with conflicts, arouses only joy in us. When we read the life of Rama, however, we are filled with sorrow. From the depths of this sorrow wells a poetic outflow which only grief can evoke. As Valmiki himself admitted, "from *shoka* (suffering) comes *sloka* (verse)." Poetry streams from sorrow. This is true of almost all poetry, in all cultures and at all times. Much of Greek drama is tragic, for the Greeks believed that only the tragic events of human life, alone, can bring about a catharsis in human nature, which will help the person to evolve. Pain and grief touch a deep chord in the depths of every human being, in a way which happiness and joy cannot. The knife can penetrate into depths which the finger cannot reach. The baby comes into this world with a cry of pain and the aged depart from life with a sob. In between these two traumatic events, we live in an ocean of tears, in which we are hard put not to drown. We keep ourselves afloat by clutching at the straws of so-called happiness which keep floating past us, in our make-believe world, pretending that we are happy. Most of the time we are in the grip of some misery or other. This being the case, what doubt that some of the most exquisite poetry of the world has gushed forth from the spring of sorrow? The

Ramayana is no exception. It is an epic of compassion and wrenches at your heart-strings, in a way that few other books do.

Before we actually go into the story, it would be good to clear some doubts which will arise in the reader's mind about many of the situations encountered in the book.

There are almost no controversies surrounding Sri Tulsidas' re-telling of the story of Rama, since it is an obvious treatise on *bhakti* alone, or devotion to a personal God, which is Rama. However, controversies rage around Valmiki's *Ramayana*, since there are so many incidents which do not seem to fit our conception of a perfect human being, which is what Valmiki tries to portray in Rama. One thing which we must realize before going into these controversies is that Valmiki was not a fool. He must have realized that the recounting of these incidents would surely taint the character he wanted to depict as perfect. So then the question arises—why did he do it? He could easily have avoided such ambiguous situations, as Tulsidas did, and recounted only those incidents which would highlight his hero in a most favorable way. Since Valmiki did not do so, we must conclude that there was a very good reason for him to have kept those events in his book. In fact, we should try to probe the mystery of these very situations, for in them will lie the key to Rama's character and a true understanding of the *Ramayana*.

Controversies start with the date on which the poem was composed, whether the historical figure of Rama ever existed and whether the poem was an attempt to profess the superiority of the Aryans and their conquest of the southern tribes. These questions have not made much sense to me. I am not an erudite scholar who finds it difficult to connect with a book unless it is dated and tabulated. I am only a *bhakta* (devotee) of Lord Vanamali. His commands are my desires. He is the *antaryami* (indweller). He alone inspires me to write. I have no will or particular desire of my own. He has inspired me to try and project the character of Sri Rama as Valmiki saw him. Whether Rama existed or not is immaterial. What is more important is that he has exerted more influence on the Indian mind than many other characters, who undoubtedly did exist. The character of Rama has molded the mind of a whole nation and he has been held as the ideal of manhood and Sita as the ideal of womanhood from Valmiki's time to the present day. Therefore, it is meaningless to ask whether he was a true figure or a figment of Valmiki's imagination. Whoever he was, the impact he has had on the life of this nation has been profound and cannot be denied by any scholar, however learned, and that should be enough for any reader. If the purpose of the *Ramayana* was to educate the public and to place before the masses a story which they could integrate meaningfully into their own lives, then Valmiki has succeeded, as perhaps no other author has done. Sri Rama is the *maryada purusha*, the perfect man, whose actions are shown as worthy of emulation. Sri Krishna, however, is the *uttama purusha*, or the Supreme Soul, and His actions can never be emulated.

Now, let us try to analyze the controversial situations in this book. For this, we should try to probe the mind of the author, Valmiki himself, and try to find out what he considered to be the main characteristic of Sri Rama. Only by doing this will we be able to understand the reason for Rama's apparently strange behavior, which has provoked criticism from all sides and which even the staunchest of his supporters find difficult to explain.

The invincible, rock-like foundation of Rama's character, around which Valmiki has built the entire story, is his absolute and unequivocal adherence to dharma. His first and last love was dharma. All the other loves of his life paled into insignificance before this all-consuming passion for dharma, which sometimes amounted to fanaticism. This is the basic fact of his character which we have to keep in mind before we can begin to appreciate many of his actions, which seem to conflict with our ideas of a noble human being. As he told Bharata, "I will follow the path of dharma, and obey the will of my father. A person of dharma should obey the guru, be true to himself and keep his word."

According to Hindu tradition, the triple laws which govern the universe are *rita* (order), *satya* (truth) and dharma (righteousness). The first two are universal laws which, when translated to human life, are called dharma. One who bases life on this dharma would be true to himself and to the laws of the universe, and therefore such a person could well be called a perfect human being. Sri Rama is the personification of such a character. He is dharma incarnate. In the *Mahabharatha* it was Yudhishtira who portrayed this role, though not as perfectly as Rama.

The universal laws of *rita* and *satya*, when reflected through the medium of the human mind, become distorted and that is why we find that though many of us struggle to become totally *dharmic,* we don't always hit the mark. Even God Himself, when he takes on a mortal body, appears to come, at least a little, under the sway of *maya*. That is why we often find even Sri Rama falling prey to the frailties of human emotions. He is totally bereft at the loss of Sita and weeps like any infatuated husband who has been parted from his beloved wife. There is also another reason why Valmiki showed him in this state. Despite his overwhelming love for Sita, he was prepared to banish her, so as to be true to his dharma as a king. Rama shows that a king's first loyalty should be to his country and to the citizens. A king should always place public duty before personal satisfaction. This is true of anyone holding a government position. If our politicians followed this rule, every country would be a *Ramarajya* (perfectly governed, leading to harmony in the lives of the people). It is to prove this point that Valmiki lost no opportunity to describe Rama's great attachment to his wife. In fact, contrary to the custom of the age, when it was quite common for kings to have many wives, Rama refused to marry again, after the banishment of Sita. The lesson Valmiki tries to teach us from this is, "not that Rama loved Sita less, but that he loved dharma more."

In fact, Rama was the epitome of all types of love—love of a son for his father, love for a brother, for a friend, for a wife and for the country. But soaring above all these loves was his love for the abstract principle of dharma. As mentioned above, the life of Rama shows that when a human being tries to uphold dharma at all costs, he must be prepared to sacrifice all other loves. Dharma is a stern disciplinarian and brooks no straying from its strict path. One who adheres fanatically to the path of dharma will find, like Rama, that even the strongest of material attachments will have to be sacrificed for the sake of his beliefs. The *Ramayana* is a fascinating story because in it one sees the terrible anguish and pain that Rama felt as a mortal when the time came to sacrifice his greatest loves, one by one, on the altar of dharma. On the other hand, one also sees that despite this agony, he did not deviate from the strict ideal he had set for himself and did not flinch from making the final sacrifice, of even his beloved brother, Lakshmana.

We, who live in an age of casual morality, where ideals are conveniently renounced for the sake of self-interest, where greed and selfishness alone are the standards to be followed, may consider Rama a fool, but to the ancient Indian society, he was God, for none but God could act in this fashion, with absolutely no trace of self interest. This is why Rama was deified in Tulsidas and why one finds his picture on every Hindu altar. The morals which have been instilled in the Indian people from the Vedic times help us, at least, to appreciate godliness, even though we may not be able to emulate it.

One finds, unfortunately, the younger generation has not tried to understand the reason why Valmiki portrayed such a character. They denounce certain of Rama's actions without understanding the tremendous moral purpose which motivated him. He has been held up as the model son, model husband, model friend and model brother. He played each role to perfection, no doubt, but eventually, he was forced to sacrifice each of the persons he loved so dearly. The *Ramayana* is a story of utter pathos, which ascends to sublime heights of glory—the pinnacle of divinity—for no ordinary mortal could be so utterly selfless, to the point of being considered heartless. Whatever role he played, he followed only this rule, "Am I acting according to dharma?" In following this path of fire, he burned himself time and again and was instrumental in bringing about the death of all his dear ones, beginning with his father. Each person whom he loved had to be offered as a *yajna* (ceremonial sacrifice) to that implacable law of dharma, which he was bent on following to the bitter end.

In the Ayodhya Kanda, we find that his stepmother Kaikeyi prevails on the king, his father, to grant her the two boons which he had promised earlier, and asks him to appoint her own son, Bharata as the Prince Regent and banish Rama to the forest for fourteen years. Rama did not flinch when he heard this harsh order of his stepmother, delivered to him on the eve of his coronation as heir apparent. His father could not even speak, due to his overwhelming sorrow, but Rama cheerfully agreed to this proposal and was quite prepared to renounce the golden throne of the kings of Ayodhya, to uphold his father's word to Kaikeyi. He was fully prepared to discard the glory of life as a king to be parted from his newly wedded wife, his beloved brothers, and his parents, and to wander alone in the forest for fourteen years, true to his role as *dharmanuchara* (one who is a practicer of righeousness). His father however could not bear the loss and died of a broken heart.

Another controversy concerns his killing of Tataka and the disfigurement of Surpanekha. How could he have done this to women? Again, one has only to refer to his role as the upholder of dharma to understand. One of the duties of a king was to see that the *rishis* were not molested during their spiritual practices. In fact, this was imperative, because the prosperity and well-being of the country depended on it. The *rishis* were no doubt powerful enough to protect their territory against evil forces but if they killed any-one, it would be a violation of their vows of nonviolence, which in turn would lessen the psychic powers which they had gained through their austerities. So they always sought the help of the rulers whose dharma it was to give protection. This was the reason why Vishwamitra had asked for Rama's support. Rama had agreed to protect the sacrifice at all costs and it was immaterial whether the culprit was a man or a woman.

In the case of Surpanekha, it was different story. The *rakshasi* was so enamored of Rama that she was determined to have him. Since she took Sita to be the only obstacle in her path, she pounced on her and would have gobbled her up, had not Rama intervened. Naturally, it was his duty to protect his innocent wife. However, he did not relish the task of killing Surpanekha, since she was a woman and her only crime was wanting him. But he could not afford to let her go unpunished, since she was sure to return with more proposi-tions and would most probably bide her time to kill Sita when he was not around to protect her. Therefore, he told Lakshmana to dis-figure her and thus teach her a well deserved lesson.

The next ambiguous incident is the one in which Rama kills Vali, jumping from behind a tree. To understand this, one has to recall his promise to his friend Sugriva. When Sita was abducted by Ravana, the demon king, Rama was bereft. Obviously, his foremost dharma at the moment was to his wife. He had to rescue her at all costs. In order to do so, circumstances forced him to get the help of Sugriva, the deposed king of the *Vanaras*. Hanuman told him to forge a friendship with Sugriva, by which Sugriva would be bound to help him. This solemn pact of friendship was sealed in front of the blazing fire. Rama and Sugriva went three times around the fire and Rama swore to help Sugriva defeat Vali and restore his kingdom, while Sugriva promised to help Rama rescue Sita. According to the ancient laws of dharma, death was the penalty for a man who committed adultery with his own daughter, his daughter-in-law or with the wife of his younger brother. Vali had abducted Ruma, Sugriva's beloved wife, just as Ravana had abducted Sita, and Rama was bound to kill Vali in order to uphold dharma. He was also honor bound to keep his promise to his friend, to depose Vali and place him on the throne of Kishkinda and restore his wife Ruma to him.

One may ask why he did not face Vali in a straightforward combat. Vali was also a *bhakta* and Rama would never have been able to kill him in a duel, since Vali would have thrown himself on Rama's mercy. Rama would then have been placed in a dilemma, where he would not have been able to kill Vali, as he deserved to be killed, for having misappropriated his younger brother's wife, nor would he have been able to keep his pledge to his friend, Sugriva. All things considered, Rama decided that the only way was to kill Vali from behind a tree. In this fashion, he would be able to uphold his dharma as a king, to see that justice was done, as well as his dharma to his friend, by keeping his pledge.

The last and most inexplicable episodes, which have aroused much criticisms, are the two concerning Sita. Why did he ask her to undergo the ordeal of fire and why did he banish her to the forest when she was with child? Before we consider this question, we should remember that Valmiki has given us countless instances before the fire ordeal, which should prove to us, beyond doubt that Rama was madly in love with his wife. There never was, and never would be, another woman for him. In fact, there are many scenes when we feel amazed at the way he lamented the loss of his wife. A couple of times even Lakshmana gently points out to him that this sort of behavior is not worthy of him. Valmiki has deliberately depicted these scenes, to show us how much Rama loved Sita. No woman was ever loved as much as was Sita. Naturally, it is understood that Rama himself entertained absolutely no doubts about her chastity, even after living in the city of the lustful Ravana. He knew quite well that her own innate purity would protect her. But his dharma as a king necessitated that he make a public demonstration of her purity. His dharma as a king demanded that his wife not be above the law, or else he would be guilty of setting a bad example to his people, whom he was bound to rule as a benevolent patriarch. Future events were to prove that he had, indeed, been right in suspecting there was gossip and even this test of fire was not enough to subdue the envious voices of human beings, who are always thirsty for another scandal, especially one connected with royalty. Rama knew that "Caesar's wife should be above suspicion." In order to try and forestall any such criticism, he asked his beloved Sita to step into the fire. Had he suspected even for a minute that she would be consumed by the fire, it is to be doubted whether even he would have had the courage to ask his love to undergo this ordeal. Sita knew all this and that is why she fearlessly agreed to enter the fire.

The next incident is the one where he asks Lakshmana to abandon Sita in the forest when she is pregnant. We of the modern age find it difficult to appreciate this, for we are so obsessed by the so-called infatuations, which are purely sensual and have no basis in dharma, that we are unable to understand, much less appreciate, a person who is prepared to sacrifice the one he loves above everything in order to uphold the abstract ideal of a king's dharma.

We can appreciate the English king who gave up his kingdom for the sake of a woman, but we cannot esteem a Hindu king who gave up his most beloved wife for the sake of his people. An individual who is prepared to sacrifice personal happiness at the altar of public interest is totally alien to modern culture, used as we are to politicians who use their office only to feather their own nests. We have strayed so far from this ancient code of righteousness that we are unable to see the godlike nobility of such a character. As has been said before, there never was, and never would be, another woman in Rama's life. He was in the prime of life when he forsook his wife but he refused, absolutely, to marry again, for he could not bear the thought of living with any woman other than Sita. He was prepared to sacrifice his own pleasure and become a lifelong celibate for the sake of his dharma as a king. He placed his duty towards his subjects before his duty as a husband, since the latter

xxiv · The Song of Rama

was personal in nature. For a king, public duty should always take
precedence over private pleasure. When the time came for him to
perform the *aswamedha yajna* (a royal ceremony), his own Guru
urged him to take another wife, for a *yajna* was incomplete unless
it was conducted along with a consort, but he refused to do this and
made a golden figure of Sita to stand beside him during the ceremony in lieu of a live woman. One cannot but feel a sense of awe
in the face of such an overwhelming sacrifice. Valmiki has given us
enough incidents during their sojourn in the forest to allow us to
imagine the years of loneliness and pain Rama must have gone
through, after having sent his beloved away.

The next question is, why did he not tell her of his decision
before banishing her, and why did he make Lakshmana do this
painful task instead of doing it himself? Both these questions can be
answered if we put ourselves in Rama's place on the night of the
impending abandonment. Could any man, as much in love with his
wife as Rama was, ever have been able to sustain the agony of seeing her weep when he made his dire pronouncement? Even Rama's
great determination would have broken down in the face of his darling's tears and he would have been forced to break his adamantine
resolve of observing his kingly dharma at any price.

The same reason dissuaded him from taking her to the forest
himself. How could he bear to desert her in those sylvan glades,
where they had sported so happily during their forest sojourn? How
would he be able to resist his dear one's tears, as she pleaded with
him not to abandon her? He had not been able to do so many years
before, when she had begged him to allow her to accompany him to
the forest. At that time, had he crept away at daybreak without
telling her, perhaps he could have spared her this agony now, but he
had given in, and he knew that even now he could not be sure of
keeping his resolve in the face of her tears. Even his mighty heart
would have broken and he would never have been able to forsake
her, as it was his duty to do. Thus we see that, far from condemn-
ing him as a heartless wretch, we would do better to stand back in
amazement and exclaim, "Can such a man ever have existed?" No
wonder he was deified, for only a God could behave in such an
exalted manner.

The incident of Shambuka is again a painful one to modern

eyes. We will never understand it without understanding the strict caste system which was followed in those times. The ancient Vedic caste system ensured a peaceful coexistence of all the castes, thus ensuring a faultless running of the machinery of society. Each caste had its own strict code of conduct. Any attempt to violate these codes was strictly squelched and the culprit chastised immediately. The smooth running of the society depended on this. The laws were based on the mutual cooperation of all parts of the society and not on unhealthy competition, as it is today. It was the king's duty to see that the social machinery ran on oiled wheels. Sometimes it so happened that he might even have to act ruthlessly. For the sake of the society an individual might have to be sacrificed. The decapitation of Shambuka was an instance of this. Rama had sacrificed his entire happiness for the sake of the people of Ayodhya. It is only natural that he was prepared to kill an individual who was transgressing the laws of the land, thus jeopardizing the smooth running of the society. It may seem ruthless to us, but this incident is shown by Valmiki in order to place before us the picture of a hero, who was invincible in his resolve to uphold the king's dharma.

Thus we see in Rama the portrait of a mighty superman, who based his entire life on strict adherence to the implacable law of dharma. It is a blind law and, like all the laws of Nature, it knows no compassion and brooks no disobedience. An ignorant child is burned by fire, just as an adult who knows the danger. There is no question of granting mercy on grounds of ignorance. All of Nature follows this rule, without question. Human beings, however, allow their greedy minds to overrule their heads. Rama was the one exception and he had to pay a heavy penalty for his utter loyalty to a blind law.

His life is one of sheer pathos, from beginning to end. One by one, he was forced to be instrumental in the death of each of his loved ones. His father died because of the separation from his beloved son, Sita gave up her life when she was asked to undergo the test of fire for a second time, and finally at the end of his life, he was forced to banish his beloved brother, Lakshmana, who was as close to him as his own shadow, in order to keep his word to the ascetic. Lakshmana left the city and walked into the Sarayu river and ended his life. This was the final straw and even Rama's mighty xxvi · The Song of Rama

heart could not stand the strain anymore. Lost in deep thought, he murmured to himself, "Nothing will remain, nothing will remain."

Taking leave of the citizens for whom he had sacrificed so much, he left for his higher abode, followed by all the faithful ones, who could not bear to live after his departure. His was a life spent only for the sake of others—for the sake of the people of *Bharathavarsha* (classical name for India) over whom he had ruled and cared for, like a father, caring for his children. Really, the only happy years he ever knew, were the thirteen years he spent in the forest with Sita and Lakshmana before Sita was abducted by Ravana. He bore under all his trials with heroic fortitude, and firmly abided by the high code of conduct he had set for himself, despite insuperable odds. What wonder that this nation has held him up as the glowing example of human perfection!

A reading of the *Ramayana* has the effect of cleansing us of our negative emotions and charging us with the moral fervor and grace of the great characters of the poem—Rama, Sita, Lakshmana, Bharata, Hanuman and the others.

In this rendering of the immortal classic, I have relied mainly on Valmiki's narration. I have also included stories from the wealth of oral tradition, which have been interwoven into the poem through the ages. Lord Vanamali alone has guided me and to Him goes all credit. May the story of Sri Rama guide and inspire us to act with justice and honor at all times.

Hari Aum Tat Sat.

INTRODUCTION

We feel both pleased and privileged to be offering to the reading public Devi Vanamali's inspired retelling of the *Ramayana*. This is the second book by Devi Vanamali that Blue Dove Press has published, the first being *The Play of God—Visions of the Life of Krishna*. As was the case with the earlier volume, this book also was experienced by Devi as a work given to her by God, her Lord Krishna (or Vanamali), not as something written by her own effort. We are inclined to accept this report. The work has an unearthly, inspired quality, such that it might well be approached as scripture rather than simply the creation of a human author.

The *Ramayana* is the story of Rama, worshiped by millions of Hindus as an avatar or incarnation of God. Rama is said to have incarnated with Sita, his eternal, divine consort, Lakshman, his brother in the story, and Hanuman, the monkey who becomes the exemplar of perfect devotion to God. Ravana, the demon king who threatened and burdened Earth, also figures prominently in the narrative. More than just a story, however, the *Ramayana* evokes and encompasses a whole spiritual path, to which people devote their entire lives as a vehicle of God realization.

In the West, this story and this path became better known through Ram Dass (Richard Alpert), whose guru was Neem Karoli Baba. Many of Neem Karoli Baba's devotees believe he was an incarnation of Hanuman. Ram Dass tells of a time in India when he was worshiping an image of Hanuman in a temple, absorbed in the universe of spiritual meaning embodied in this icon and in the *Ramayana* itself. He reflected that if some of his colleagues at Harvard could have seen him prostrating to this "monkey-god," they would have thought he had gone off the deep end. But he, like many other Westerners, had seen beyond the initially exotic, culture-bound externals and found profound depths of meaning in the spiritual universe expressed in the *Ramayana*. Ram Dass went on to teach us to appreciate and be inspired by the blissful heart of this story.

Like the great Hindu epic, the *Mahabharata*, and other sacred texts such as the *Srimad Bhagavatam*, the story of the *Ramayana* can be read on many levels. On the most superficial, it is a about a prince who is banished to the forest for a period of time, whose beautiful wife is kidnaped there by a demon king, and who must mount an epic struggle to rescue her. On another level it is about the separation of a soul from God because of its momentary attraction to some illusory worldly glitter, the soul's cry for help to its beloved, and God's rushing to the soul's aid. On a still deeper level, the entire story takes place in each of us: We are all Sita, separated from God in the Divine's own cosmic play or *lila*, but destined to be reunited.

Finally, let me say something about the author, Devi Vanamali. I first met her in 1993 in Rishikesh, by the banks of the Ganges. India has some wonderful but well kept secrets and at the time she was one of them. It was baffling to me that someone as incredible, inspiring and wonderful could be so unknown. Well, the secret is getting out. Now many people know who she is and have visited her at her ashram in Rishikesh. She is simple and unassuming, even childlike, yet a diamond where things of the spirit are concerned.

May you be blessed and enlightened by this inspired work.

Jeff Blom
Blue Dove Foundation

The Song of Rama

Sri Ganeshaya Namah!

O god, of huge body and curled trunk,
With the brilliance of a thousand suns,
Let me never encounter any obstacles,
At any time, in anything I do.

Sri Hanumanthaya Namah!

I bow to Lord Hanuman,
the sole witness to the story of Rama,
the Ramayana
May He bless us with ears to listen
and hearts to understand.

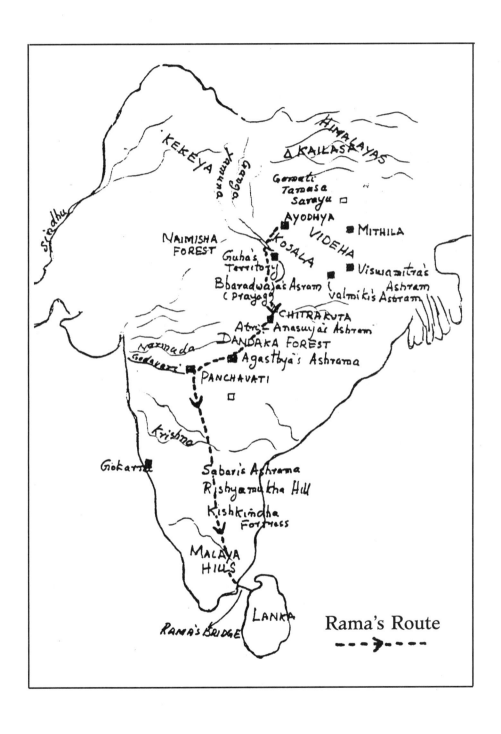

Rama's Route

BOOK ONE

*Sri Ramachan-
draya Namah!*

Salutations to
Rama the auspi-
cious one.

BALA KANDA

THE BOOK OF BOYHOOD

ONE

THE STORY OF SAGE VALMIKI

Shaswathaya Namaha!

Homage to the eternal one.

I bow to Rama, the scion of the race of Raghu, husband of Sita. To Ramachandra I bow along with Sita, Lakshmana, Bharata, Shatrugna and Hanuman.
—RAMAYANA OF VALMIKI

Before we go into the story of the *Ramayana*, let us listen to the story of the Sage Valmiki who was the author. It is said that he was born of *Brahmin* parents, who abandoned him in the forest at birth. He was found and brought up by a hunter and thus became a hunter—and a robber—by profession. He was known as Ratnakar. He was a wild and savage man who knew nothing of culture or civilization. All those who went into the forest were in fear for their lives, for he was known to be ruthless. He lived with his wife and his brood of children in the depths of the forest and had never gone near a town.

One day he saw a man approaching. With the ferocity of a wild animal, Ratnakar pounced on him, with a view to kill the man and rob him of his money. He was surprised to find that the man did not show any signs of fear but stood absolutely still. He was quite intrigued by this strange behavior as Ratnakar had only seen two types of animals before in his life—those who turned tail and ran away as soon as they saw him and those who bared their teeth and pounced on him. It was the first time that he had seen a creature who looked at him fearlessly, with eyes that were filled with compassion. Love and compassion were emotions to which he was an utter stranger, and for a minute he faltered in his tracks, his upraised arm holding a brutal knife, freezing in the air.

Slowly he brought his hand down and asked the man, "Who are you that you show no signs of fear? Everyone I know runs away as soon as they see me and I catch them easily. Why don't you run?"

"I'm Narada, the heavenly sage. I don't run because I'm not afraid of you."

"Why aren't you afraid of me?" asked Ratnakar. "Don't you know that I can kill you?"

"Then why didn't you kill me?" asked the sage curiously.

"Because I saw something in your eyes which is bothering me."

"What did you see?"

"I don't know. I've never seen it before in any other eyes but it's very pleasant."

"I will tell you," said the sage. "What you saw was love and compassion."

"Why should you feel love for me?" asked the savage, surprised, for he had never seen that look before, not even in the eyes of his wife.

"Because I love everybody and everything."

"Why should you do that?" asked Ratnakar.

"Because everything and everyone is a form of that Supreme Being whom I worship. Now let me ask you something," said the sage. "Don't you know that by killing all these creatures and people, you are incurring great sin?"

"Yes, I suppose I know it," said the hunter doubtfully.

"Then why do you do it?" asked the sage.

"Because I have to support my family," said the hunter.

"Will they share at least part of the sin which will accrue to you by these acts?" questioned the sage.

"I'm sure they will," said the hunter.

"Why don't you go and ask them," asked Narada, "and I'll wait for you till you to return."

The hunter ran back to his home and asked his wife and children if they would take their share of his sins, as they were taking more than their fair share of ill-gotten goods. They were quite surprised at this question and asked him what he meant by this. He explained to them that since he was committing so many crimes for their sake, it was only fair that they should also share his sins. They were quite horrified by this request. The woman said that it was the duty of a husband to look after his wife. The children said that it was the duty of a father to look after his progeny. As for his sins, naturally they were the outcome of his own acts and he would have to bear the consequences himself. The hunter did not wait to hear any more. He ran back to the sage who was quite sure of his return and was waiting with a smile on his lips.

"Well, what did they say?" he asked. "Were they not eager to share your sins, as they were eager to share your spoils?"

Ratnakar hung his head and admitted that no one was willing to share his burdens. Then Narada gave him a discourse on the law of karma and told him that he alone would have to bear the consequences of his actions. To commit sinful acts for the sake of another was quite foolish.

The hunter looking lost and unhappy asked the sage, "Now what should I do?"

"Meditate on the Supreme Being," he said. "Only then will you be able to attain salvation. He alone is your relation; He alone your friend. I will give you a mantra, by using which you will be able to do *tapas* (spiritual austerities)."

"I am your servant; please guide me," said the hunter and knelt before the celestial sage.

Narada whispered the glorious mantra "Rama" into his right ear but the poor savage was so untutored that he was unable to repeat it. Then Narada asked, "Can you repeat the word '*mara*.'?"

"Of course I can," he said, since the word *mara* means "tree" and that was a thing he was always cutting down.

So Narada blessed him and taught him how to sit in a meditation pose and to repeat the word constantly. The word *mara*, when repeated fast, becomes "Rama" and thus, without knowing, the hunter started repeating the word "Rama" instead of *mara*. Due to his past *samskaras* (soul tendencies carried from past lives), he went into deep meditation for many years, until he was covered by a hillock of mud brought by ants.

Many years later, Narada returned and found the anthill in the exact place where he had left the hunter. He broke open the mud cage and woke up the person seated within.

"Arise, O sage!" he said. "Do you remember who you are?"

"Yes, Your Holiness," he answered, "I'm the poor hunter whom you took pity on and advised to repeat the glorious mantra, 'Rama.'"

"Now you are no longer a hunter but a sage, and from now on you will be known as Valmiki, since you have emerged from this anthill or '*valmeekam*.'"

"Why have you awakened me, O divine sage?" asked Valmiki. "I would prefer to meditate for another few years."

"Your time for meditation is over. Now is the time for action. You have many more things to achieve in your life. Go to the banks of the river Tamasa, where it meets the Ganga (Ganges River), and there make your hermitage. Very soon, Sita, the beloved wife of Rama, will be coming there. She is with child and has been abandoned by her husband. It is your duty to look after her and the babies, till they are old enough to return to their father."

"O holy one," Valmiki said, "I find that this world is a wicked place filled with ignoble people. If I could find at least one human being who possesses the qualities of a noble soul, then I would feel like returning to the world. Otherwise, it would be better for me to remain within the security of my anthill. Tell me, do you know of such a one?"

Narada asked him to enumerate these qualities.

Valmiki said, "Integrity, bravery, righteousness, gratitude, truthfulness, dedication to one's principles, concern for all living beings, learning, skill, beauty, courage, ability to keep anger under control, lack of jealousy and undaunted heroism. O sage, pray tell me, am I expecting too much? Can anyone have all these qualities at the same time?"

Narada was pleased to answer this question and said, "Indeed, I do know of such a person. He is born in the line of Ikshvaku and his name is Rama."

Narada then proceeded to acquaint Valmiki briefly with the story of Rama, who possessed all the qualities of a perfect man. He concluded the story by saying, "This Rama now resides in the city of Ayodhya and rules the kingdom with all righteousness. He is born to establish dharma (righteousness) on earth. Very soon, as I said, his wife Sita will be coming here and it is your duty to take care of her."

Thus saying, the sage departed, strumming his lute.

After he had left, Valmiki went to the land near the Tamasa river and made his hermitage. Soon he had many disciples. One winter morning he went to the banks of the river for his bath. On the way, he saw two cranes mating. As the sage gazed in joy at their spontaneous love for each other, a hunter aimed a fatal arrow at the male bird and shot him, contrary to all rules of dharma. Pierced by that cruel arrow in the midst of the act of love, the bird fell to the ground with a heartrending cry. Wrenched from her lover, the female bird screamed piteously, beating her breast with her wings. She fluttered around, terrified and bewildered. Her heartbreaking cries brought a gush of compassion into the heart of the sage and he cursed the hunter. As soon as the curse left his lips, he felt great remorse. He was horrified that his compassion for the bird had made him break his vow of nonviolence by cursing the hunter, who was, after all, only a helpless victim of his own karma, as he himself had been a long time before. He felt very unhappy about the whole episode. Then he realized that his curse had flowed from his lips in a spontaneous verse of four lines with eight syllables each. He was struck by the beauty of the verse and told his disciple Bharadvaja to memorize it. The sage then continued his interrupted ablutions and returned to his *ashrama* (a place devoted to spiritual pursuits). Just then, two young *brahmacharis* from the neighboring *ashrama* ran to him and told him that a beautiful woman had been abandoned near the river and appeared to be contemplating jumping into it. Valmiki ran to the woman and knew that she was Sita, the wife of Rama, as foretold by Narada. He escorted her home and told the wives of the sages to look after her, for she was carrying the heir to the throne of the Ikshvakus.

Later, when he sat for meditation, he was filled with sadness over the episode of the two cranes and remorse over his involuntary curse of the hunter. Brahma, the Creator, appeared to him and told him not to brood over this strange event, because from this incident would arise the inspiration to narrate the story of Rama, Sita and Lakshmana. Brahma spoke thus.

"You will be inspired, O *rishi* (sage), to compose a most memorable poem, on the exploits of Sri Rama. The whole life of Rama will be revealed to you. Everything that you say in your poem will be based on facts which you have witnessed. You will be able to see each and every one of the glorious episodes in the life of Sri Rama. You will achieve great fame as the first of all poets. The story of Rama will endure as long as these mountains and rivers stay on the face of this earth. Your fame will resound in the realms of heaven above and the kingdoms of the earth below."

Having thus blessed Valmiki, Brahma departed. Valmiki then sat down and meditated on the Lord and out of his mouth gushed the immortal poem, called *Ramayana*—the way of Rama.

This is how the *Ramayana* came to be written, from the depths of Valmiki's sorrow at the fate of the two birds who were so much in love with each other and who were parted so cruelly. It does not need much imagination to see the parallel between this story and the fate of the two lovers, Rama and Sita, who were parted time and time again, despite their intense love for each other.

The poem took twelve long years to complete and by then, the twins that Sita had given birth to had reached twelve years of age.

Having composed this remarkable poem consisting of 24,000 verses on the life of Sri Rama and Sita, the seer looked around for a person with a prodigious memory who could memorize the entire story. Just at that moment, the twin sons of Sri Rama himself—called Lava and Kusa, who were being brought up by Valmiki in his own hermitage—appeared before him, clad in hermit's garb. Knowing them to be endowed with great intelligence and mastery of music, the sage forthwith proceeded to teach them the entire poem, which they mastered with ease. At an august assembly of sages, the twins sang the whole poem exquisitely, in one voice. The sages were charmed and gave them many boons.

It was at this time that news was brought to the *ashrama* that the king was going to hold the *ashvamedha yajna* (the Vedic horse sacrifice ceremony), which would last for one whole year at the forest of Naimisharanya. When he heard this, Valmiki told the two boys, Lava and Kusha, to go to the *yajna* and recite the whole of the *Ramayana* in front of Rama and the assembled sages. The children did as they were told. As the melodious voices of the children rose in unison with faultless rhythm and perfect harmony, tears poured down the cheeks of Sri Rama, and the whole court became totally absorbed in the narrative. This is the story of the *Ramayana* which they sang.

Thus ends the first chapter of the glorious Ramayana of Sage Valmiki *called "The Story of Sage Valmiki."*

Hari Aum Tat Sat

TWO

BIRTH AND BOYHOOD

Janakivallabhaya Namaha!

Homage to the beloved of Janaki (Sita).

Rama had the glory of the moon
And Sita its beauty.
Rama had the gait of an elephant
And Sita that of a swan.
—SOURCE UNKNOWN

LONG, LONG AGO in the beautiful land of Kosala, on the banks of the river Sarayu, was situated the magnificent town of Ayodhya. Ruled by the wise and just king called Dasaratha, he belonged to the solar dynasty in the lineage of Ikshvaku, who was the son of Vaivasvatha Manu, the first of all created beings. Dasaratha had one sorrow and that was that he had no son to carry on his line. As he was brooding over this, his Guru, Sage Vasistha, exhorted him to perform the horse sacrifice (*ashvamedha yajna*), as well as the *putra kameshti yajna*, a ritual for the sake of begetting a son. Sage Vasistha told Dasaratha to approach the famous sage, Rishyasringa, and request that he be the chief priest in conducting the *yajna*.

It was at this time that the gods approached the creator Brahma and begged him to intercede with Lord Vishnu on their behalf to kill the demon king, Ravana, who was harassing them sorely. Brahma conveyed the message to Lord Vishnu, who agreed to descend to the earth, taking on four forms, as the sons of Dasaratha. At that very moment, King Dasaratha had successfully completed his *ashvamedha yajna* and had begun his *putra kameshti yajna*. Rishyasringa had raised the ladle high and poured the ghee into the flaming fire, invoking

9

the presence of Lord Narayana, protector of the world. Just then out of the sacrificial fire there appeared the striking figure of a divine figure carrying a golden vessel containing an ambrosial confection of rice, milk and honey. The celestial being handed the vessel over to the king and told him to give it to his three queens. The king gave half of this nectar-like sweet to his eldest wife, Kausalya. He divided the remaining half into two portions and gave one portion to his second wife, Sumitra. The remaining quarter he split into two and gave one part to his third wife Kaikeyi and the remainder again to Sumitra. As soon as they ate the pudding, the queens became pregnant with the spirit of Lord Narayana.

In course of time, they gave birth to four sons, each of whom manifested the power of the Lord in proportion to the amount that their mothers had partaken of the divine confection. The first to be born was Kausalya's son, Rama, who contained within him one half of the power of the Lord. He was born in the month of *Chaithra* (March-April) when the star *Punarvasu* was in ascendance, a most auspicious time, when five of the planets were in an exalted state. Next, Kaikeyi, the youngest queen, gave birth to Bharata, who possessed a quarter of the Lord's powers, and finally, the second wife, Sumitra, delivered twins who were called Lakshmana and Shatrugna. The king's joy knew no bounds. In place of the one son he had wished for, he had been given four. Gifts were distributed in abundance to all. The city of Ayodhya went crazy with joy. There was month-long rejoicing and all kinds of festivities.

As the children grew up, they were given all the training necessary for royal princes. Their guru was the great Sage Vasistha. Even as a child, Rama exhibited extraordinary powers of intellect as well as great nobility of character. Though the other three were all devoted to him, Sumitra's son Lakshmana followed Rama like a shadow and could not bear to be parted from him for even a minute, whereas his twin, Shatrugna, kept close to Bharata.

After their return from the hermitage of their preceptor, Rama wished to go on a pilgrimage around the holy land of *Bharathavarsha* (the ancient name of India). Dasaratha was pleased to grant his request and the four brothers went on a tour with their retinue. After his return, his father and brothers noticed a great change in Rama. He became very pensive, took no delight in the various sports and pastimes of his brothers, shunned all social contacts and even refused to eat unless coaxed by one of his mothers. He became pale and emaciated. He politely evaded all the questions of his anxious father.

At this time, it so happened that Sage Vishvamitra came to the court with a request. The king assured the sage that his wish would certainly be granted. Vishvamitra then asked Dasaratha to send his son Rama to kill the two demons, Maricha and Subahu, who were disturbing his *ashrama* and preventing him from completing his sacrificial rites. The king was stunned to hear this request and he feared for the safety of his son, who was barely sixteen years of age. He offered to send his entire army to help the sage or even to come himself, but the sage refused all these alternatives, for he said that Rama alone had the power to kill the demons. At last, urged by his own guru Vasistha, who reminded him that he gave his word, Dasaratha reluctantly gave his consent and ordered an attendant to fetch Rama. The attendant came back and gave the news that ever since his return from the pilgrimage, the prince had been strangely lethargic. He seemed bereft of hope and desire and attached to nothing.

Hearing this, Vishvamitra said, "His condition is not the result of delusion but the result of wisdom and dispassion, leading to enlightenment. Let him be brought to the court."

Rama came to the assembly hall and bowed to his father and the sages. His loving father asked him, "My dear child, why have you become so sad and dejected, when you have everything in life? Who has harmed you? What has happened to you?"

Rama replied, "During my recent pilgrimage through this holy land of ours, I saw many sights which I had never seen before. Agony and suffering did I see, and poverty, disease and death. A new kind of thought has taken hold of me. What happiness can we have from this ever-changing world? All beings take birth only to die, and die only to be born again. I see no meaning in this transient phenomenon which has its roots in suffering and ignorance. Everything in the world depends on our mental attitude, but the mind itself seems unreal, although we are bewitched by it. We are not bonded slaves, yet we have no freedom. Ignorant of the world, we have been wandering aimlessly in this forest of *samsara* (illusion) for many lives. How can this suffering come to an end? My heart bleeds with sorrow when I think of these things. I do not feel like eating or sleeping, much less engaging in vain pursuits, unless I have an answer to these questions."

He went on in this vein for some time and the whole assembly was stuck by the depth and perspicacity of the young boy's reflections. At last, he said, "I do not consider him a hero who is able to battle against an army. I regard him a hero who is able to conquer his mind. By reflecting on the pitiable state of living beings who have fallen into this pit called *samsara*, I am filled with grief. My mind is confused. I have rejected everything but I am not yet established in wisdom. Hence, I'm partly caught and partly freed, like a tree that has been cut but not severed from its roots. Pray tell me how I am to reach that supreme state of bliss!"

All the assembled sages and people were thrilled to hear Rama's speech and settled themselves down to hear the reply of Vishvamitra and Vasistha.

Vishvamitra said, "O Rama! You are indeed the foremost among the wise and there is nothing further that you need to know. However, your knowledge needs confirmation and I earnestly request sage Vasistha to instruct you so that all of us who are assembled here may also be inspired. Vasistha is truly a liberated sage, who is not swayed by sensual pleasures and who acts without motivation of fame or any other incentives."

On hearing Vishvamitra's request, the great *Brahmarishi* Vasistha proceeded to instruct Rama on *Atmic* (soul) knowledge and *Brahmic* (the formless Supreme) bliss. This discourse came to be known as the *Yoga Vasistha*. Though many people had listened to this marvelous talk, it was only Rama, of mighty intellect, who could grasp in its totality the essence of Vasistha's teachings.

This was how Rama at the tender age of sixteen became a truly liberated being, steadfast in his quest of dharma, caring not for the pursuit of personal happiness but only for the pursuit of righteousness, for he realized that only in dharma could a person find eternal bliss.

At the end of this learned discourse, Rama's father gave him permission to accompany Vishvamitra and accomplish whatever the sage had in mind. Lakshmana followed him. The king watched them go with anxious eyes, but did not dare to say anything, for he did not want to incur Vishvamitra's wrath.

When they reached the river bank, Vishvamitra gave them two

mantras which would make them invincible and protect them from all fatigue and hunger. Proceeding further, they came to a forest in which many hermits lived. They travelled in fear of the demoness called Tataka, who, Vishvamitra told the princes, though born a woman, was endowed with the strength of a thousand elephants. She and her sons Maricha and Subahu roamed the forests and killed anyone who went there. They also harassed the sages who lived in that forest and stopped them from performing their sacrificial rites. Every time they raised their ladle to pour the oblation of ghee into the fire, they would find that their fire had gone out due to the blood, bones, and fecal matter which had been thrown into it. Vishvamitra asked Rama to kill her and save the forest dwellers.

Since she was a woman, Rama was reluctant to do so and decided to maim her instead so that she would no longer trouble the sages. Taking up his bow, he twanged it loudly. This infuriated Tataka and she rushed toward the sound. Seeing the princes, she showered rocks and uprooted trees on them and kept appearing and disappearing in the sky, in order to confuse them. Rama was sorely perplexed as to what he should do. Vishvamitra then told him to kill her immediately, before she could wreak further havoc. She deserved no sympathy and she was far from being a weak woman. Thus, commanded by Vishvamitra, Rama did not hesitate anymore, for he realized that this was his duty, since Vishvamitra had brought him there for that express purpose. As she rushed toward him with the intention of making an end of him and Lakshmana, Rama shot a deadly arrow at her and she fell down lifeless in her tracks. Thus, he earned the gratitude of all the sages and other forest dwellers. It was a king's dharma to protect the people under him and thus Rama was forced to kill Tataka, even though she was a woman.

That night, the forest dwellers slept peacefully without fear of being bothered by Tataka. In the morning, Vishvamitra gave Rama many powerful missiles by which he could defeat all enemies, as well as knowledge of how to recall them. Then he took the boys to his own *ashrama*, where the hermits were delighted to see them. The next day Vishvamitra commenced his *yajna*, after having instructed the two princes to be strictly vigilant for the next six days to see that the sacrifice was not interrupted. Just as the ceremony commenced, there was a fearful clamor in the sky and the two demons, Maricha and

Subahu, swooped down on the sacrificial altar, scattering blood, pus and bones. Rama ran out and hurled a missile at Maricha, which sent him hurtling eight hundred miles away to the ocean. Next he killed Subahu without difficulty and thus saved the ritual as he had promised.

Next day, the sages apprised him of the sacrifice of the bow, which was being held in the town of Mithila by the great sage-king Janaka. All of them proceeded towards Mithila and on the way, the sages regaled the boys with an account of Vishvamitra's birth and history, as well as the story of the Ganga. They also told them the story of the churning of the Ocean of Milk by the gods and the demons.

On their way, they reached a deserted hermitage which had belonged to the Sage Gautama. His beautiful wife, Ahalya, had been cursed by him and turned into a stone for having unwittingly betrayed him. As Rama entered the *ashrama*, he placed his foot on the stone and Ahalya was immediately released from her curse, rising up in all her beauty. Gautama also returned and the reunited couple paid joyful homage to Rama.

As the party entered the flower-bedecked town of Mithila where the festival of the bow was being held, Vishvamitra told the story of how the bow had belonged to Lord Shiva and was so huge that none could lift it. However, when Janaka's daughter, Sita, at a very young age, was playing with a ball, it had rolled beneath the bow. The king was astonished to find the child effortlessly lifting the bow to get the ball. Then and there he decided that anyone who aspired for his daughter's hand would have to lift the bow, bend it and string it.

Many princes had come to try their luck and had gone away disappointed. Vishvamitra knew that Rama was the one to wed Sita and that is why he took him to Mithila. As they entered the palace gates, Rama's gaze was drawn to an open window in the palace through which he could see the head of a young girl. As if drawn by his look, she turned and looked straight into his eyes. So intense was her gaze that he felt as if he had received an electric shock. His heart left him forever and flew into her beauteous eyes. She was just a child, but child though she was, she also knew that in him she had found her life partner. The boys walked on and the girl kept hoping with all her might that he would be able to bend the bow and marry her, for she was none other than Sita, the adopted daughter of King Janaka.

Once when the king had been ploughing the ground for a *yajna*, he heard the gurgling chuckle of a baby. He stopped the plough just in time and found a beautiful baby girl in the furrow. He gathered her up tenderly and decided to adopt her for she was so charming. He called her "Sita," which means a furrow.

Vishvamitra and the princes were welcomed by King Janaka with great joy. He told them the story of the bow and of his daughter, Sita. Vishvamitra assured him that Rama, the son of Dasaratha, would easily bend the bow. Five thousand able-bodied men were needed to carry the chest containing the bow into the hall. The lid was opened and the bow was revealed to everyone. Urged by Vishvamitra, Rama took up the gigantic bow as if it was a mere toy and bent it till it broke. There was a thunderous noise, like the breaking apart of a mountain. The whole earth shook and shuddered with the impact. All the spectators fell to the ground, except for the two princes, the sage and the king. Everyone gazed at Rama in wonder. The king was delighted, for he had almost despaired of finding a husband for his daughter, since all the mightiest kings of the land had come and tried their luck with the bow and failed. He immediately sent speedy messengers to Ayodhya to invite Dasaratha to his son's wedding.

When the king arrived accompanied by Bharata, Shatrugna and a vast retinue of followers carrying loads of gifts, he was met with all due honor by Janaka. Janaka suggested that his younger daughter Urmila should be given in marriage to Lakshmana and his brother's two daughters, Mandavi and Srutakirti, would make suitable brides for Bharata and Shatrugna. Dasaratha was delighted to accept such beautiful brides for his sons.

At the auspicious hour called *Vijaya*, the nuptials took place. Vasistha prepared the altar in the center of the marriage pavilion and decorated it with sandal paste, golden platters, vases filled with flowers, incense burners, conchs, bowls filled with offerings and golden ceremonial vessels containing unpolished rice, roasted and smeared with turmeric powder. Scattering *darbha* grass on the altar, Sage Vasistha began the ceremony with the recitation of the sacred marriage mantras given in the *Rig Veda*. King Janaka now led his beautiful daughter, bedecked with ornaments, into the marriage pavilion. He took her hand and placed it firmly in Rama's. Sita looked up shyly at her husband and as their eyes locked, they both realized that they had already seen each other and chosen each other some days ago, when Rama had arrived in Mithila. Neither of them could bear to tear their gaze away from the other and hardly noticed that the king was giving his daughter Urmila to Lakshmana, and his nieces Mandavi and Srutakirti to Bharata and Shatrugna. Clasping the hand of his bride, Rama led her three times around the sacred fire, thus pledging his love. His brothers followed suit. The combined wedding took place with great pomp and style.

The wedding party left the very next day for Ayodhya. On the way they were accosted by the invincible Parasurama, who, though born a *Brahmin*, was yet a *Kshatriya* (member of the ruler/warrior caste) in his valor and might. Parasurama had sworn to exterminate the whole race of *Kshatriyas*, since one of them had killed his father. Vasistha and the other sages tried to placate him, but the irascible Parasurama, who was supposed to be another *avatara* of Lord Vishnu, ignored all of them and addressed himself to Rama alone.

"I have heard of your great prowess in breaking the mighty bow of Lord Shiva. I have with me the even mightier bow of Lord Vishnu. If you are indeed a true *Kshatriya* and a man of valor, take this bow and string it and come for a duel. Dasaratha was devastated when he heard this challenge and begged Parasurama to let the boy go, but Parasurama totally ignored him and challenged Rama again. Undaunted by the fierce aspect of the sage, Rama took up the bow and strung it with ease and turning it towards Parasurama, asked him in an authoritative voice, 'O holy *Brahmin*! Tell me at whom I should discharge this arrow?'"

Recognizing his Master, the fierce Parasurama became meek as a fawn and said, "O Rama, I realize that you are none other than Lord Vishnu, for no one else can string this bow. I surrender all my powers to you and will now retire to Mount Mahendra for further austerities."

After Parasurama left, Rama handed over the bow of Vishnu to Varuna, the god of waters, and the wedding party proceeded without interruption to the city of Ayodhya, which had been richly festooned to welcome the princes and their brides.

For the next twelve years Rama and Sita delighted in each other's company. Sita was as good as she was beautiful and Rama came to love her even more for her nobility of character than for her charm and beauty. As for Sita, she was enchanted with her handsome and noble husband and thanked the gods who had given her such a boon. Their love for each other grew with every passing day and they could not bear to be parted for even a moment. Thus the days and months passed like minutes for the radiant couple and time ceased to exist while they gazed into each other's lotus petal eyes.

Thus ends the second chapter of the glorious Ramayana *of Sage Valmiki called "Birth and Boyhood"*

Hari Aum Tat Sat

This story of Sri Rama has millions of verses.
Each word is capable of freeing us from terrible sins

–INDIAN SAYING

BOOK TWO

*Rajeevalochanaya
namaha*

Homage to the
lotus-eyed one.

AYODHYA
KANDA

THE BOOK OF AYODHYA

THREE

IMPENDING CORONATION

Raghuttamaya Namaha!

Homage to the best of the Raghus.

Rama, the light of the race of Raghu,
Sita, the lamp of the race of Nimi.
One was born in the solar dynasty,
The other, in the lunar line.
—INDIAN POPULAR SONG

THE CITIZENS OF AYODHYA loved all four young princes of the realm, but they took special pride and pleasure in the eldest—Rama, as indeed did the king, his father. Rama was an extraordinary person. Nature had been lavish in her gifts to the young prince. Not only was he handsome of stature and mien but, even at this young age, was a fully enlightened being. The discourse given by Sage Vasistha had been fully understood by him alone and he shone among the rest, as a diamond in the midst of pebbles. Not only was he possessed of great physical beauty, but his manners were also charming. He had a keen intellect and could be tender and sympathetic when the occasion merited it. Though he was soft and kind with the weak and the poor, he could also be stern and inflexible when it came to wrongdoers. Always self-controlled, and ever immersed in the Self, he was even tempered, never flaring up in anger nor giving in to unseemly mirth. In fact, he was a paragon of all virtues, yet he was never puffed up with pride or arrogance, accepting everything as the gift of God.

For twelve years after his marriage, Rama led a carefree life, enjoying the company of his charming wife and learning to handle the multifarious affairs of state.

21

It was at this time that Kaikeyi's brother came to take Bharata, along with Shatrugna, for a holiday to his home.

Seeing his son Rama so full of noble qualities, King Dasaratha felt that it was his duty to install him as heir apparent as soon as possible, for he himself was getting weak and old. Having once decided on this, he was in a desperate hurry to accomplish it. He consulted his ministers and decided on a day for the installation. Invitations were sent to all the kings but by a strange twist of fate, the king forgot to send invitations to two of his closest relations—his father-in-law, the king of the Kekayas and his son's father-in-law, King Janaka. Had the former been invited, Bharata and Shatrugna would naturally have accompanied them and the whole course of the story would have changed. By the time Dasaratha became aware of the omission, it was too late to send for them. Whether the fateful oversight was intentional or accidental, we cannot say. He consoled himself with the thought that they would soon hear the delightful news.

There in the presence of all the kings and prominent citizens of the city, Emperor Dasaratha proclaimed his intention of crowning his son Rama as Prince Regent the following morning. The most auspicious time was chosen by the astrologers, when the planet *Pushya* was in ascendance. All the kings acclaimed the decision as a wise one.

King Dasaratha then turned to his guru, Vasistha, and asked him to get everything ready for the installation on the following morning, for the function was to start at break of dawn. The minister Sumantra was sent to escort Rama to the Assembly. Rama was the object of all eyes as he walked into the hall with his stately gait. He prostrated before his father, who in turn embraced him and bade him be seated on a special seat. He then apprised him of the honor in store for him on the morrow. Rama was neither elated nor displeased by this pronouncement, but took the news calmly, as was his nature. He returned to his own palace, cheered by the populace who had thronged to the palace gates as soon as they heard the news.

The Assembly now broke up and the King retired to his own quarters. Then he again sent his minister Sumantra to fetch Rama. The king was feeling agitated, since he had been told by the astrologers that he was passing through a very bad time, which might even end in his death, so he was anxious that Rama's installation should take place without delay. Moreover he had remembered that at the time of his marriage with Kaikeyi, he had promised his father-in-law that Kaikeyi's son would become king after him. He was frightened that if Bharata happened to be present at the time of the installation, he might demand his rights.

When Rama arrived, King Dasaratha told him that he should observe a fast along with Sita for the duration of the night and should keep vigil on a seat of *darbha* grass with a stone for a pillow. Rama agreed to everything and returned quickly to his own palace to give the news to Sita. However, she was nowhere to be found. He went to his mother's quarters and found both Sita and Lakshmana's mother, Sumitra, with Kausalya. She had heard the news and was praying for the well-being of her son. Rama was blessed by his mother and Sumitra. He turned to Lakshmana and invited him to share the good fortune which was to come to him on the morrow. Then he and Sita retired to their own apartments.

News of the impending coronation had spread like wildfire and people from all over the suburbs started pouring into the city of Ayodhya, excited at the event to which everyone looked forward with great joy, since Rama was loved by all. Decoration of the city commenced immediately.

Thus ends the third chapter of the glorious Ramayana *of Sage Valmiki called "Impending Coronation"*

Hari Aum Tat Sat

FOUR

KAIKEYI PLOTS

Rajendraya Namaha!

Homage to the king of kings.

Rama, Lord of Ayodhya,
Sita, Princess of Mithila.
Rama, jewel of the line of Raghu.
And Sita, the treasure of Videha.
—POPULAR SONG

KAIKEYI WAS THE KING'S youngest and favorite wife. When she came to Ayodhya, she was accompanied by her maid, a hunchback called Manthara, who had been selected to look after her interests. That evening Manthara happened to climb to the battlements and look down at the festivities going on in the town. She was quite astonished to see the city decorated so quickly, as if for a big occasion.

Seeing Rama's old nurse standing nearby, Manthara asked, "Why has the city of Ayodhya gone mad with joy overnight? What is the special event?"

The nurse gave her the news of the impending installation. Hearing this, Manthara was shocked and rushed to her mistress, who was relaxing in bed.

"Rise up, O deluded queen!" she said. "Your husband who professes to love you has cheated you. Having sent your son away to his maternal grandparents, he is now set on crowning Kausalya's son Rama as heir apparent tomorrow. Beguiling you with sweet words, your husband has behaved like a treacherous serpent!"

Kaikeyi rose up, filled with delight at the news of Rama's impending installation. She presented Manthara with a beautiful jewel, since she was the first to bring the good news to her, and said, "Thank you for letting me know this. In my eyes there is no difference between Rama and Bharata. I'm

25

delighted with the king's decision."

Manthara was shocked at Kaikeyi's reception of her news. She threw away the jewel and spoke in a scornful tone. "I cannot believe that you can be so blind to the misfortune that is to befall you. Once Rama becomes king, you will be only a maid to Kausalya, and your son too will be degraded to the status of a servant to Rama."

The hunchback ranted and raved over the calamities which she foresaw for her mistress and would not listen to Kaikeyi's praise of Rama. Kaikeyi could not foresee any of the dire possibilities which Manthara kept insisting would happen, but at last, after listening to her tirade for a full hour, Kaikeyi also began to believe that all that Manthara said was true and the king had indeed plotted to deprive her son of his lawful position. This shows us how important it is to keep the company of noble people. This is why there is so much emphasis in scriptures on the value of *satsang* (the community of devotees to God, a saint or a spiritual path). Once we start mixing with wicked people, even the most elevated mind will slowly succumb to their poisonous insinuations.

At last, the agitated Kaikeyi begged Manthara to tell her how she could save her son from this dire misfortune which was to overtake him. Manthara reminded her of the two boons which Dasaratha had promised her long ago. Once, he had taken her along on one of his military sorties. At that time, he had been sorely wounded and fell into an unconscious state. Kaikeyi had skillfully maneuvred the chariot and taken him to a safe place. When he regained consciousness, he was so grateful to her for having saved his life that he asked her to choose two boons. She had kept the offer open and had almost forgotten about it. Manthara now reminded her of these boons and asked her to demand first that Bharata be crowned heir apparent and second that Rama be banished for fourteen years to the forest, which would be enough time for Bharata to consolidate his position in the country. Manthara advised the queen to enter the apartment specially reserved for sulking wives, and lie there with hair disheveled and torn clothes, thus indicating to her husband the unhappy state of her mind. Goaded by the hunchback, Kaikeyi proceeded to carry out all her orders, her own good sense completely vanished.

At nightfall, the King entered Kaikeyi's chamber, eager to share the news of the forthcoming event with his favorite consort. He was quite dejected to see that she was not awaiting his arrival as she usually did and to hear that she was in the sulking chamber. He hurried to that room and was horrified to see his beauteous wife writhing on the floor with her jewels scattered everywhere, her hair unkempt and face dark with anger.

"What is it my dearest one?" the old king inquired in distress. "Who is it that has dared to offend you? What is it that you lack? Whatever be your wish, don't hesitate to ask. You know that I will gladly give you anything you ask for."

Kaikeyi then spoke, "I have neither been insulted nor treated with disrespect, but I desire something which only you can give me. Promise me that you will fulfill my desire; only then will I rise up."

The infatuated monarch smoothed her disheveled locks with his hands and placed her head on his lap, and solemnly swore that he would grant her whatever she wished.

The queen, knowing full well what effect her request would have on him, cruelly spoke the following words, as prompted by Manthara.

"O king! Do you remember the time when I saved your life in the war and guarded you till you regained consciousness? At that time you promised me two boons. The time is now ripe to redeem your pledge. I request you to install my son Bharata as Prince Regent and to banish Rama to the forest for fourteen years. These are my two wishes and if you do not grant them, you will be proving yourself a traitor to the noble family into which you have been born and will be guilty of the great sin of breaking your solemn word!"

The king could not believe that he was hearing such cruelty coming from his beloved's mouth. Unable to bear the anguish which her words had caused him, he fainted.

Coming out of his swoon at last, the king said, "What has possessed you, O wicked woman, to ask for such terrible boons? What has the innocent Rama ever done to you? When the whole of the country is extolling Rama's virtues, why are you alone bent on ruining him, as well as this noble race? You know full well that I cannot continue to live without seeing Rama, even for a day. Are you bent on killing your husband as well? What demon has possessed you, O Kaikeyi? Have I been nurturing a viper in my bosom all these years? I beg of you, I will fall at your feet, but please spare me from going against my word, for I cannot agree to this most terrible request." Thus saying the agonized king fell at her feet.

But the queen, whose good sense had been completely stilled by the wicked words of Manthara, retorted cruelly, "How can you, who claim to be the scion of the Ikshvaku race, break your word to me not once, but twice, for you not only gave me your word at that time, but also just now. Shame on you, that you should be so false to your own race and have no pride in your status as a king! Hear this, O perverted king. If Rama is installed as Prince Regent, I shall surely drink poison in front of your eyes and die here this very minute." Saying this, she sank down and refused to utter a single word.

The demented king now ranted and raved about how all the other kings would despise him when they heard that he had canceled his own command to have Rama installed and placed Bharata in his stead and also sent the peerless Rama to the forest. What would he say to Sita? What could he say to Kausalya?

"O wicked woman! Do you want to kill your husband and enjoy the kingdom with your son? How will my darling and delicate Rama survive in the forest? How will the daughter of the king of Videha bear separation from her beloved husband?" Thus wailing, the unhappy monarch writhed in pain on the floor, beside his cruel consort.

The night passed and the auspicious day on which the installation was to take place had dawned. Sage Vasistha entered the city with his disciples and requested the minister Sumantra to apprise the king of his arrival. Sumantra was astonished to see the king on the floor and Kaikeyi sitting in a dishevelled state beside him. She ordered him to go and get Rama. Sumantra left immediately and brought Rama to the king's chamber. As the chariot with Rama and Lakshmana seated within passed through the streets thronged with people, Rama was hailed on all sides and showered with flowers and jewels. Entering the royal palace, Rama bowed before the dejected king and Kaikeyi. He was surprised to see his father, who was usually so happy to see him, sitting with eyes cast down.

"Have I caused you any unhappiness, O father? In what way have I displeased you?" he asked.

The king could not speak or even raise his eyes to look at him. Kaikeyi said, "The king is neither angry nor displeased with you. He is unhappy because he does not wish to keep the promise he gave me long ago. It is your duty as an obedient and loving son to see that your father does not break his word. One who breaks his word will have to go to a special hell, reserved for such people."

Rama was astonished to hear this and said, "How can my father doubt that I would not obey his commands! I would jump into the fire if he so ordered me."

Kaikeyi now spoke again, "Well know this, O scion of the Raghus, the two boons I have asked for are these: that my son Bharata should be installed as Prince Regent in your place and that you should be banished to the forest for fourteen years! Your father cannot bear to carry out these wishes of mine and that is why he has such a sorrowful look and refuses to look at you."

Not by a flicker of an eyelid did Rama betray the fact that the news was a great shock to him. He had come there expecting to be feted and fawned over and instead he had been stung as if by a venomous serpent, yet his countenance showed no anger or hatred.

In an even voice, he asked, "How can you doubt, O princess of Kekaya, that I would be disobedient to my father's wishes, even though I have not heard this command from his own lips. Yet your wish is my command. Just give me time to take leave of my mother Kausalya and the princess of Videha and I shall do your bidding and go to the forest with matted locks this very day as desired by you."

Thus saying, Rama circumambulated his father and Kaikeyi thrice and backed out of the room. The agonized king was choking with grief and could not utter a word. Rama walked out of the palace without a backward glance. Nothing in his mien or behavior gave an inkling to his waiting friends and citizens of the shocking news which he had just received. Waving aside the white umbrella and fan of royalty, he strode into his mother's apartments, in complete control of himself and his emotions as befitted a *sthitha prajna*, a master yogi, who had risen above all the pairs of opposites.[1] But Lakshmana strode after him, eyes blazing with anger, and face suffused with fury, his hand clutching and releasing the sword at his side, as if ready to draw and kill even his father if Rama so desired it.

Rama entered his mother's apartments accompanied by Lakshmana and saw her seated for *puja* (worship). She rushed to

---

[1] *risen above all the pairs of opposites*—Hindu's (and Buddhists) believe that a master yogi rises above opposites such as good and bad, big and small, out and in etc. to the ground on which all pairs of opposites rest.

greet him, embracing him fondly and offering him a jeweled seat. Rama merely touched the seat. He was sad at having to upset his mother but there was no way of breaking the news gently to her.

"O mother!" he said, "I fear I have to give you some bad news. This jeweled throne is not for me, nor the white umbrella, for by my father's orders I am to proceed directly to Dandaka forest, clad in bark and existing on fruits and roots for the next fourteen years, while Bharata rules in my stead."

Hearing this shocking news, Kausalya fell to the ground in a dead faint. When she recovered, she began to lament, "O my beloved son! Can I be hearing aright! Can the king give such a shameless order. How can I live without you! For many years after he married Kaikeyi, the king had treated me with scant respect, but at least after you were born I had some claim to merit. But now without you I shall surely be despised and treated like Kaikeyi's servant. I will not stay, but will follow you as a mother cow follows her calf."

Hearing this, Lakshmana, who was in a furious mood, spoke up. "O brother, who will follow the orders of a man in his dotage who is completely under the thumb of a woman. Who but a fool would forsake a son as godly as you and listen to the prattle of his wife. Before anyone comes to know of this shameful fact, take up the reins of administration in your own hands and install yourself as Prince Regent. Both the priests and the people will support you, and I will stand guard over the gates of the city, ready to kill anyone who thwarts you, even if it be the king himself or Bharata. On what authority does the king dare to give the kingdom to Kaikeyi's son, when you alone have sole right over it? I shall kill my aged and wretched father, who is in his second childhood, and hand over the reins of government to you this minute!"

Hearing this, Kausalya added, "Indeed Lakshmana speaks rightly. I will not grant you permission to go to the forest. If you go, I shall fast to death."

Knowing her agony, yet unable to help her, Rama spoke to his mother, "O noble lady, please try to understand that I cannot flout the command of my father, even if it brings grief to you and to me. Our land is filled with stories of great men who, at the behest of their fathers, were ready to carry out any order. It is my duty as a son to do this. Moreover, I have already given my word to mother

Kaikeyi and will not back out of it. It is your duty to bless me and give me leave to carry out my duty."

Then turning to his brother he said, "O Lakshmana, I'm well aware of your great love for me, as well as your valor, but remember that I have pledged my word to do my father's bidding and, in so doing, I'm also redeeming the pledge he made to Kaikeyi, which must be honored by me. O gallant Lakshmana, I have taken my stand in righteousness and it is your duty to help me to carry out the royal command. This is not the time for violence, my dear brother. It is not worthy of you to sink into unrighteousness."

Once again he turned to his mother and said, "Grant me leave, O mother, to carry out my father's wishes. After fourteen years in the forest, I shall return. It is your duty as well as Sita's and mother Sumitra's to abide by the commands of my father. Such is the eternal law of dharma."

Even after he said this, Kausalya wept and begged him not to go. Time was running out and Rama was impatient to leave before anyone else tried to dissuade him.

Once again he turned to Lakshmana, saying, "O Lakshmana! I know of your everlasting devotion to me but both you and my mother have failed to understand me fully and you are both harassing me most painfully. Dharma, *artha* and *kama* are the three goals of human life but all these will lead to *moksha*[2] (liberation) only if a person follows the path of righteousness. Which is the man of righteousness who would fail to perform, as a sacred obligation, a command given by his aged father? My mother is his wife and so long as her husband is alive, she cannot follow me to the forest like a widow. It is her duty to remain here and pray for my successful return. Therefore I beg of you to give me leave to depart to the forest. Life is of short duration and I will certainly not accept the trivial sovereignty of the world if I have to resort to unrighteousness in order to get it!"

Thus saying, he circumambulated his mother and said to his brother, "Curb your anger against my father and Kaikeyi and be joyful that you have helped your father to keep his word. The only way you can help me is to see that all the materials which have been brought

---

2 *dharma, artha, kama* and *moksha*—Hindus consider these the four goals of life. Dharma is living a righteous life according to spiritual precepts. *Artha* is goods and wealth that result from right livelihood. *Kama* is pleasure resulting from physical relationship. *Moksha*, said to be beyond the other three and the fruition of them, refers to enlightenment or God realization.

for the coronation ceremony are sent back. Without wasting any more time, see that everything is ready for my departure to the forest. See to it that Kaikeyi's mind is not in the least agitated by the fear that I shall back out of my promise. I hold nothing against her. It is fate alone which has decreed that I should go to the forest and that the kingdom should have been snatched from me at the last moment. Kaikeyi and Manthara are only instruments in the hand of providence. How else could my gentle mother, Kaikeyi, ever have conceived of such an idea? To the best of my knowledge, I have never offended her at any time, and I have never made any distinction between my three mothers. A decree of providence cannot be set aside by anyone. Joy and sorrow, fear and anger, gain and loss, birth and death will all come in their time. An individual who comes under the sway of these pairs of opposites will always be unhappy. Only he who can surmount the pain and pleasure caused by them can be called a man of enlightenment. Despite the shock which I received this morning, I feel no agony and no anger. Therefore, O Lakshmana, take my advice and do not give way to remorse over my loss of fortune. To me, it makes no difference if kingship or exile falls to my lot. In fact, the latter is more favorable, for it gives me an opportunity to redeem my father's pledge."

All these words failed to convince Lakshmana, for he was of a fiery temperament, but Kausalya realized that Rama was firm in his resolve and could not be shaken and she said, "I see that you will not waver from your high resolve and therefore I give you my blessings. Let good befall you at all times, my beloved son. Destiny is all powerful and cannot be averted. As for me, I shall have no peace of mind until I see you return, safe and sound. How can I sleep on my silken bed when you are sleeping on rocks and stones? How can I eat the palace fare when you are living on roots and fruits? How can I wear satin clothes when you are clad in bark? I will sleep soundly only after you return to my arms once again, my darling son. May that dharma which you follow so scrupulously protect you. May your path be smooth and may your every undertaking meet with success. Depart happily, my beloved son, and return safely, protected as you are on all sides by my constant prayers." So saying, Kausalya controlled her grief and blessed Rama, who fell at her feet. Rama now proceeded to his own palace to convey the unwelcome news to his wife.

Sita was waiting joyfully for the arrival of her husband,

accompanied by bards and waving of the ceremonial fans. She was shocked to see him come alone, looking pale, for he was not sure how to break the news to his dearest wife.

"What is troubling you, my noble Lord?" she asked. "How is it that you have come alone and unaccompanied by minstrels? The auspicious time has come and yet you have not gone to the hall. Tell me what is the cause of this change of plans?"

Rama briefly narrated to her the story of his father's promise to Kaikeyi and of his banishment to the forest and Kaikeyi's demand that her son Bharata should be installed as Prince Regent.

"It is your duty, my dearest wife, to stay with my aged mother and look after her, as well as your father-in-law, and pass your time in prayer and penance until my return. Do not displease Bharata in any way for he will be king in the future, and be sure to treat all three mothers equally."

Hearing Rama's words, Sita, though a docile and meek wife, could not bear the thought of separation from her beloved husband and spoke out forcefully.

"What you have just said is unworthy of you, O scion of the race of Raghu! Fathers and mothers all reap the consequences of their own destiny. It is only the wife who actually shares the fortunes of her husband. For a wife, her husband alone is her refuge. Therefore I shall follow you wherever you go, my darling. I shall go before you and crush the thorns in your path. Accompanied by you, the forest will be as secure for me as my parental home. Without you, this palace will be a forest for me. I too long to see the mountains and the lakes and flowers of the wilderness, my darling one. I can spend hundreds of years with you in this fashion without any sorrow. Heaven itself has no charms for me without you. I assure you that I shall not be a burden on you. I shall serve you as I have served you here and we shall delight in each other's company and rejoice in the beauty of nature."

Rama said to her, "My dearest wife, you have painted a rosy picture of life in the forest but, believe me, this is far from being the case. You are a tender and frail princess, totally unfit for life in the harsh jungle, filled as it is with wild beasts, *rakshasas* (a kind of demonic being) and other poisonous creatures. There will be none of the delicacies which you have been used to and no one to wait upon you. You cannot imagine such an existence and that is why you are speaking like this. But please heed my words and desist from this idea. I say this for your benefit and not because I think you will be a burden to me."

None of this could deter Sita from her firm resolve. "My Lord," she said, "how many times have I begged you to take me for a trip to the forest and now when the opportunity has come, why are you denying me? I have been told by *Brahmin* soothsayers that I was fated to go one day. The time has now come for the prophecy to come true. In fact, I feel quite delighted at the prospect of a prolonged stay in your enchanting company. I cannot live even for a minute without you, my dearest love. If you refuse to take me, I will take poison and give up my life here and now in front of your eyes. Nothing can deter me from my resolve to follow you, so please don't waste your time trying to convince me of the rigors of forest life."

Rama was actually delighted to hear her words. He had been dreading the thought of parting from her and had tried to deter her only from a stern sense of duty but now that she was so adamant in her resolve to accompany him, he gave in gladly.

Folding his agitated wife in his arms, Rama spoke soothingly to her and kissed away her tears. "Not knowing the strength of your purpose, O Janaki (daughter of King Janaka), I tried to stop you, not because I wanted to leave you, but only because it was my duty to point out to you the dangers of forest life. You know that I cannot bear to cause distress to you, my lovely princess. O beloved Sita, heaven has no charms for me either without your bewitching presence. I too would love to frolic with you in the woods and glades and on the mountain tops, so make haste and give away all your jewels and costly clothes and prepare yourself for a long journey with me."

Sita was overjoyed that Rama agreed, and hurried to do his bidding.

Lakshmana, who had been listening to this dialogue between Rama and Sita, could not bear the thought of being separated from him and said to Rama, "O brother, I cannot remain in Ayodhya without you. I will go with you and clear the path for both of you so that you can blissfully enjoy the beauties of the forest."

Rama tried to deter him with these words: "Who will look after our aged mothers and father if you come with us, O Lakshmana? I know of your great love for me but it is your duty to stay here and be a support to our aged parents."

"How can you doubt, O brother, that Bharata will look after both our mothers as if they were his own! Shatrugna will be there to help him, so have no fears on that score. Kindly condescend to take me as your attendant. I will bring a sword and spade and my bow and arrows and cut the creepers and trees which stand in your path. I will stand guard over you and Sita day and night so that you can sport with her on the mountain tops, undisturbed by any evil forces. Please do not stop me from coming with you, my dear brother, for my mind is made up."

Rama knew it was useless to try and dissuade Lakshmana, so he agreed to take him. He told him to go and take leave of his dear ones and to collect his two heavenly bows and quiver of inexhaustible arrows and his two invincible swords and return immediately. As soon as Lakshmana returned with the weapons, Rama instructed him to call Suyajna, the son of his preceptor Vasistha, so that he could worship him and give away all his wealth and thus get his blessings before departing to the forest.

Thus ends the fourth chapter of the glorious Ramayana *of Sage Valmiki called "Kaikeyi Plots."*

Hari Aum Tat Sat

FIVE

THE BANISHMENT

*Sathyavrathaya
Namaha!*

Homage to the
upholder of Truth.

*Rama was the son of Dasaratha
Sita, the daughter of Janaka.
Rama followed the advice of Vasistha,
And Sita of Shathananda.*
—SOURCE UNKNOWN

RAMA, SITA AND LAKSHMANA all gave worthy presents to the *Brahmins* and to their servants, as well as to the afflicted, the destitute and the impoverished. Then they proceeded to their father's palace to take leave of him. As the three of them walked through the streets, without a chariot and attendants, the people exclaimed in sympathy.

"What dreadful misfortune has befallen our noble prince that he should walk unescorted like this through the streets! Look at the princess of Videha, whose face has never been seen by anyone, walking like an ordinary woman. How could the king banish a son like this whose character has been acclaimed by all! Strange are the ways of destiny." Thus spoke the citizens of Ayodhya who were heartbroken to see the condition of their beloved prince. "Let us also follow him into the forest, and let Kaikeyi and her son rule over a deserted land. Let rats and mice play havoc, eating the grains and foodstuffs which are stored here. Let Ayodhya turn into a forest while we convert the forest into a city with Rama."

Though he heard the laments of the citizens, Rama was unperturbed and continued his journey to Kaikeyi's apartments to see his father. The king ordered his minister to fetch his other wives before Rama entered. Both Kausalya and Sumitra came, accompanied by their attendants. As Rama entered, the

37

king rose and went forward to meet him but he was so overcome with emotion that he collapsed. Rama and Lakshmana ran forward and helped him to his couch.

With folded palms, Rama said, "Kindly grant me permission to leave for the forest, O king! And kindly allow Sita and Lakshmana to accompany me. They refuse to be left behind even though I have tried to dissuade them from coming."

The wretched king now spoke in tortured accents, "Because of the pledge I had made to Kaikeyi, I have been forced to act in this senseless fashion. I beseech you to take me captive and ascend the throne yourself, this minute."

Rama smiled and said, "I have no desire for sovereignty, Sire. I will proceed to the forest and redeem your pledge. I shall clasp your feet once again after my return."

Urged by Kaikeyi, the afflicted monarch said in faltering accents, interspersed with tears, "I give you leave to proceed to the forest, my dearest son, but remember, this promise has been extracted from me by Kaikeyi, by a trick. I cannot bear to see you go. At least stay this night with me and your mother so that we might delight in your presence for a few more hours before you depart."

Rama was pained to hear this request of his father and said, "Please do not try to deflect my intention, Sire. Neither kingship nor comforts can give me the joy which I gain by carrying out your wishes and thus ensuring that you keep your word. Do not worry about us, dear father. We shall play with the deer in the forest and have the association of sages and saints. I have promised Kaikeyi that I shall leave this very day and I must keep my word. Do not give way to grief, my Lord. Let the land be given to Bharata. I bear him no ill will. Do not grieve on my account. I shall live in the forest as happily as I have lived in the city."

The bereft king now clasped his beloved son to his bosom and blessed him, crying all the while. As Rama backed out of the room, followed by Sita and Lakshmana, Dasaratha told Sumantra, his minister and charioteer, to take a contingent of the army together with all precious articles and provisions and drive the three of them to the forest. Hearing this command, Kaikeyi remonstrated and said that this was very unfair since Bharata would inherit a barren land if the king insisted on sending all the precious articles in the treasury with

Rama to the forest. The king was wounded to the quick by these words but Rama intervened and said in his gentle fashion, "Father, what is the use of burdening me with the wealth which I have already forsaken? A forest dweller does not need wealth nor an army. It is the monarch who needs protection, so let Bharata enjoy all these luxuries. I want none of them."

Kaikeyi now asked her maid to bring pieces of bark, which was the correct apparel for forest dwellers, and very kindly presented a set to each of them. Rama immediately took off his silken apparel and donned the bark. Ill clad though he was, nothing could mar the nobility of his towering personality. Lakshmana followed suit. Sita looked dismayed at the pieces of bark in her hands and did not know what to do with them. She looked appealingly at her husband. Rama took the bark from her hands and tenderly fastened them over her clothes. All those present wept at this. The women spoke up and begged Rama not to take Sita.

"Kaikeyi cannot demand Sita's banishment. Let us at least rejoice in seeing her countenance, even though we cannot see yours. If Sita goes, we will also come with you." Turning to Kaikeyi, they continued, "The whole state of Kosala will accompany Rama to the forest and you can rule over a barren land. Even your son, for whose sake you are doing all this, will curse you, for he is devoted to Rama. You should be giving Sita jewels, O queen, and not the bark of a tree. Are you not ashamed of yourself? Infamy will be your lot if you persist in this wickedness."

Sita, who was listening to all this, was not in the least put out, for she was quite excited at the prospect of following her husband to the forest. Dasaratha also exhorted Kaikeyi not to insist that Sita wear the clothes of an ascetic.

"O wicked woman," he said, "what do you gain by forcing the delicate princess of Videha to wear such clothes? Let her go if she insists, but let her be allowed to wear clothes befitting a princess."

He told his minister to go and take the costliest jewels from the treasury and personally decked his daughter-in-law with finery. He then ordered Sumantra to fetch the chariot and take Rama to the forest. All the ladies started to wail. Kausalya then clasped her daughter-in-law to her bosom and gave her words of advice. Rama requested his father to take special care of his mother Kausalya, for he feared she would not be able to bear the parting. The three of them circled their father thrice and then turned to their respective mothers.

Sumitra was the bravest of them all. Clasping Lakshmana to her bosom, she said, "You have my permission to accompany your brother to the forest, my son. May all go well with you. Look upon Rama as your father, Dasaratha. Regard Sita as myself, your mother. Let the forest be your Ayodhya. Depart happily, my son. My prayers will always be with you."

Luckily for Lakshmana, his wife Urmila did not seem to have put up much resistance to his going, nor did she insist that she accompany him. No doubt the thought of going into the forest for fourteen years was intimidating for a delicately nurtured girl like a princess of Videha. As for Sita, she was obviously an extraordinary woman, as Rama was an extraordinary man. An ordinary woman would never have had the courage to forgo the comforts of her regulated life in the palace and embark on a life of rigorous discipline in the wilds. That is why all the sages extol her fidelity and love for her husband, which enabled her to dare anything for his sake. Lakshmana's character, as indeed Bharata's too, is marked by the fact that they were totally devoted to their brother. Nothing seemed to give them as much pleasure as service to Rama. Indeed, this is another point to be remembered when we analyze Rama's character. His charisma was such that no one who came within his orbit could resist him. Everyone, including monkeys and bears, were drawn irresistibly to him. Such was the power of his commanding personality and such the power of his love, which he gave to all without discrimination—blood brothers or adopted ones, he was beloved to all.

Requested by Sumantra, the three of them entered the golden chariot in which were kept the weapons of the two brothers and the glorious raiment and jewels which had been bestowed on Sita by her loving father-in-law. As the chariot started to move, the citizens clung to its sides, praising Rama and bewailing their lot. Rama told the charioteer to move faster. Looking back, he was most distressed to see that even the aged king and his mother were following the chariot along the dusty road. Though he was sorely grieved at the sight, he knew that it would be fatal to stop and turn back to comfort them. Even Rama's strong mind wavered at the sight of his mother, bereft and weeping, running after the chariot. Sternly controlling his emotions, he ordered Sumantra to drive faster so that the painful scene would not be prolonged.

He left behind a city in which life was frozen into immobility. The fires in all the hearths died down, for no one cared to attend to them. No food was cooked that day in Ayodhya, for no one could eat a morsel. Cows lowed piteously and refused to feed their calves. All shops remained shuttered and closed. No one could think of either food or recreation. Even the sun was obscured by clouds, so that it appeared as if darkness had fallen on the city soon after Rama left. The city of Ayodhya which had been festooned and gay earlier that same day appeared to be in deep mourning—the banners were fluttering forlornly in the wind, the garlands were torn and flowers scattered, clouds of dust rose up in the streets and citizens with sad, unhappy faces wandered about, lamenting malevolent luck which had robbed them of their savior at the last minute.

They cursed Kaikeyi, who was the root cause of the problem. Dasaratha kept his eyes glued to the fast vanishing chariot until at last only the dust raised by the wheels remained. Then he turned and tottered back to the palace, refusing Kaikeyi's help and leaning heavily on Kausalya's arm. The whole night the bereft parents sat and lamented their lot, until at last Lakshmana's mother Sumitra came and gave wise counsel. She told them that they should be proud to have a son who was such a *dharmatma* (righteous soul), one who was so committed to righteousness, who was prepared to give up a kingdom so that his father's word would be honored.

The next evening the charioteer Sumantra returned to Ayodhya at dusk. Dasaratha was anxiously waiting for information about Rama but the only news which Sumantra could give him was that Rama had crossed the river at night and had asked him to return to town. He believed that Rama had proceeded to the forest of Chitrakoota.

Both Kausalya and Dasaratha were greatly agitated on hearing this news and Dasaratha related the story of how, in his youth, he had once inadvertently killed a young ascetic in the forest who had been filling his pot with water in the river. Mistaking this gurgling sound for the sound of an elephant, he had killed the boy with his arrow. The parents of the boy were blind and had no one to help them and when they heard of this heinous act, they cursed the king, that he too would meet his death in his agony of separation from his son. Then they gave up their lives.

After the griefstricken king had narrated the entire episode to Kausalya and Sumitra, he fell into a swoon from which he never awoke. When the bards came to wake him up the next morning, they found him dead. The consorts of the king started wailing and lamenting their loss. The whole city was immobilized with grief. The sages urged Vasistha to send for Bharata and Shatrugna immediately and to install Bharata as king, for a land without a ruler would be an easy prey to invaders. Messengers were forthwith sent to the land of Kekeya to recall the princes.

Thus ends the fifth chapter of the glorious Ramayana *of Sage Valmiki called "The Banishment"*

Hari Aum Tat Sat

He who protects himself with the name of Rama,
Can never be harmed by the denizens of the nether worlds.

—RAMAYANA OF TULASIDAS

SIX

BHARATA'S VOW

I bow to this divine couple
Who look like each other,
I worship them for fulfillment.
—DEVOTIONAL SONG

Pithrubhakthaya
Namaha!

Homage to the
one who was true
to his ancestors.

IN THE MEANTIME, ALL THE citizens who were able to follow had run after Rama's chariot, determined not to be left behind. Rama tried his best to persuade them to return but they refused, so the three exiles alighted from the chariot and walked with them, until they reached the banks of the Tamasa river. Here all of them spent the night. A bed of leaves was made for Rama and Sita and here they slept, while Lakshmana and Sumantra kept watch. Waking up well before dawn, Rama observed that the tired citizens were still fast asleep. He feared that they would keep urging him to return. So he called Sita and Lakshmana and requested Sumantra to drive them to the forest before the others woke up. In the morning, the citizens were heartbroken to find Rama gone and they sadly traced their way back to Ayodhya.

Meanwhile, the chariot quickly crossed the boundary of Kosala and arrived at the banks of the Ganga, where they were met by the Nishada chief Guha, who was delighted to meet the young princes and Sita. The tribal chief did all he could to host the royal three. That night was spent on the banks of the sacred river. At dawn, Rama woke and requested Guha to take them across the river. He asked Sumantra to return to Ayodhya, for from there he preferred to proceed on foot. The charioteer was very unhappy to hear this and begged him to return with him, for the king had made him promise to bring Rama back. However, he had no option but to obey him.

Rama said, "Sumantra, it is up to you to take care of my father. There is no one so devoted to our family as you. Please bring back Bharata immediately and then my father will feel better. Tell the king that I am not in the least unhappy at leaving Ayodhya and living in the forest. Sita and Lakshmana also are not unhappy. After fourteen years, I shall return and take the dust of his feet. Convey my respects to my mothers and love to Bharata and Shatrugna. Sumantra, it is your duty to return and give what comfort you can to my aged parents. Please don't worry about us." Reluctantly, with tears streaming from his eyes, the noble Sumantra returned to Ayodhya.

In the meantime, Guha had arranged a boat and soon the three of them were rowed across the sacred river, Ganga. From there they proceeded on foot, much to Sita's delight. The next day they reached the hermitage of Sage Bharadwaja, picturesquely situated at the holy spot *prayaga*, the confluence of the rivers Ganga and Yamuna and Saraswati. Having spent the night at that delightful hermitage, they proceeded the next day to the sacred hill of Chitrakoota, as directed by the sage. Rama was very conscious of the duty he owed to Maithili Sita, the dainty princess of Mithila, who was prepared to brave the dangers of the forest in order to be with him, and he tenderly helped her over the rough patches and kept up her spirits. She, on the other hand, was filled with delight at seeing all the wonderful plants and flowers of the forest and kept exclaiming with delight at everything, pointing out many new things to Rama and asking him about them. Rama said, "O Lakshmana, please walk in front of the princess of Videha and clear a path for her so that her tender feet will not be hurt by the sharp stones and thorns. I will come after and guard her from the rear. If you see any beautiful flowers or fruits, please pluck them for her."

Lakshmana was delighted to do this service and soon Sita was loaded with bunches of flowers and fruit, so that she looked like a wood nymph. As they approached the region of Chitrakoota, made holy by the sages who lived there, Rama pointed out to Sita the various interesting things to be seen.

"Behold these trees, my love, heavy with fruits and nuts, this huge hive filled with honey and all these delicious roots. We will never go hungry. Though you may not have the delicacies of the palace, you will feast on the abundance of nature. You shall sleep on a bed of fragrant grass and flowers and have the nightingale to sing a lullaby for you. You will be awakened by the cooing of the wood pigeons. Tell me, are they not more melodious than the bards of Ayodhya?"

Thus beguiling Sita with many interesting stories, the party soon reached the holy mountain of Chitrakoota. Rama requested Lakshmana to build a hut of wattle, for he felt that this was the right place for them to live. Lakshmana made a beautiful cottage for them and for three months they lived comfortably and happily at this charming place.

Sita and Rama used to roam the mountains hand in hand while Lakshmana kept watch. Tiny wildflowers carpeted the hillsides, and silver cascades tumbled down the rocks. One day Rama and Sita bathed in the Mandakini river and then relaxed on the banks, tired by their walk and the swim. Sita leaned against a tree while Rama slept on her lap. Then an incident occurred which she was to narrate to Hanuman long afterwards.

Rama dropped off to sleep, and a sharp wind came and whipped off her top scarf. Just at that time, a crow who was flying by saw the beauty of her breasts and flew down and pecked at them, as if he suspected them to be berries. Sita screamed and shooed it off again and again. Rama, who had been sleeping, had not witnessed the incident. Hearing her cries, he woke up but he didn't realize the extent of her injury and told her not to distress herself and went back to sleep. Again the crow swooped down and pecked her hard. Rama woke up when drops of hot blood fell on his face. Then he realized that this was no ordinary crow but Jayanta, the son of Indra. He became very angry when he saw Sita's tearful face and taking a reed, he muttered the fierce incantation of Brahma and aimed it at the crow, who flew off in great fright. The empowered reed followed the crow to all the worlds and at last, in great terror, Jayanta returned to Rama and begged his forgiveness. As usual, Rama could not resist a person in distress, so he agreed to spare his life. But the reed, once discharged and made potent with the mantra, had to find a target, so instead of killing him, it blinded the crow in his right eye. Rama then comforted his frightened wife, who was sobbing with pain and rage.

While the three exiles were, for the most part, having a comfortable sojourn in the forest, the messengers sent by Vasistha brought back the two princes, Bharata and Shatrugna. As they entered the city of Ayodhya, they were surprised to see the gloomy looks of the citizens. They went first to the king's apartments and, not finding him there, Bharata then went to his mother's abode. Kaikeyi rejoiced to see her handsome son. When questioned by him about the sorrowful looks of the citizens and the absence of his father, she told him the entire story and waited for his look of joy at the thought that he would soon be installed as king. Bharata couldn't believe his ears. He was amazed to see how little his mother knew him.

"Surely my eldest brother Rama should be king and not me!" he exclaimed.

Now Kaikeyi told him the whole story of the king's promise and Rama's exile. She waited expectantly for her son's words of appreciation at his mother's cleverness. She was shocked at his reaction. He jumped back as if stung by a wasp and exclaimed in horror, "Can you really expect me to rejoice at this news? Having deprived me of the two people I value most in life, my father and my brother, do you imagine that I will seize the throne for myself and rejoice at my good fortune? O wicked woman! I cannot bear to call you 'Mother'! It was my misfortune to have been born in your womb. You have brought nothing but calamity on our race. And now you are bent on exterminating it? What possessed you to act in this insane fashion!" Having ranted and raved at his mother thus, Bharata rushed to Kausalya's apartments, for he could not bear to look at Kaikeyi's face.

Kausalya turned her head away when she saw him approach. He was totally bereft at this treatment and fell at her feet, pleading his innocence. At last she was convinced of his ignorance of his mother's plot and comforted him. Controlling his grief, Shatrugna and he proceeded to perform the last rites for his father.

The next day Sage Vasistha requested Bharata to come to the court and urged him to accept the kingdom. Bharata refused the offer and said that he had decided to go to the forest to try and persuade his brother to return and take up his rightful heritage. When this news leaked out, the whole city decided to accompany him. A huge cavalcade, consisting of elephants, horses and chariots, soldiers and even the three dowager queens, set out happily, determined to persuade Rama to return. When they reached the banks of the Ganga, the Nishada chief, Guha, gave orders that they should be stopped from crossing the river, for he suspected some foul play on Bharata's part. But when he realized that Bharata's intentions were completely honorable, he allowed him to proceed. From there, they went to the hermitage of Sage Bharadwaja, who apprised them of Rama's whereabouts. The sage, with his extraordinary powers or *siddhis*, proceeded to feed the entire army in a lavish manner, much to the amazement of all, for such a feast could not be had, even in a palace.

The next morning the entourage proceeded to Chitrakoota. Rama had been sitting outside the hermitage with Sita, beguiling her with his graphic descriptions of forest life, when he realized that the whole woodland was in an uproar. Birds were screaming and animals running about and a cloud of dust could be seen rising in the distance. He asked Lakshmana to climb a tree and find out the cause of this disturbance. Lakshmana was horrified to see the approaching army with Bharata at its head and decided that Bharata had followed them with the sole intention of killing Rama, thus ensuring that there would be no contender to the throne. He swore that he would kill him before they dared to approach. Rama pacified his impetuous brother and they awaited Bharata's coming, with some trepidation on Lakshmana's part and full confidence on Rama's.

Bharata's eyes were so full of tears at the sight of his brother with matted locks and bark clothing that he stumbled and would have fallen had not Rama run forward and caught him in a tight embrace. Seating Bharata next to him, Rama tenderly inquired about the welfare of his father and others. He was greatly upset to hear of his father's death. Bharata begged Rama to return and take up the reins of government, for he felt himself unfit for the task. Rama advised him to do his duty, as he himself had done, and return to Ayodhya and rule for fourteen years till his return. Bharata tried many methods to persuade Rama to come back. He even said he would fast unto death unless Rama returned However, Rama, with his usual conciliatory and pacifying words, persuaded the griefstricken prince to do his duty. Then Bharata begged that he be allowed to stay in the forest in lieu of his brother but to this Rama also gave a negative reply and said that, in this case, there was no question of proxy. It is rare indeed to find such a noble soul as Bharata, especially in those times when it was quite common for the younger brother to kill the elder and usurp the throne. If Rama was the soul of dharma, Bharata was in no way inferior to him and was the very soul of honor. The *Ramayana* is thus an inspiring narrative where characters vie with each other to sacrifice their interest for others.

In the meantime, Vasistha led the royal ladies to Rama's presence. Rama hugged his mother and bemoaned the loss of his father. Rama and Lakshmana then performed the last rites for their father. Bharata was at last reconciled to the fact that he would have to play the role of Prince Regent, for that appeared to be the only way that he could serve his beloved brother. From the many beautiful articles which he had brought for his brother, Bharata took out a pair of polished, wooden sandals, embellished with gold. These he put before Rama and requested him to kindly place his feet on them. He swore that he could never ascend the throne of his father, which rightfully belonged to his brother, but would place the sandals on the throne and be only an instrument for carrying out the orders of his brother. He also swore that as long as his brother lived in the forest, he himself would also live outside the city, wearing the bark of trees, with matted locks and subsisting only on fruits and roots as his brothers were doing. This he would do for fourteen years, at the end of which, he would immolate himself in the fire, if Rama did not return.

Rama embraced his noble brother and tenderly stroked his head as Bharata sobbed on his shoulder. He blessed him and told him that he would certainly return the moment the fourteen years were over and take up the reins of government. He then placed his holy feet on the sandals and stood for a few minutes in contemplation and then removed them and gave them to his brother. Bharata placed the footwear on his head and circumambulated Rama thrice. Then he walked away while Rama bade farewell to his mothers, for he could not bear to see them weep. Having paid obeisance to the elders and his guru, Rama walked into the hut, eyes filled with tears, for he could not watch them depart.

The royal party returned to a forlorn and bereft capital. The citizens wore gloomy faces, for they had failed in their endeavor. Having taken his mothers back to the palace, Bharata decided to take up his residence at the village of Nandigrama, a few miles away from Ayodhya. The golden throne of the kings was brought to Nandigrama and he placed the wooden sandals on the throne and bowed low before them.

He said to his ministers, "The kingdom will be ruled by me as a sacred trust till my brother returns. Hold the white umbrella of sovereignty over these sandals, for they will rule and not me. Until I see his royal feet placed once more on them, I will live like an ascetic." All those who had assembled applauded these noble sentiments.

For the next fourteen years Bharata lived a hermit's life. Every day the ministers came from Ayodhya and they were also clad in bark. They would bow low to the sandals, as they would before the king, and all matters of state would be discussed before them. For fourteen years there was no sound of mirth or music in Ayodhya. The chariot wheels were removed and all the people walked, since Rama had to go on foot. Only the gardens around the empty palace was kept watered and alive, waiting for Rama's return. At least Rama had Sita and Lakshmana with him and they enjoyed the simple pleasures of forest life until Sita was kidnapped. Bharata is not even mentioned by Valmiki till Rama returns. But we can imagine what a strict life he led, denying himself even the simplest of pleasures. With the tangled hair and rough clothing of an ascetic, he refused even the pleasure of eating good food. It is said that his only fare was a few grains of wheat soaked in water. He would talk to the sandals and report everything to them. He did nothing without consulting them. It is impossible for us to even imagine such character. Such sacrifice and self-denial are not seen even in sages. No wonder that Bharata has been extolled as a paragon of virtue.

An aura of gloom covered the *ashrama* after Bharata left. The tear-stained eyes of his brother haunted Rama. None of the three could forget the painful episodes connected with Bharata's visit. The cottage which had once been a scene of joy, was now filled with sorrow.

At this time, Rama noticed that the sages who lived in the other *ashramas* seemed to be troubled about something. When he enquired into the matter, he was told that the *rakshasas* living in their settlement, called Janasthana, had begun to harass them. The *rakshasas* were cannibals and would swoop down on the *rishis* (sages) and carry off many of the ascetics. Their leader was called Khara and he was the cousin of their king, Ravana. Due to this harassment, the sages decided to leave Chitrakoota.

Hearing of these events, Sita and the two brothers also decided to leave. They proceeded to the well-known *ashrama* of Sage Atri and his wife Anasuya, who was famous for her chastity and for her *tapas*.

They were welcomed with great love by the old man and his wife. She took Sita inside the hut in which they lived and praised her for her fidelity and love for her husband and her courage in renouncing the comforts of palace life for the rigors of life in the forest.

Sita, in turn, said, "Mother, if you only knew the wonderful qualities of my husband, you would not marvel that I prefer to be with him rather than live in the luxurious apartments of the palace." Anasuya was delighted to hear this reply. She caressed Sita fondly and told her to ask for any boon. She had done so much of *tapas* that she was capable of giving boons.[1] Sita was surprised. This was the first time that she had met a lady ascetic who had accumulated so much power by austerities.

Sita smiled and said, "Mother what need have I for boons? Am I not the most fortunate woman alive? Have I not got the noblest living being as my husband?"

Anasuya was charmed by this reply. She brought all the garments and jewelry which she had and adorned Sita like a bride. She also gave her specially prepared perfumes which would make her smell sweet and keep her fresh all the time. Then she made Sita recount the events of her *swayamvara* (ceremony where groom is chosen), which she did with great joy. By this time, night was falling and the old lady blessed her and told her to go to her husband. Rama's eyes lit up with appreciation when he saw his beloved, dressed as she had every right to be.

They spent that night at the hermitage. In the morning, Atri asked Rama to go to the Dandaka forest. He said that the forest was infested with *rakshasas* who delighted in harassing the *rishis*. He asked him to go there and protect the sages from the torments of these cannibals and allow them to continue their life of simplicity and renunciation. Rama willingly agreed to this and the three exiles entered the dark and forbidding forest called Dandaka.

Thus ends the sixth chapter of the glorious Ramayana *of Sage Valmiki called "Bharata's Vow"*

Hari Aum Tat Sat

---

[1] *capable of giving boons*—Hindus (and some Buddhists, Catholics, Eastern Orthodox Chistians and other religions) believe that performing spiritual austerities and penances of various kinds (*tapas*) gives powers, including the power to grant blessings (boons).

Meditate on the long-armed Sri Ramachandra,
Who is cloud blue in color, has matted hair,
And is adorned with all accoutrements.
Who wears yellow clothes and is holding,
The bow and arrows and sitting in the lotus pose.
His lotus petal eyes are turned to his left,
And are gazing at the lotus face of Sita.

—SOURCE UNKNOWN

BOOK THREE

*Danadakaranya-
karthanaya
namaha!*

Homage to the
Lord of the Dan-
daka forest.

ARANYA
KANDA

THE BOOK OF THE FOREST

SEVEN

THE FOREST DWELLERS

Raghupunghavaya Namaha!

Homage to the most illustrious of the Raghus.

Rama, Born of the womb of Kausalya.
Sita, Born from the womb of the earth.
Rama, With eyes like a lotus petal.
Sita, Gaze, sparkling like the moon.
—POPULAR SONG

THOUGH THE FOREST LOOKED DARK and gloomy from the outside, as they went into it, they were amazed to find that it was filled with *ashramas* in which many sages lived. The pleasant aroma of sandalwood and incense coming from the sacrificial fires assailed their nostrils. They noticed that even the wild animals walked about freely without fear.

Rama and Lakshmana unstrung their bows for they realized that they had nothing to fear in this place. There were lakes and flowers in plenty and the trees were laden with fruits and nuts. The spiritual energy which permeated the place could be physically felt by all three of them. Rama's fame had spread before him and the sages welcomed him with love and invited him to spend the night at one of the hermitages.

The next morning the three of them set out once again, penetrating deeper into the forest. It was only now that they understood why this forest had been called fearful. The ground was rough, trackless and deserted. The trees were twisted with lianas trailing their tentacles down, ready to catch the throat of the unwary traveler. Bamboo thickets infested with snakes creaked in the dry, hot wind. Wild animals like tigers, wolves and bears roamed at large. The birds seemed to have been struck dumb for they no longer chirped happily as they had done at Chitrakoota. Even the lakes looked deep and forbidding with dark waters in which no lotuses grew.

Sita crept closer to her husband and timidly caught the end of his bark garment. He turned and gave her a reassuring look and held his hand out to her. She clung to his strong arm and shivered at the ominous sounds coming from the thickets. He knew that this was not the type of forest which she enjoyed and held her comfortingly close. Sometimes he carried her across swamps and dying trees.

They passed many heaps of white bones belonging to hermits who had been killed and eaten by the cannibals. They proceeded cautiously, with Lakshmana in front, and Sita, clinging to Rama, coming after him. Lakshmana hacked his way through the fierce undergrowth of poisonous roots and vines.

Suddenly an enormous figure sprang up in front of them and blocked their path. It held a trident in its hand on which were impaled the carcasses of lions, deer and an elephant, all dripping with blood. A long red, hairy arm reached out and grabbed Sita around the waist and held her high above the branches of a tree while she screamed and struggled. The creature roared at them.

"Who are you who have been foolish enough to enter the dreaded Dandaka forest? You are dressed like *rishis*, yet walk around with weapons and a woman in your midst. My name is Viradha and I live by eating those *rishis* who are stupid enough to enter this forest. You shall provide my fare for today and this woman I shall make my wife."

Seeing his beloved trembling like a leaf in the vile hands of the monster, Rama lost his courage for a minute. Tears welled up in his eyes as he thought of the injustice he had wrought on his princess by bringing her here. But Lakshmana was undaunted. He sprang at him with upraised sword. But Viradha laughed scornfully and said, "Desist from this foolishness, O stupid mortal. Know that I have a boon by which I cannot be killed by any weapon. So leave this woman with me and I'll let you go unmolested."

Rama was furious when he heard this and sent seven scorching arrows at the monster which simply fell off his chest. He dropped Sita on the ground and rushed at Rama with trident upraised. Rama split the trident in two and Viradha lifted both brothers on his shoulders and marched off into the forest, leaving Sita bereft. She sobbed loudly and begged the monster to take her and leave her beloved alone. Rama and Lakshmana proceeded to chop off the monster's arms. Thus maimed, he fell to the ground but they were unable to kill him.

At last Rama said, "Lakshmana, let us strangle him and bury him. That's the only way he can be killed."

As soon as he heard these words, Viradha said, "Ah, now I know who you are. You are Rama. You are the one who has been ordained to rescue me from this curse. I am actually a *Gandharva* (celestial singer) who has been cursed by Kubera (god of wealth). Please hurry up and bury me. Then I can leave this dreadful body and regain my own form. After burying me, you should proceed to the hermitage of the great Sage Sharabanga and take his blessings."

Rama and Lakshmana did as he told them and the *Gandharva* was released from his curse and returned to his heavenly abode.

Night was falling by now, and Rama took Sita's hand in his so that she would not be frightened. She forgot her fatigue and they hurried towards the *ashrama*.

When they arrived, they saw a divine chariot waiting outside. They waited and soon saw Indra, the king of the gods, coming out of the hermitage and leaving in the golden chariot. The old sage was waiting for their coming, his heart filled with joy. In fact, it is said that he had refused Indra's offer of taking him alive to heaven, for he did not want to leave this earth without having a glimpse of the Lord in the form of Rama. He asked Rama to bless him with his loving gaze while he shed his mortal frame and entered the blazing fire.

The next day all the *rishis* living in the neighborhood came with a supplication to Rama. They showed him a heap of bleached bones and told him that it belonged to the hermits who had been killed and eaten by the *rakshasas*. They begged him to rescue them from the constant threat of these creatures. Rama gave his assurance that he would kill the *rakshasas* and enable them to perform their austerities in peace.

The three of them proceeded to the *ashrama* of the Sage Sudeekshana, who was expecting them, having known by his intuitive powers of their coming. He invited them to stay there as long as they liked but the three of them decided to continue onward and check on all the other *ashramas* in the forest, as they had promised the sages.

After a good night's rest, they set out once again, penetrating deeper into the dark forest. As they walked on Sita, spoke gently to her husband.

"My Lord," she said, "for a long time I have been wondering about the meaning of the word 'dharma'. It is not always easy to know what one's dharma is. To act without swerving even a hair's breadth from it is possible only for one who is absolutely without desire. I'm frightened, my Lord, of the possible consequences of your promise to the ashramites, to protect them from the *rakshasas*. They have done you no wrong, yet you are prepared to kill them. Is this not against the dictates of dharma? I don't think we should go further into this forest. If you see some *rakshasas*, your fingers will itch to string your bow, for that is the duty of a *Kshatriya*. But now you have adopted the garb of a hermit. Don't you think you should live like one? Forgive me for presuming to speak to you like this, for I know that you are the very soul of dharma. It is only my fear of the unknown that has prompted me to speak."

Poor Sita, little did she realize that what she spoke was the truth and she herself was going to be victimized for Rama's killing of the *rakshasas*.

Rama was pleased to hear this discourse on dharma by his dutiful wife. He replied lovingly to her. "O Janaki, you are the daughter of Janaka, one of the wisest men of the age. It is not surprising, therefore, that you should know all the nuances of dharma. But consider the predicament of these sages, my love. They have abandoned all worldly pleasures only for the sake of *tapas*. By their *tapas*, the country itself gets purified. All negativity will be cleared. At present, they are unable to perform their austerities due to the harassment of the *rakshasas*. They have begged me to save them and since I'm a *Kshatriya* and their king. Don't you think it is my duty to protect them? Even if they had not requested it of me, it would have been my duty to do so. Now, of course, after having given my word, I cannot dream of breaking it. I know well that it is only your wifely concern for me that made you speak as you did and I thank you for it, but, my dear, I cannot stand by and see these poor ascetics being devoured by these cannibals, even if it brings their wrath on my head."

Thus saying, Rama walked ahead with Janaki following and Lakshmana in the rear.

Thus ends the seventh chapter of the glorious Ramayana of Sage Valmiki called "The Forest Dwellers"

Hari Aum Tat Sat

Meditate on the blue-colored Rama,
With lotus eyes,
Who carries the sword, bow and quiver in his hands.
Who exterminates the night wanderers.
Who incarnated himself in order to save the world,
even though he is the ever-full Unborn.

—SOURCE UNKNOWN

EIGHT

THE GROVE
OF FIVE TREES

*Janardanaya
Namaha!*

Homage to the
one who removes
the evils of birth
& death.

Rama's Chest smeared with sandal paste.
Sita's Breast with saffron powder.
His hand, splendid with the bow.
And hers, with the lotus.
—POPULAR SONG

THUS THE MONTHS AND YEARS passed in happy companionship as the three of them wandered in the forest of Dandaka, going from *ashrama* to *ashrama*. Everywhere they were welcomed with delight, for Rama's fame had spread to all the far corners of *Bharathavarsha* and everyone longed for a chance to see him and offer them hospitality. At some places they stayed for six months, at others a few days, and sometimes even a year. Fortunately they were not accosted by *rakshasas* at any of these stops.

Sita forgot her fears and wandered happily behind her husband, enthralled by the beauty of the peaks, the lakes, the birds and the animals. She would exclaim in delight at many of the small things which had escaped the notice of Rama and Lakshmana. She would pick a twig here and a leaf there and put a flower into her hair. She would peer curiously into the nest of a small bird and run after the deer. The beauties of nature were always a delight to her and she did not pay heed to the hardships which such a life would naturally bring, nor did she miss the sophistication of palace life. As she had told Anasuya, even the most luxurious life would have been torture to her without the presence of her beloved husband. To her, nothing was as wonderful as walking hand in hand with her beloved, lying in the sun

61

on the mountain tops with him beside her, allowing him to place a flower garland in her hair, or just sitting beside him listening to his voice. Lakshmana too never seemed to miss his own wife and derived maximum joy from serving the two of them.

One day Rama had gone to the forest for hunting and Lakshmana had gone to collect firewood, leaving Sita alone. It was getting dark and cold and she began to feel frightened so she decided to go after Rama. It was the first time she had ventured into the dark forest alone and she kept tripping over roots and getting caught in brambles.

She walked on and on, crying out "Rama! O Rama! Where are you?" Soon tears started rolling down her cheeks and falling to the ground. She heeded them not and walked on. At last, she heard his answering call and saw him resting beneath a tree. She ran towards him and was caught in a fierce embrace.

"Why did you come here, my darling?" he asked, holding her close.

"It was getting so late and I couldn't find you and I felt so frightened!" she whispered into his broad chest, where her face was smothered.

"Wasn't Lakshmana there to keep you company?" he asked. "I had particularly told him never to leave you alone."

"He had gone to bring firewood, and I couldn't bear to be alone any longer."

He didn't have the heart to scold her and they started to walk back home, but the way was long and Sita was weary. Seeing her distress, Rama took her in his arms as one would a baby, and strode along, while her arms entwined themselves around his neck. It was a hot summer night and drops of perspiration rolled down his thighs onto the ground. At last, they reached the *ashrama* where Lakshmana was anxiously awaiting their return. Rama chided him gently for having left Sita alone.

The next week, Sita wanted to go back along the path they had taken, since that was her first, and perhaps only, solo venture into the forest. As they walked hand in hand, they noticed that some strange new saplings had grown up in those spots where Sita's tears had dropped and another type of saplings where Rama's drops of perspiration had fallen. Within a few months, the saplings had grown into bushes and Sita was delighted to find that one set of trees had strange-looking green fruit and the other set had reddish colored fruit.

Both types tasted delicious. They had never seen such fruit before so Rama laughingly told Sita "These green fruits shall henceforth be known as 'Sitaphal.'"

Then Sita retorted that the reddish fruit should henceforth be known as "Ramphal." To this day, these fruits are found in India and are called by those very names.

Twelve years thus flew by without any of them feeling the weight of them. However, to poor Bharata, residing at Nandigrama, those twelve years were like twelve aeons, for the burden of kingship lay heavily on his shoulders and he did not have the exhilarating presence of Rama to keep up his spirits.

Now Rama remembered his promise to Sudeekshna to visit his *ashrama* once again. So they decided to return to that place. The sage was very happy to see them. Rama asked directions to the *ashrama* of the famous sage known as Agastya. Sudeekshna gave them directions and the next morning the three of them set out to pay their obeisance to him. It was in the thirteenth year of their exile that they crossed the Vindhya hills and walked down the southern slopes. They first came to the hermitage of Agastya's brother, who told them many stories about his wonderful exploits.

Agastya was a very slightly built man and he had been doing *tapas* up in the Himalayas. At one time, the Vindhya hills became jealous of the Himalayas and began to grow so high that none could cross them. They blocked even the passage of the rain-bearing clouds to the north. Agastya remedied this. He came from the Himalayas and requested the Vindhya hills to lower themselves to allow him passage to visit the South and to remain thus until his return. They bowed their heads low to allow him to pass. He never again went back to the North and the Vindhya is still waiting with bowed head for him to return. Agastya also subdued the might of the two demon brothers, called Vatapi and Ilwala. After staying the night with Agastya's brother, they proceeded to their destination.

All of them were excited at the prospect of meeting this eminent sage about whom they had heard so much. As they neared the *ashrama*, they noticed that the deer were very tame, the bark garments of the ascetics were drying in the sun, and perfume arising from the sacrificial fires was pervading the air.

Rama told Lakshmana to go and announce their arrival.

Lakshmana did as he was told. Agastya was apparently expecting them, and told his disciple to bring them in immediately. Though the sage was slightly built, he was aglow with the fire of intense *tapas*, and as he came toward them, they were not even aware of his small stature. He welcomed them with great cordiality and, after finishing the fire ceremony, gave them food and presented Rama with many divine weapons given to him by the gods: the bow of Lord Narayana, the inexhaustible quiver of arrows given by Indra and a sword with a silver scabbard, which Narayana had used to fight the demons. With all humility, Rama accepted the wonderful gifts though he didn't know of what use they would be to him in this forest life. Agastya, however, knew that the time was fast approaching when Rama would need all his weapons.

He said, "O Rama, the time of your exile is drawing to a close and your hardships in the forest will soon be over. May you return with all glory and take up the reins of the kingdom once again."

Rama replied, "O Holy One, our life in the forest, far from being unpleasant, has actually been a very happy time for all of us. We have delighted in the freedom and informality of our life here and have been blessed by our contact with great sages like you and charmed by the simplicity of life in the *ashramas*. However there is one thing I would like to ask you. Could you please let me know of a suitable place where we could stay for the remainder of our exile? It should be beautiful, with a river and flowering shrubs, so that my wife will be happy, yet it should not be crowded."

Agastya said, "Rama, it is right indeed that you should always think of your wife's happiness, for very few women would have been ready to forego their comfort and pleasures, to go forth into the forest with their husbands. Sita is indeed an exemplary wife and you should take great care of her. You have been brought into this forest in order to rid the place of the *rakshasas*, the night wanderers who have made it their home. There is a place not far from here called Panchavati. Fruits and roots are in abundance there. There is plenty of water and deer can be seen bounding all over the place. I'm sure Sita will be delighted with that spot. You can make an *ashrama* there and live happily till it is time for your return. I would have asked you to remain with me until your exile is over but I can see that there are many things left for you to do and Panchavati is the place from where these will be accomplished."

Taking leave of the great sage, the three of them followed his directions and soon came to the beautiful grove known as Panchavati. On the way, they noticed an enormous eagle perched on the very tree which Agastya had given as a landmark. The bird was greatly excited at seeing them and introduced himself as Jatayu. He said he had been a friend of Dasaratha. He said that he had a brother called Sampati whom he had not seen for many years. Jatayu promised to live with them and guard them and give warning at the approach of *rakshasas* and wild animals. Rama was delighted to hear this and Jatayu showed them the way.

Panchavati was a wonderful place surrounded by mountain peaks and filled with fruit-laden trees and flowers. The sound of the river Godavari close by and the gurgle of its stream were delightful to the ears. Having chosen a level spot, close to the stream, with five flowering trees—*champaka, parijatha, ashoka, kadamba* and sandalwood—Rama requested Lakshmana to build a small cottage for them.

Lakshmana first plucked some flowers and offered them to the gods for protection, requesting that they give him leave to build on that terrain. Then he built a beautiful cottage with twigs and wattle and a grass roof and invited Rama and Sita to enter. They were charmed with the place. He had made separate partitions for eating, sleeping and *puja*. Everything was made to look fresh and beautiful with an eye to utility as well as asthetics.

Rama laughingly asked him, "My child, where did you learn the art of construction? I can't remember ever having learned anything like that from our tutors at the *gurukula* (school run by the guru)!"

Lakshmana answered, "When love fills the heart, there is no task which is onerous or difficult. The magic of love overcomes all difficulties and gives all knowledge."

Rama's eyes filled with tears as he embraced him and said, "My dearest brother. How can I ever repay you for the loving service you have rendered to me all these years. My life during this exile would have been unbearable but for your constant and vigilant care and attention."

The three of them spent a long time in that beautiful spot. Sometimes Jatayu would join them and narrate tales of their father and they would talk of their past life in the palace, which felt as if it were a dream. Jatayu was always on guard against wild beasts and *rakshasas*, and would shriek wildly if any beast of prey came within fifty yards of the place.

Once, on a misty autumn morn, when the brothers were taking their bath in the Godavari, Lakshmana said, "I don't know why, but today my mind is filled with thoughts of our dear brother, Bharata. He must be also taking his bath in the cold waters of the Sarayu and perhaps thinking of us. What a noble soul he is! Instead of enjoying the pleasures of palace life, he is living like a hermit in Nandigrama in order to show his love and respect for you. Poor thing, I fear he does not know the happiness that I enjoy, for he is denied the felicity of your company. How is it that such a noble soul was born in the womb of such a wicked woman as Kaikeyi."

Rama's eyes filled with tears as he replied, "My child, speak more to me of our glorious brother, Bharata, but don't let me hear you speak ill of our mother. After all, she was only a tool of fate. I too cannot rid myself of the memory of Bharata's tear-filled eyes as he pleaded with me to return with him. I can still see him placing my footwear on his head and going back, with tears streaming from his eyes. How can I forget that scene? Very often it haunts me in the night. I fear that I am fated to bring unhappiness to those I love!" These were indeed prophetic words which Rama spoke.

Thus the three of them spent many blissful days at Panchavati, each doing his allotted task, offering their daily prayers and enjoying the beauty of nature. Sita spent the happiest years of her life there. She would roam through the forest with Rama, clutching his hand, while he plucked flowers for her. She would sit still while he braided her hair and twined it with blossoms. At night, they would lie close to each other on the hill tops, watching the stars above.

One day while they were walking hand in hand, Rama lifted his hand to point to something and inadvertently wiped off the vermilion mark on her forehead. He was most apologetic and searched for a red stone, which he crushed into powder and applied it once more with great care on her forehead and then he smeared the rest of the powder on her cheek, in order to tease her. Sometimes if a stream was too deep, he would carry her in his arms and when they reached the other bank, she would refuse to get down and he would pretend to throw her into the sky and she would laugh and nestle closer to him. She was in a blissful dream all the time and Rama too found great happiness in the beauty of nature, as well as the beauty of his charming bride and the companionship of his brother. Little did they realize that the time was inexorably coming close for the purpose of his *avatara* to be fulfilled, and the reason for his exile to be completed.

Thus ends the eighth chapter of the glorious Ramayana *of Sage Valmiki called "The Grove of Five Trees."*

Hari Aum Tat Sat

He who chants the name of Rama,
Will never be touched by sin,
And will get both material wealth and liberation.

—*Ramayana of Tulasidas*

NINE

THE NIGHT RANGERS

Kharadwamsine Namaha!

Homage to the one who killed Khara.

I bow to Sri Ramachandra,
Who has a beautiful dark color and lovely eyes.
Who is full of wonderful qualities and who is sweet spoken.
To whom the entire universe bows
And who fulfills the desires of his devotees.
—*RAMAYANA OF TULASIDAS*

O NE DAY WHEN THE THREE of them had finished all their small chores, done *puja* and eaten their simple meal, they sat outside in the shade of a beautiful *champaka* tree. Rama and Sita were sitting close together and he was teasing her about her fear of a small bear which they had seen when they went for a bath that morning. Lakshmana was sitting a little further off, whittling a piece of wood he had picked up from the river.

At that time, a *rakshasi* called Surpanekha, who was the sister of the demon king Ravana, happened to be passing by and she spied the two extraordinarily handsome men sitting under the tree. She was fascinated by the beauty and virility of Rama's body. Though he wore the matted locks of a sage, he had the stature of a *Kshatriya* and the nobility of a king. She gazed and gazed at him with delight. She could not bear to tear her eyes away from him, even though he did not notice her and seemed to be engrossed in talking to the girl beside him. Surpanekha decided that this was the man for her. The *rakshasas* were a race of cannibals and their morals were barbarous. What they desired, they took, regardless of the consequences and the propiety of such behavior. It didn't even cross her mind that he might find her offensive.

69

She was enormous, with flaming red hair and small cruel eyes. She had mottled, yellow, horny skin, like a toad, a belly like a cauldron with a protruding navel, flapping elephant ears and talons on her fingers and toes. She had just killed and eaten a rabbit and blood was dripping from her fangs. Throwing away the leg of the rabbit which she had been gnawing, she went towards Rama. She did not care about the fact that he was sitting with another woman who might well have been his wife. She was determined to have him and she approached with her elephantine gait and spoke in a harsh and raucous voice.

"Who are you, O handsome one? You are dressed as a *rishi*, yet your looks belie your appearance. Moreover, you have weapons at your side. How did you happen to come here?"

Rama replied politely, "I am Rama, the son of King Dasaratha. That is my brother Lakshmana who is sitting there and this is my wife Sita, the princess of Videha. Now tell me who you are and what I can do for you."

She replied, "I'm a *rakshasi* called Surpanekha and I'm the sister of Ravana. I happened to be passing by and saw you and fell in love with you. You are a fitting mate for me. Look at this puny little creature beside you. She is certainly not worthy of you. I will gobble her up in a trice, and your brother too, and we will roam around happily in this beautiful forest."

Saying this, she stood before him with arms akimbo, drawing herself up to her full height so that she towered like a mountain above them. Sita shuddered and crept closer to her husband. He put his arm reassuringly around her and laughed. He really could not believe that this woman was actually soliciting him in broad daylight, in front of his wife and brother. He was sure it was a joke.

Laughingly, he said, "My dear lady, I'm quite honored by your offer but you must understand that I'm a married man. Moreover, puny though she is, I happen to love my wife very much, even though it might surprise you. Sharing a man with another woman will not appeal to one like you, I'm sure. Look over there at my younger brother, who is fair and handsome and does not have his wife with him. Why not approach him?" Surpanekha thought this over and decided that he spoke the truth, so she approached Lakshmana and asked him in the same way to be her husband.

Lakshmana was also amused by her and decided to keep up the joke. He replied, "My dear lady, I'm only a servant of Rama. How can a princess like you be happy with a servant? You say that you can change your form at will. Why not take a beauteous form and press your suit with Rama with increased vigor? I'm sure he can be persuaded to leave his ill-favored wife and marry a beautiful woman like you."

Surpanekha was not used to this particular brand of humor. She returned to Rama and said, "I see that you are not interested in me only because this ugly woman is sitting beside you. I'll devour her and thus you can be rid of her and we will be able to consort together without any fear of this creature."

With this ultimatum, she turned her eyes, like burning hot coals, on the trembling Sita and rushed towards her. Sita screamed and clung to Rama. He stood up and put her behind him and spoke to Lakshmana.

"It was wrong on our part to sport with such a being. Look how frightened my Sita is. Please punish this woman and send her away, O Lakshmana. We will not kill her, since she is a woman but we should teach her a lesson, so that she will go away and leave us in peace, or else she might come back when we are not here and harass poor Sita."

Lakshmana immediately took his sword and sliced off the tip of Surpanekha's nose and ears. Roaring with rage and pain and swearing revenge, she ran off into the forest. The ground shook with the weight of her steps and the birds flew off with shrill cries of fear. She ran to the *rakshasa* settlement, called Janasthana, where her cousin Khara lived, and poured out her whole story. Of course, she omitted that she was responsible for the whole incident, having invoked the wrath of the Kosala brothers in the first place.

Khara swore to take revenge and called fourteen of his best soldiers to go and put an end to the intruders who had dared to harm his sister. Surpanekha then led them to the *ashrama*. The three exiles were sitting and discussing the extraordinary events of the day, when the *rakshasas* arrived. Rama turned to Lakshmana and said, "It looks as if we are in for a bit of fighting. Guard Sita while I go and finish them off."

So saying, he went toward them and killed them in no time, as he had promised to do. Surpanekha could not believe her eyes. She had never seen human beings who could stand up to even one *rakshasa*, let alone fourteen. She ran back and stood, howling like a jackal before Khara.

"What's upsetting you now?" he enquired. "I have sent my men as I promised and by now Rama must have been devoured by them."

Surpanekha said scornfully, "You are a disgrace to your race. I think you are frightened to go and face them yourself. Your men are all lying in a lake of blood, killed by Rama, single-handed!"

Khara was amazed by this and ordered his commander, Dhushana, to lead fourteen thousand warriors to fight this man. The army poured out of the fortress, armed to the teeth, in order to kill two puny humans.

Far away in the *ashrama*, Rama saw many omen and heard the roaring sound of the approaching army, coming like a tidal wave.

He told Lakshmana, "I'm afraid I'll have to deny you the chance of using your weapons, O brother, but I think it is better for you to take your weapons and go to that cave with Sita. I dare not leave her alone, even for a minute. That woman may come and devour her while we are both engaged in fighting. Please do as I tell you."

Lakshmana reluctantly took Sita and left his brother to fight alone. Rama saw that they were safe inside the cave. He then strung his bow and prepared himself for battle. Twanging the string of his bow he challenged the *rakshasas* to battle. Khara drove his chariot up to where Rama stood ready to fight and let loose hundreds of arrows, tridents, sickles, axes and many different types of weapons, while the rest of the army did the same. Rama stood like a rock, unmoved by the onslaught. Though wounded in many places, he fought on calmly, ably resisting the attack. The dexterity with which he handled his bow evoked the admiration of even his enemies. His arrows charged with mantras were so painful that the first onslaught of *rakshasas* turned tail and ran back, screaming with agony. Again and again, Khara sent his warriors, only to be decimated by Rama's deadly arrows. At last, only a few remained to tell the tale. Khara worried when he saw that his brave commander Dhushana had been killed. He then sent Thrishiras, another great general, who managed to wound Rama on the forehead. Rama admired his prowess but was forced to kill him in the end. At last, Khara began to worry whether he would also be killed. He advanced toward Rama in his chariot.

Rama, who was fighting from the ground, broke the demon's chariot and said, "No one who has been perpetrating such cruel deeds as you have has a right to live. How many innocent *rishis* have you killed? This is your last day, O Khara! Prepare to die."

Khara rushed at him with mace upraised and flung it at him but Rama splintered it into a thousand pieces with his arrows. Next Khara uprooted a huge tree and flung it at Rama, who warded it off easily. Blind with rage, Khara rushed toward Rama, determined to throttle him with his bare fists. Rama invoked the power of Indra into his arrow and sent it hurtling at Khara. It entered his chest and Khara fell down dead. Seeing their leader fall, the rest of the *rakshasa* army, including Surpanekha, fled in terror. Sita's peaceful and beautiful garden was totally devastated, strewn with arms, legs and heads, blood and bones.

Lakshmana now returned with Sita and congratulated his brother. Sita rushed to Rama and embraced him. She was so happy to see him alive. Tenderly, with her upper garment she wiped off the droplets of blood from his face and body. Her voice was choked with emotion and she couldn't speak a word. Though proud of her husband's prowess in combating so many *rakshasas* single-handedly, she had some foreboding that this was not the end of the affair and that their peaceful days were over.

Thus ends the ninth chapter of the glorious Ramayana *of Sage Valmiki called "The Night Rangers."*

Hari Aum Tat Sat

TEN

THE DEMON KING

I bow to Sri Ramachandra, the essence of the world,
Who is extolled in the Vedas,
Who is Dharma incarnate, born to decrease the load of the earth.
Who is the immutable ocean of goodness.
—SOURCE UNKNOWN

Dhushana- Trishiro Hantré Namaha!

Homage to the one who put an end to Dushana and Trishiras.

THE ONLY ONE WHO MANAGED to escape from the fray at Janasthana was a *rakshasa* called Akampana. Seeing that it was a lost cause, he had hidden himself behind a tree and watched all his friends fall. At last, he returned quickly to Ravana's capital on the island of Lanka and reported the whole matter. The *rakshasa* king could not believe that his best commanders had been killed and his entire army wiped out by one single individual.

Ravana glared at him and roared, "Who is this foolish person who has dared to meddle with my outpost at Janasthana? It is obvious that his end is near. Even Indra, the king of gods, is afraid of me, so also Kubera, the god of wealth, and Yama, the god of death. I spell death to Death himself, and my wrath can burn up even Agni, the god of fire. Name the person who has dared to defy me!"

Akampana shivered with fear and stammered, "My Lord, it was a man who did it."

"A man! A human being! I cannot believe it. I haven't heard any report of an army marching to Janasthana, so how can this have happened?"

"There was no army, Your Majesty. It was one single individual who routed the entire army and his name is Rama. He is the son of king Dasaratha, of the clan of Ikshvaku, the ruler of Ayodhya. He and his wife and

75

brother have been exiled and are now living in the forest at Panchavati. He is dark and handsome and is as strong as a lion. He is an amazing archer and he decimated the entire army single-handed."

Ravana could not believe this story. He said, "I'll go immediately to Janasthana and kill this man."

Akampana said, "I would not advise you to do so, my Lord. Rama is invincible. He can destroy this universe and create a new one if he wants. He has command of all *astras* (a kind of missile) and weapons. You will never be able to beat him in a fair combat. But I can tell you of a means by which you can defeat him. He has a wife called Sita, whom he loves dearly. She is his weak point. Her beauty is unparalleled in all the three worlds. Even the gods are bewitched by her charm. She is the daughter of King Janaka of Mithila. You will never be able to withstand her beauty. I suggest that you go to Dandaka and abduct her. If she is lost, Rama will not be able to live. He will pine away and die. This is the only way you can destroy him."

Ravana's eyes gleamed with green fire at the thought of another conquest to his harem. "Your idea is very good, O Akampana," he said, "I will go to the forest of Dandaka tomorrow and capture this beauty for myself. As you know, I am a connoisseur of women's beauty so let me add another jewel to my collection."

Ravana called for his golden aerial chariot, yoked to magic asses with the faces of fiends, and went to the *ashrama* of Maricha, the son of Tataka, whom Rama had sent hurtling off for a few hundred miles in his very first battle, when he went to save the *yajna* of Sage Vishvamitra. Maricha had now become an ascetic and was living a simple life at a place called Gokarna. He was honored that the king had come to visit him and paid him all respect.

Ravana did not waste time in idle talk. He came straight to the point. "My dear uncle," he said, "did you hear that the entire *rakshasa* encampment at Janasthana has been totally wiped out?"

Maricha was amazed that such a thing could have happened and wanted to know how it took place.

"It was wiped out by a mere mortal—a man called Rama!"
At the name of Rama, Maricha trembled like a leaf and began to perspire.

Ravana pretended not to notice, saying "Evidently, Rama possesses some sort of extraordinary powers or else this could not have happened. I hear that his wife Sita is amazingly beautiful. I wish to capture her and for that, I need your help. That is the only way to punish Rama."

Maricha said, "My Lord. Have you offended or insulted someone? For it is clear that someone wishes to see your downfall. The person who has suggested this to you is indeed your great enemy. Trying to steal Sita from Rama is like trying to extract a poisonous tooth from the mouth of a cobra. He is like a wild elephant who will crush you if you taunt him. Please don't attempt this foolish thing. I have had personal experience of his great strength and that at the age of sixteen. What will he be like now? That is why I took to a life of *sannyasa* (renunciation). I am old enough to give you advice and I have nothing to gain or lose from you, so listen to me and leave Sita alone. Let them live happily in the forest and be content with your own harem of wives. Do not lust after another man's wife."

Though Ravana was not put off by the tales of Rama's valor, he valued the advice of Maricha and decided to give up his plan and return to Lanka.

The next day, when Ravana was sitting resplendent on his golden throne and holding court, Surpanekha rushed in with her tale of woe. Ravana was extremely noble looking—the hero of many wars. There was no end to his glories. He and his son Meghanatha had even defeated Indra, the king of the gods. Ravana was the son of Vaishravas and the half brother of Kubera, whom he had defeated and from whom he had stolen the beautiful flying machine called Pushpaka, made out of flowers. He had obtained a boon from Brahma that he could not be killed by demons, gods, celestial beings or beasts. In his arrogance, he had not asked for immunity from humans, since he thought they were not worthy of his might. His atrocities and inequities had become so great that, at last, the gods were forced to approach Brahma and ask for protection. Vishnu had appeared before the gods and agreed to incarnate as a human being, in order to kill Ravana. This had happened just at the time when King Dasaratha was holding his great *yajna* for the sake of progeny and Rama, the seventh incarnation of Vishnu, had been born as his son.

Surpanekha now stood before Ravana and started howling like a mad dog about her bad luck. The story she told was totally different from actual fact. She began with a burst of venomous insults hurled at her brother.

"What sort of a king are you?" she shrieked. "You sit here indulging in wine and women, totally oblivious of your duties. Don't you know that your outpost at Janasthana has been wiped out by a mere mortal called Rama?"

Ravana let her rant and rave for some time. Then he interrupted her, "Who is this Rama? What does he look like? What are his weapons?"

"Rama is the son of King Dasaratha of Ayodhya. He looks like the god of love incarnate but he is deadly in combat. He shoots forth arrows which are like cobras. He has a brother called Lakshmana who is as valiant as he and who is completely devoted to him. He also has a wife called Sita, a woman whose beauty is beyond compare. He loves her very much and she is devoted to him. She has one of the most captivating figures that I have ever seen. Her color is that of molten gold, her waist is slender and can be spanned by your hand, her breasts are full and her hair is long and lustrous. Her eyes are like lotus petals and her beautiful hands have rounded, pink-tipped nails. There is no woman to equal her in all the three worlds. Seeing her, I thought that she would make a perfect mate for you. I tried to capture her and bring her to you as my gift and this is what Lakshmana did to me.

Rama was furious when I tried to capture his beloved wife and would have killed me, had I not been a woman. As it is, he has maimed me for life. If you have any compassion for me, if you want to avenge the death of your people at Janasthana, if you want to own that beauty for yourself, then go immediately and kill those two and capture her for yourself!"

Ravana dismissed the court and pondered his sister's words. He knew that Rama would be no mean match for him but his heart beat fast at the thought of getting Sita for himself. At last, his lust overcame his caution and he went again to Maricha's *ashrama*. Maricha saw him coming and was filled with foreboding, but he masked his feelings and welcomed the great personage.

"What has brought you once again to this humble abode, my Lord?" asked Maricha.

Ravana replied, "I told you already about this mean creature Rama who has killed my general and his forces at Janasthana and mutilated my sister. Obviously, he is a wicked fellow or else his father would not have banished him. Uncle, you are the only one who can help me now. My sister has pointed out that Sita is Rama's weak point. If I capture her, he is as good as dead. Now this is where you come in. I want you to take the form of a golden deer and go near Rama's *ashrama*. You should frisk and frolic in front of Sita and beguile her so that she will ask Rama to catch the deer for her. You should then lead him far away from the hermitage so that Sita will be left alone. Then I will go and capture her. What do you think of my plan?"

Maricha shivered at the thought of invoking Rama's wrath once again. His mouth had gone dry and he could hardly speak. At last, he stammered out a few words. "My child, you are an emperor and you are surrounded by sycophants. They will speak only what is pleasing to your ears and not what is good for you. Rama is full of noble qualities. He is more powerful than Indra and Kubera. His wrath will surely fall on your head if you steal Sita. She is dearer to him than life. She will surely be the cause of your death. You are now the happy and powerful emperor of the *rakshasas*. If you want it to last, let Rama alone. You have many women in your harem, all equally beautiful. Why should you lust after another man's wife?"

Ravana remained silent and Maricha thought he had almost convinced him. So he went on with his story.

"I will tell you of my first encounter with Rama, when he was only a boy of sixteen. Once when Sage Vishvamitra was performing a *yajna*, I was bent on disturbing it, so Vishvamitra brought Rama to protect his *yajnashala* (place where ceremonies are performed). I remember him vividly. What a wonderful picture he presented, young and handsome, with a huge bow in his hands. But I thought he was only a boy and continued with my act of desecrating the *yajnashala*. For some reason, Rama did not kill me, but his arrow pierced me and carried me many miles out and dropped me into the ocean.

A few years ago, I had my next encounter with him in the Dandaka forest. You know how we *rakshasas* love to eat the flesh of the *rishis* living in the forest. I had gone with two others, taking on the form of a deer, and we killed many *rishis* before I saw Rama. I thought that I would gore him to death to punish him for what he had done to me. I went near and charged at him with lowered horns. He shot just three arrows at us and my companions died on the spot. Somehow I managed to escape.

Since then, I decided to turn over a new leaf and take to the life of a recluse. I live here alone in this forest and shun all company. I have given up eating flesh and killing people and live only on fruits and roots. I am old and tired and all I want is to be left in peace and do penance for my sins. The very mention of the name Rama frightens me out of my wits. If you persist in this foolish plan, both of us will surely die. As for the tragedy at Janasthana, I'm sure Surpanekha must have instigated Rama's wrath. By listening to her lies, you will also come to a bad end."

Ravana now gave up all pretense of trying to coax Maricha. He had made up his mind to go on with his suicidal plan. Fate was beckoning him to his approaching doom.

In an angry voice, he said, "Maricha! You are overstepping the limits of decorum in talking to your king like this! I don't need any advice from you about what I should do. All I want is implicit obedience. Go immediately to Rama's *ashrama* in the form of a golden deer and entice him deep into the forest. If Lakshmana remains behind to guard Sita, you should imitate Rama's voice and cry in a loud voice, 'Ha Sita! Ha Lakshmana.' Sita will be frightened and send Lakshmana after Rama. At that time, I will enter the hermitage and capture her. After having done this, you can return to your own abode. If, however, you refuse to obey me, I will send you straight away to the abode of Yama (god of death)!"

Maricha was in a sorry plight but he realized that there was no way out. He knew he was doomed to die either way, so he thought to himself that it was better to die at Rama's hands than at the hands of this wicked nephew of his. He said sorrowfully, "Ravana, I see that we are both doomed. If you capture Sita, remember, you will be capturing death in your arms. As for me, this will be my third and last encounter with Rama."

Ravana scarcely heard what he said. "Come! Let us go," he said. "I will drop you near the *ashrama* so that no time will be lost."

He took Maricha in his aerial vehicle drawn by the magic asses and they soon came to the vicinity of Rama's *ashrama*. The chariot landed and Ravana told Maricha to make haste and change his form.

Thus ends the tenth chapter of the glorious Ramayana *of Sage Valmiki called "The Demon King."*

Hari Aum Tat Sat

Those devotees of mine who constantly repeat these names,
Rama, Daasharathi, Shoora, Lakshmananuchara,
Bali, Kakuthsa, Purusha, Poorna,
Kausalyeya, Raghuttama, Vedantavedya,
Yajnesha, Puranapurushottama,
Janakivallabha, Sriman,
And Aprameya parakrama,
They will have more benefit than those
Who have performed the horse sacrifice.

—Source unknown

ELEVEN

THE GOLDEN DEER

Mayamareecha hantré Namaha!

Homage to the slayer Maricha.

I bow to Sri Ramachandra, the scion of the race of Raghu,
Who, though of playful form, could annihilate all enemies,
Who was invincible in battle, and had a powerful voice.
—RAMAYANA OF TULASIDAS

MARICHA CHANGED HIMSELF into a most captivating deer. Its face was like a glowing golden topaz from which gleamed its amethyst eyes. Its hair was golden in color, with spots which looked like silver and glistened in the sun. Its dainty branching antlers were dazzling and seemed to be set with gems. Its hooves looked like black polished onyx. Its neck was long and curved and it had a tantalizing way of tilting its head at an angle and gazing sideways through its beautiful eyes. It appeared suddenly on the lawn in front of the *ashrama* and frisked and danced around, giving long looks in Sita's direction. At times, it would stop and pretend to be nibbling at the grass and at times, it would step softly, as if afraid of being caught. The other deer which were grazing nearby sensed that this was no ordinary deer and ran away in panic.

In his old days, Maricha would have loved to eat one of them. He kept looking at the *ashrama*, for Sita was not outside. Just then, she came out to gather flowers for their morning worship. The deer came close to her and stood still with bent head as if grazing. The morning sun fell in golden shafts on its skin and brought it flaming to life. Sita stood absolutely still when she saw it. She could not believe her eyes. She had never seen such a fascinating creature in all her days in the forest. Though her hand went automatically

83

to pluck the flowers, she could not tear her gaze away from the little deer, who took care to see that it was always within her gaze. It did the most absurd things to beguile her. It pranced and frolicked and turned its long neck to look sideways at her. It appeared almost human in its enchanting ways. She ran forward to try and catch it but it avoided her grasp adroitly and skipped off and stood just a few feet in front of her. Again and again, she tried to grasp it, but it skillfully avoided her. She tried to tempt it with bits of grass and leaves. Sometimes it would pretend to nibble but the moment her other hand came up to catch it, the deer would prance off like a filly, with a playful backward glance. She chased it round and round the lawn, forgetting the flowers she had come to pluck. Her flower basket had fallen to the ground and the flowers were lying forlornly on the grass. At last, she was quite dejected and called out to Rama and Lakshmana. Hearing her voice raised in appeal, both of them came running out of the house.

Raising her charming face to him, she said, "Rama, please capture this deer for me. Look how beautiful he is! Such an enchanting figure. I've never seen anything like it. I must have him for myself. Please catch him for me. He's so clever that he has dodged my every effort to catch him, but I'm sure you can do it."

Lakshmana peered closely at the deer and said, "Brother, I'm sure this is not a deer. This must be our old friend Maricha in disguise. Remember how clever he was in taking on the disguise of a deer, in order to kill the *rishis*. This must be him. No ordinary deer could be so extraordinarily beautiful."

Rama looked at Sita's excitement and was moved. He had never seen her so excited. He could deny her nothing. Moreover, there was no doubt about it. The deer was indeed enchanting. He looked at her tenderly and said, "My love, I shall surely capture this deer for you if that is your wish." Then turning to Lakshmana he said, "I think that your suspicions are correct and this deer could well be a *rakshasa*, but even so, it is my duty to kill it. Whatever it is, I must chase it, for Sita wants it and I can deny her nothing. If even a man like me should feel so attracted to this deer, then why not she? She loves all animals, as you know. I will either capture this deer alive or kill it and be back soon. Please stay with Sita. Do not leave her even for a single moment. Be on the lookout for danger. I can sense danger. It is close by. I feel that some crisis is imminent in our lives. Guard Sita with your life and I will return with the deer, dead or alive."

He strapped his sword to his waist and took up his bow and quiver. He turned to smile reassuringly at Sita. She looked adoringly at him. She was sure that her beloved Rama would get the deer for her. As he reached the edge of the forest, he turned round once again to look at her. It was the last time he was ever to see her so happy. Her wide-eyed, excited look and enchanting smile was to haunt him for many months before he saw her again.

Rama turned toward the deer. It was just in front of him, prancing and cavorting in its cute fashion. Rama was not unduly worried. He was sure the deer would fall to his grasp pretty soon. He followed casually but looked around for any danger, for he could sense it close by. Ravana's aerial vehicle was well hidden and he could not see it. Now the deer seemed to be playing some sort of game with Rama. It would come almost within his grasp and then dance away with a naughty look, as if to say, "catch me if you can." Rama began to get impatient and also to worry a little, for the day was wearing on and the deer seemed to have some deliberate campaign to lure him deeper and deeper into the forest. Like the moon playing hide-and-seek between the clouds, the deer would appear for some time in front of his gaze and then disappear within the forest. At times, it would turn and look at him with terror, then it would pause as if exhausted and pretend to rest, but as soon as Rama stretched his hand to catch it, it would dart away like an arrow, looking mockingly back at him.

Rama realized that he had come a long way from the *ashrama*. He also realized that this was no ordinary deer, but a *rakshasa*, just as Lakshmana had suspected. He stood still for a while and it suddenly appeared before him. He rushed toward it and the animal fled in panic. This was the end. He decided to kill it since it seemed impossible to capture it. Fixing an arrow to his bow, he let it fly. With unerring accuracy, the arrow entered the body of the animal and split it in two. Maricha howled and fell to the ground. As he fell, he regained his hideous *rakshasic* form. So Lakshmana was right, thought Rama, and this is indeed the wicked Maricha. His life was ebbing away fast and with his last breath he let out a cry. Imitating

Rama's voice perfectly, he called out loudly, "Ha Sita! Ha Lakshmana!"

Rama was deeply disturbed when he heard that cry, imitating his voice. He realized that the whole enterprise had been a trick to lure him away from the *ashrama* and now this cry was, no doubt, to bring Lakshmana to his aid. All of a sudden, he was terribly frightened. He feared for the safety of his beloved. What if some harm should come to her? Of course, he could depend on Lakshmana to guard her with his life but this cry was most disturbing. He knew that Sita would be distraught with grief when she heard it and perhaps she might even believe that he was in danger. He started to run back as fast as he could but he was a long, long way from the hermitage.

Far away in the *ashrama*, Sita heard that piteous call for help from Rama, as he thought, and she froze with fright. She was sure that it was her beloved and that he was in great danger. She forgot that he was an invincible warrior and there was no one who could defeat him. That pathetic cry took away all her capacity to reason and she turned to Lakshmana with an agonized look, saying, "Did you hear that call of My Lord? He is in distress. I want you to go to him immediately. He must be surrounded by *rakshasas* and his life must be in danger, otherwise he would never have cried out like that. Don't hesitate a moment. Hurry to his assistance!"

Lakshmana did not move an inch from his place. He was unmoved by that shout of Maricha's for he knew that it was only a ruse.

Sita was trembling with fear and anger and begged him repeatedly to go. Lakshmana did not know what to do. At last, he said, "O Sita! Don't you know that Rama is invincible in battle? Didn't you see with your own eyes how he slew so many hundreds of *rakshasas* single-handedly? Have you no faith in his prowess? As soon as I saw the deer, I knew it must be a *rakshasa* and I warned Rama but he paid no heed to me, for he wanted to please you. He will be back soon, I assure you. The voice we heard was not his, but Maricha's. Rama has asked me to stay by your side and guard you. I cannot disobey him, even if you entreat me. It would be very dangerous to leave you alone here at this moment. I feel that there is some danger lurking here. Rama felt it too; that is why he made me promise to stay with you, no matter what happened."

Sita was furious with him. Her fear had made her lose all sense of proportion. All she could think was that her Lord was in danger and this man was refusing to go to his aid. She rushed out of the *ashrama* and said, "If you don't go, I will!"

Lakshmana jumped up and caught her as she was running out. For one startled moment, they looked into each other's eyes. It was the first time in his life that he had ever touched her or even looked fully at her face. Both of them were shocked. Hurriedly, he dropped his hands and begged her pardon. Her unreasonable fear for her husband made her speak in the most unbecoming way to Lakshmana. Poor girl, driven by destiny, she spoke in a most taunting way to him.

"You are a traitor to Rama. You have followed him to the forest with some ulterior motive. Either you are a pawn of Bharata or else you have evil designs on me and you hope that if Rama dies you can have me for yourself. But let me tell you once and for all that I will kill myself, here and now, if you do not go immediately. I will not let you touch me."

Lakshmana recoiled in disgust when he heard these cruel words from the gentle Sita. He stood with folded palms before her and said, "Sita, I have always looked upon you as a mother. My own mother has given me this advice when I left Ayodhya—that I should regard Rama as my father and you as my mother. You are like a goddess to me and I refuse to be angry with you for what you are saying. Your words are, no doubt, prompted by your fear for your husband. I have never heard you talk like this. You are attributing a heinous crime to me, when I am completely innocent. I cannot bear to stand and listen to such talk. I will go after my brother but I fear that something is threatening you. Please don't force me to go."

Behaving like a common woman, Sita beat her breast and swore to kill herself if he did not go. She berated him severely and threatened to throw herself into the river or jump into the fire. Lakshmana was in a panic. He didn't know what to do. At last, with tears in his eyes, he said.

"All right, I will go, but first I will draw this magic circle around you. Please see that you do not step out of it. As long as you remain within it, you will be safe. I go with the greatest reluctance.

My brother is sure to be most displeased with me. But it looks as if I cannot please both of you at the same time." So saying, he took the tip of his bow and made an enchanted circle round her with mantras. He bowed to her and walked away with unwilling steps.

All Sita could say was, "Go, go, go!" Reluctantly and with many a backward glance, poor Lakshmana walked away from the *ashrama* with slow, unhappy steps.

Thus ends the eleventh chapter of the glorious Ramayana *of Sage Valmiki called "The Golden Deer."*

Hari Aum Tat Sat

Hail to the darling of the Raghus,
Who stands with Lakshmana on his right,
The daughter of Janaka on his left,
And Hanuman in front.

—RAMAYANA OF TULASIDAS

TWELVE

THE ABDUCTION
OF SITA

Sumitraputra
Sevithaya Namah

Homage to the
one who was
served by the son
of Sumitra

Bow to Sri Ramachandra who is extolled in the Vedas,
Who is worshipped by all.
Who humbled the pride of his enemies,
Who is foremost in conducting sacrifices.
Who saved the elephant Gajendra and is without pride.
—MEDITATION VERSE FOR RAMAYANA OF VALMIKI

LAKSHMANA WAS FILLED WITH sorrow and anger at the way he had been forced to leave his post and betray Rama, but he had been unable to bear Sita's harsh words, as she knew only too well. In fact, she had repented her accusations as soon as she had uttered them, but her anxiety and fear for Rama had clouded her reasoning.

Ravana had been hiding close by, waiting for Lakshmana to go. He was anxiously watching the proceedings between the two. There was no time to be lost. He had to capture her and leave before Rama returned. He had no desire to have a close encounter with Rama at the moment. As soon as he heard Maricha's voice, he knew that his uncle had died but he felt no remorse at all for having sent him to his death. Maricha had served his purpose and that was all Ravana cared about.

He had a few anxious moments until he saw Lakshmana leave. As soon as Lakshmana had gone, Ravana donned the garments and makeup of an aged *sannyasi* (renunciant). His hair was matted and he wore

ochre-colored robes (orange-colored; signifies the fire of renunciation)
and wooden sandals. He held an umbrella and a staff in one hand and
a water pot in the other and walked with eager steps towards the
ashrama. Ravana couldn't afford to step inside the magic circle made
by Lakshmana, so he stood outside and shouted out, *"biksham dehi"*
which was the normal call for alms, made by all mendicant *sannyasis*.

Timidly, Sita came to the door of the *ashrama* and looked out.
Ravana gave a gasp of pure delight. He was a connoisseur of beauty
and had captured many of the most beautiful women in the world
for his harem but never had he come across any woman as lovely as
this one. She stood framed in the doorway, eyes wide open and long
black tresses falling almost to the ground. Her complexion was
golden, her lips soft and red and parted in anticipation of her Lord.
She was so bewitching that Ravana couldn't move or speak. He
could only stand stock still and devour her with his eyes. He knew
that she was the most beautiful woman he had ever seen and his
hunger to possess her became an urgent need. Controlling himself
with the greatest difficulty, he announced his status by chanting
some vedic mantras. Ravana was a past master in the art of
beguiling women but, in this case, he did not have to pretend
anything which he did not actually feel, for Sita's alluring looks had
hypnotized him.

His green eyes shooting golden flames of desire, he said, "O
beautiful one, who are you, who lives alone in this forest? Your dark
eyes hold magic in their depths. Your form is perfectly made. I wonder
what divine hands sculpted your tantalizing breasts. Your face, your
smile, your teeth, are all fascinating and have captivated me. Your
waist is so slim that I can span it with one hand. The perfume of
lotuses emanates from your lovely hair. I cannot believe that you are a
mere mortal. You must be Parvati, the consort of Shiva or Sachi, the
consort of Indra. I am struck dumb by so much beauty, but tell me
how it is possible that you are living alone in this dark forest. This is
not a fitting place for you. You should be living in a palace with
terraces and beautiful gardens. Who is the cruel one who has
abandoned you in this dreadful forest, infested with *rakshasas* and
wild beasts?"

Ravana's impassioned words and looks were quite embarrassing
to Sita but she took him to be an elderly *sannyasi* and it was against

the code of conduct to be rude to those who wore the ochre robe of spiritual renunciants. She was beside herself with anxiety about Rama and kept watching the little path to see if he was coming, but at the same time she could not afford to neglect this holy man who might curse her if she did not entertain him.

So she said, "I am the daughter of Janaka, king of Mithila and the wife of Rama, son of Dasaratha. I have come to this forest with my husband, who has been banished for fourteen years from his kingdom. His brother Lakshmana has also come with him. I cannot bear to live without my husband, neither can he bear to be parted from me and that is why I accompanied him to this forest. At the moment, he has gone with his brother to capture a deer which I desired. If you like, you are welcome to wait for his return. You may sit outside this circle for no one can enter it. However, I will bring you some food."

So saying she went inside to get some edibles for the holy man. Ravana was watching her every gesture and movement with hungry eyes, sparking green fire.

She returned with water to wash his feet, as well as a seat for him to sit and some refreshments. It was the custom to honor a *sannyasi* in this fashion. She was not suspicious of the character of the person who stood before her, so she innocently came out of the magic circle and kept everything ready for the holy man and respectfully stood beside him and asked him to partake of the repast.

Ravana did not have much time to waste on civilities, so he immediately stated his purpose in coming there. "O princess!" he said, "You must have heard of the king of the *rakshasas*, called Ravana. His very name strikes terror in the hearts of all. Well, I am he. Ever since I heard about your beauty from my sister Surpanekha, I have not been able to think of anything else. Now that I have seen you, I am filled with delight. If anything, her description did not do you justice. You are far more charming than what she said. You have captivated me and I don't want any other woman but you. Come with me and I'll make you my foremost queen. My city is called Lanka and it is situated on an island. It is the most beautiful city in the world. You can have the most wonderful palace for your own and wander about in lovely gardens instead of this terrible forest. Cast away this miserable life and come away with me and be my queen."

Sita was furious when she heard these despicable words coming from the lips of a man whom she thought was holy. At first it didn't occur to her to be frightened.

With flaming eyes and scornful look, she said scathingly, "Listen to me, O wretch! I am the wife of the noblest man in the world and you are a most despicable person. Do you really think I will leave my husband and go with you? How dare you talk to me like this! What do I care for your name and fame and wealth. My husband is the home of all virtues and I would never look at another man. Give up these sinful thoughts and go away fast, before my noble husband returns and kills you."

Though she spoke boldly, her mind was suddenly filled with fear for she realized her state of utter helplessness. She was alone and at the mercy of this man, who appeared to be a veritable devil.

Ravana saw her trembling but he was loathe to use violence and thus cause her to hate him. Though time was running short, he tried to beguile her with stories of his glory. "Ah Sita," he said, "you don't understand what a great personage I am. There is nothing that I cannot do. I have conquered all the three worlds. Even the gods bow to me. I have a fantastic chariot which can fly in the air. I can take you over land and sea and show you wonders you have never dreamed of. What can that puny mortal Rama do? He was banished to the forest by his father and did not have the guts to go against his stepmother. You are too beautiful to be wasted on such a coward. Come with me and live a life of pleasure in my city. I will shower you with whatever you desire."

Sita replied hotly, "You say you are born in a noble family, yet not even the lowest of the low behaves like you. If you touch me you will not be able to live. Rama's arrows will split your chest. You are putting your head into a noose. Depart from here this instant if you value your life!"

Ravana was slowly losing his temper. He had never been thwarted before, especially by a woman! He had thought to make an easy conquest, but time was running out. He made one last attempt to convince her of his worth.

"For the last time, I'm pleading with you! Listen to me and be my wife. I promise I will never displease you. Rama is far inferior to me. He is only a wandering mendicant, without even a kingdom. Forget him and come with me." Speaking thus, he shed his disguise and stood in all his *rakshasa* glory before her eyes, ten heads and all!

Sita was terrified to see him in his *rakshasa* form but she did her best to hide her fear. She cursed herself for not having listened to Lakshmana and stayed within the circle. She knew that if she could only get back into the magic circle she would be safe. Slowly, she started backing her way towards it. If she tried to turn and run, he would surely catch her, so she tried to inch her way back unnoticed.

Suddenly Ravana realized what she was up to and before she could reach the edge and save herself, he lunged at her and dragged her back. Catching her long hair with his left hand, he placed his right hand under her thighs and lifted her up and put her on his shoulders. His aerial vehicle, which had been well camouflaged by the trees, now appeared like magic on the lawn. He got into it and placed Sita on his lap. The entire forest held its breath in fear. It was as if all of nature were appalled by the immensity of the crime which was being committed. The trees moaned and writhed in agony. The birds shrieked and flew back and forth. The deer on the ground were affected by their cries and they also moaned and fled into the depths of the forest, as if in an effort to call Rama.

Sita struggled and tried her best to wriggle out of his grasp but he only tightened his hold. She screamed, "Rama! Rama! Save me! Save me!" But Rama did not hear. She was like one demented. Again and again, she cried out, "O Rama! O Lakshmana! O noble brother of Rama. This evil *rakshasa* is carrying me away by force. Save me! Save me!"

The chariot was swiftly rising from the ground. She saw the trees she loved and the forest where she had roamed with her beloved. She made piteous appeals to the flowers and the birds to save her and cursed Ravana for his folly. Ravana paid no heed and the chariot sped through the air to the south. He was jubilant because his plan had succeeded. As the chariot was speeding on its way, Sita suddenly saw their good friend Jatayu perched on a tree. Unfortunately, he had not witnessed all that had taken place, for he had tucked his head into his feathers and gone to sleep.

As soon as Sita saw him, she cried out, "O revered Sir, this *rakshasa* is carrying me away by force. Please tell Rama!" Sobs stopped her from speaking further.

Jatayu woke up from his slumbers at her cry. He flew beside

the chariot and tried to reason with the *rakshasa* king. "O Ravana," he said, "what you are doing is a despicable thing. Rama has not wronged you in any way. Give up this madness or you will regret it. Even though I am old and unarmed, rest assured that I will not let you take her away. If you persist in this stupidity, you will have to fight with me first."

Ravana had hardly expected an obstacle from this direction. He was furious with the bird for trying to bar the flight of the chariot with its huge wings. Jatayu fought with his talons, beak and wings and mauled Ravana in a few places, so that blood oozed from his wounds. Ravana tried to pierce him with his arrows but Jatayu resisted manfully and slashed his bow and armor with his talons. Blind with fury, Jatayu ripped apart the magic asses which were yoked to the chariot and the chariot itself fell to the ground and was smashed. Jatayu shrieked the war cry of the eagles and swooped down on Ravana, ripping his chest with his beak. His strength and heroism was amazing. As the chariot fell to the ground, Ravana kept a firm grip on Sita. The *rakshasas* had the power to fly and so the demon king rose up into the air with Sita in his arms. Jatayu followed him but by now the old bird was tired and weak. Still he went after Ravana and valiantly pierced him with his beak again and again till he was forced to land on the ground. Ravana was amazed at the bird's prowess but he was also getting desperate. At last he took up his sword and sliced off both Jatayu's wings. Jatayu fell to the ground with a shriek. Sita wept in horror at the gory fate of her friend who had also been her father-in-law's friend. She shook off Ravana's loosened hold and ran to the bird and gathered him up in her arms and wept for him. Ravana pulled her up roughly and, placing her on his thigh, he rose up into the sky once again.

Again and again, Sita called out, "Rama! O Rama! Where are you? Can you not hear me?"

Far away in the forest, Rama felt his left eye throb. The vibrations of her piteous call were felt by him and he hastened his steps, almost running down the tiny forest track.

As Ravana rose into the sky, the sun hid behind clouds, as if he didn't want to be a witness to this outrage, the wind moaned and groaned and there was a hush of sadness in the air.

Draped in yellow silk and decked in the ornaments which

Anasuya had given her, Sita looked like a streak of lightning against the dark, broad chest of the *rakshasa* king. The lotus flowers which Rama had placed lovingly in her hair just that morning started to wilt and fall to the ground, as if they couldn't bear to be touched by that cruel hand. One of her anklets fell and lay forlornly on the ground, loathe to be parted from its partner. The shadow cast by the demon king as he carried Sita through the air was black and menacing. The wild beasts which came under the shadow growled angrily, they knew not why, and tried to claw at it. The fish in the rivers appeared to leap out of the waters, as if to help her. Again and again, Sita begged Ravana to let her go, but he only tightened his hold. He was feeling very happy that at last he had got her. He did not realize that he was holding his own death in his arms. He was sure that it was only a question of time before she succumbed to his charms. Sita spoke sometimes scornfully, and sometimes threateningly, but it was all in vain. He moved swiftly through the skies.

Suddenly when she looked down, she saw five monkeys sitting on top of a mountain. Though she did not know it, this was her first glimpse of Hanuman, who was destined to play such a vital role in her life. She was struck by an idea. Tearing off a piece of her upper garment, she took off a few of her ornaments and tied them up in the little piece of cloth and threw it toward the monkeys, hoping that someday Rama would pass by and recognize the jewels. Ravana, who was sailing along happily, did not notice what was going on. The monkeys looked up to see a beautiful woman being carried in the arms of the *rakshasa*. She was crying out, "O Rama, O Lakshmana!" in a desperate voice.

Very soon, they came to the southern straits which separated Ravana's capital from the mainland. It was her first sight of the sea but she was in no mood to enjoy anything. Ravana tightened his hold, for he felt her struggling to get free and feared that she would jump into the foaming waters below.

Soon they reached the fabulous city of Lanka, where he took her to his own private quarters and set a number of women to guard her. He gave strict orders to the women that no one should be allowed to approach her without his knowledge. He also told them to give her anything she asked for, whether it was jewels or clothes or delicious food.

"Whatever she asks for should be provided immediately," he said. He ordered eight of his vassals to go straight to Janasthana to keep an eye on Rama's movements and report to him from time to time. If opportunity arose, they were to try and kill him. Ravana heaved a sigh of relief and pleasure. He had punished Rama and gotten for himself the most beautiful woman in all the three worlds. He lay on his silken couch and pictured all the delights which were in store for him, once Sita agreed to be his wife.

Ravana couldn't lie down for long. Sita's charming face kept flashing through his mind and he decided to go and talk to her once again. He had known many women and though some of them had objected in the beginning, not one had had the guts to refuse him for long. He was sure that Sita would be no exception. Though the idea of capturing Sita had at first been only a means to punish Rama, he realized once he had met her, he had fallen prey to her charms and he couldn't concentrate on anything else. His passion was like a fire burning him up. He strode to the room in which she had been imprisoned. She was sitting on the ground, with *rakshasis* all around her, looking like a stricken deer surrounded by jackals. Her tear-stained face was cast down, her lovely eyes veiled by her long lashes. She disdained even to look up as he strode into the room.

He was determined to impress her somehow, so he started by telling her of the beauties of his palace. "Look, O beautiful one, at the glories of this city of Lanka. The palaces are made of gold with ornamental pillars. There are terraces and gardens filled with flowers, and lakes in which swans glide among the lotuses. There is no comparison between my wealth and Rama's. Who is he but a miserable wretch clad in bark, living the life of an exile? He will never be able to come here and take you away, for Lanka is impenetrable, surrounded as it is by the sea. Don't waste your youth pining for him. Accept my love and I can take you wherever you wish, give you whatever you want. We will travel through the skies and I'll show you the sights of all the three worlds. There is no one equal to me in valor in all these worlds and none dare stop me! Be my queen and I'll lay the whole world at your feet."

Sita covered her face with a cloth and cried as if her heart would break. Ravana looked at her with compassion and said, "Do not cry like this! What have you to cry for? Have I not said that I'd give the whole world to you? Not only that, I am ready to lay all my ten heads at your feet. Do you realize what that means? Ravana has never laid his head at anyone's feet before, and certainly not at the feet of a woman, but your beauty has charmed me. I am your slave. Come, my little dove, accept me and agree to my wishes."

At the end of this declaration of love, Sita looked up with flashing eyes, and said scornfully, "You do not know my Rama and that is why you dare to say such things. He is the image of dharma. He is truth incarnate. I love him with my whole life. You have dared to touch me, his wife, and he will never forgive you for that. He will never spare you. He and his noble brother Lakshmana will come here and slay you. Have no doubts about that! You call yourself brave, yet to me you are a coward. You stole me away from my husband by luring him into the forest. You were too frightened to come face to face with him. You are not only a coward but also a thief. But beware, your end is nearing or else you would never have done such a dastardly act."

Ravana was furious at these words. His lips were throbbing with anger and humiliation. "Enough of your prattle!" he shouted. "I give you twelve months to change your mind. If within that time you agree to my proposal, you will become queen of the world; otherwise your delicate flesh shall be carved and dressed for my morning meal." With this, he stormed out of the room, giving orders that Sita should be kept in the grove of *ashoka* trees with a strict guard, night and day.

Thus ends the twelveth chapter of the glorious Ramayana *of Sage Valmiki called "The Abduction of Sita"*

Hari Aum Tat Sat

THIRTEEN

RAMA BEREFT

Sitapathayé Namaha!

Homage to the husband of Sita.

I bow to the compassionate, lotus-eyed
Sri Ramachandra,
The Supreme Immaculate,
Whose body has the color of new rainclouds
Who is the friend of Sugriva, and the husband of Sita.
—RAMAYANA OF TULASIDAS

BACK IN THE FOREST, RAMA was filled with misgivings. Sita and his love for each other was so great that, even though they were parted, they were still in communication with each other and he could sense Sita's fears. He walked as fast as he could. He knew that Maricha would never deliberately have risked his life had not something stupendous been at stake. He saw terrible omen all along the way. A jackal was howling. His left eye was throbbing, which was considered to be a bad omen for men.

As he came to Janasthana, he saw Lakshmana walking towards him with a troubled look. Rama went toward him and held out his hand and asked him worriedly, "My dear child, why did you leave Sita alone and come here? Did I not tell you to stay with her? You were right. That deer was indeed Maricha, sent as a decoy to lure me away in order to fulfill some evil design. And now you have also followed me, even though I told you to stay with her. I am beginning to fear that we may never again see her alive. The moment I heard Maricha calling out in my voice, I knew that some mischief was afoot."

Lakshmana could not speak a word. He allowed Rama to go on. Rama continued, "I was a beggar without a kingdom, yet she preferred to come with me

99

rather than stay in the comfort of the palace. She could not live without me and neither can I live without her. Will my Sita be alive? If she dies, so will I. Has my exile been fruitless? Kaikeyi will be happy if she hears of our death but my poor mother will die of a broken heart."

Thus lamenting, they reached the vicinity of the *ashrama*. Rama was already tired, hungry and thirsty when they arrived, for he had been chasing the deer for a long time. He went inside the hut, calling Sita to come out, but there was no answer. Only the wind rustled through the leaves. He ran out and rushed to all her favorite haunts, calling out "Janaki! O Janaki! Where are you my beloved? Why are you hiding from me? Can't you see that I am tired and hungry. Haven't you prepared a meal for me? Why do you play with me like this. I am in no mood for games. Come to me, my darling. I cannot bear this any longer."

At last his limbs refused to carry him and he sank to the ground and murmured, "What I dreaded has happened. She has either been abducted or eaten alive." Lakshmana stood by his side and said not a word. Tears were flowing down his cheeks.

Turning to him Rama asked, "I left her only because I had entrusted her to you. Why did you leave her and come?"

His voice choked with sobs, Lakshmana said, "When she heard Maricha's dying voice emulating yours, she went into a panic and begged me to go to your aid. When I refused, she spoke so harshly to me that I could not bear it. She accused me of being your enemy and lusting after her. Even then, I refused to move, though my heart was bursting. Then she threatened to kill herself, to jump into the river or hang herself. I could bear it no longer and I ran out of the *ashrama*, leaving her alone. Before I left, I drew a magic circle around her and told her to stay within it. Had she done so she would have been safe."

Rama heard Lakshmana and said, "You did wrong, my child, to have left her alone. She was out of her wits with anxiety over me and that is why she must have spoken as she did, but you, who know me so well, must have realized that no harm could have befallen me and yet, you left her. Why did you do this?"

In his extreme grief, Rama kept on repeating the same thing over and over. The *ashrama* looked like a lotus pond in winter, desolate and forlorn. The trees appeared to be weeping and the flowers had faded and the deer stood listlessly, uninterested even in eating grass. The birds sat on twigs and gazed with dull eyes at Rama, seeming to have lost their voices.

Rama said in despair, "O my love! Where are all the flowers since you went away. Where are all the songbirds who used to sing to us so sweetly every day?"

He was inconsolable in his grief. He ran from tree to tree and asked them if they had seen her. "Didn't my darling Sita bid you farewell when she went away? Will you not tell me where she went?"

A deer came close to him and nuzzled him with her nose. He looked at her and his eyes filled with tears and he said, "My darling had eyes just like yours, so soft and kind they were! Are you trying to comfort me? Will you not tell me where she has gone?"

He ran all over, again and again crying out, "O Lakshmana, I cannot live without Sita! I cannot return to Ayodhya without her. What is a kingdom to me without her to share it? Go back, brother, and tell them that Rama is dead. She put her entire trust in me and I failed to protect her. She was my dear wife and I could not save her. What is the use of living?" Thus lamenting, his whole body on fire and his mind consumed with grief, Rama could not sit or stand.

Lakshmana had never seen him like this and he spoke gently to him, "O my dear brother! Please don't give way to grief like this. The forest is large and there are many places where she could have been hidden by someone. Perhaps in some cave. Let us go and search for her inch by inch. She used to love to wander along the river banks and sit under the trees. Let us go and see if she's there. Rouse yourself from this despondency and let's go."

Thus saying, he tried to raise his brother from the lethargy into which he appeared to have fallen. Rama tried to control himself and, with superhuman effort, accompanied Lakshmana and they began their search in a methodical manner. Lakshmana comforted him by saying that she could not have gone far, since he had just left the *ashrama*. Of course, he could not to know that she had been abducted in an aerial vehicle. They searched all available places but they couldn't find her. Rama was spent with sorrow and fatigue. His limbs felt weak and useless. He sank to the ground and did not speak for an hour. His face had lost its lustre and its habitual look of serenity and peace. Lakshmana did not know what to do with him.

He tried his best to revive him but it was of no use.

"O Lakshmana! I don't think there is a greater sinner than I am on this earth! That is why misfortune after misfortune has been heaped on me. This is the greatest calamity of all. I think I am losing my mind. I lost my kingdom, I lost my father and I am wandering around like a mendicant in this forest infested with *rakshasas* and wild beasts, but all this was bearable because of the sweet company of my beloved wife. Now my queen has been captured by some cruel *rakshasa*, who might be torturing her even now. Look at this stone. We used to sit here in the afternoons and discuss so many things. I cannot bear this grief anymore. It is tearing up my vitals and depriving me of all reason. How cruel the sun is! He must surely be knowing where she has been taken, yet he will not tell me. And this wind, he goes everywhere and even now he must be fanning my darling's face and drying her tears, yet he will not tell me her hiding place." Thus lamenting again and again, Rama cried out, "O Janaki! O Vaidehi! O Maithili! Will you not come back?"

Lakshmana was beside himself. He pleaded with him, as Krishna had once pleaded with Arjuna on the battlefield of Kurukshetra, begging him to shake off his grief, which was unmanly and ignoble, but it was all in vain.

"Come, my dear brother. Abandon this grief and arise. Victory belongs only to the brave. Only those who keep trying will achieve their goal. Arise, and let us go and search again."

But his words fell on deaf ears. Rama was sunk in gloom and did not even hear him. Lakshmana felt doubly guilty, for he had been the unwitting cause of her abduction.

Again and again, Rama lamented, "When I lost my kingdom, Sita was there to comfort me but now who is there to give me solace? O Lakshmana! How can I endure this wretched life without her?" Turning to the deer, he asked, "She was your friend. She loved you so. Will you not tell me where she has gone?"

Then Lakshmana noticed that the deer appeared to be putting on some sort of pantomime by running toward the south and running back again.

"Look, Rama!" he said, "These deer are trying to tell us something. I think she must have been taken away in a southerly direction. Let us also go that way."

Thus saying, he encouraged his brother and the two of them slowly walked toward the south, examining the ground as they went. Rama spied the faded lotus flowers and petals and he exclaimed, "Look, Lakshmana! I recognize these flowers. I had plucked them from the river and decorated her hair, just this morning. O Sita! My lovely wife! Where are you?" He took the petals in his hands and kissed them, while tears streamed from his eyes. Then suddenly his sorrow turned to rage.

With eyes wild with anger, he shouted at the mountain, "I will crush you to powder. I will burn up the waters of this river with my wrath. I will destroy the entire world if you don't tell me where my princess is!"

Lakshmana feared for his brother's reason and going forward a little he pointed out to Rama the large furrows made on the soft ground by Ravana's huge feet and the dainty footprints of Sita as she ran here and there trying to elude his grasp. Rama could not contain himself at these sights but Lakshmana went further and showed him the broken bow and the quiver and the crushed chariot.

Rama cried out her name again and again and said, "O Lakshmana! Look! These are some of her jewels and these are her flowers which have been stamped into the ground. Who could be the owner of such a magnificent bow? Here is the white umbrella, the insignia of a king. Which king would have dared to commit such a crime? Here are two donkeys lying dead. The charioteer must have been a *rakshasa*. If their intention was to avenge the annihilation of their army, they have more than succeeded, for I can never live without her. Lakshmana, you were right. Do you remember what you told me when Kaikeyi ordered me to go the forest? You said that I was too soft and that my kindness and devotion to dharma would be mistaken for cowardice. You were perfectly right. Keeping my senses under strict control, I have accepted this role of mendicant, for the good of humanity—to set an example of unflinching adherence to dharma—but even the gods seem to have misunderstood me. Beware, Lakshmana! From today on, I am a changed man. My kindliness and compassion will be cast aside and I will be a most unforgiving and terrible opponent. I will make the three worlds empty of all creatures. Even fire and air will be burned up in the holocaust of my anger and the gods will have to stand by and watch helplessly."

He took an arrow out of his quiver and fixed it on the bow. Lakshmana fell at his feet and begged him to desist from universal destruction.

"Rama, my beloved brother. You have always had only the good of the world in your mind. How can you give way to anger like this? The charm of the moon, the radiance of the sun, and the patience of Mother Earth, have all combined to make up the perfection of your personality. How can you allow your anger to get the better of you? Sita and you are both images of dharma. Evil can never befall you. Dharma must triumph in the end. Obviously, there was some sort of scuffle here. It is your duty to find out who the miscreant was and punish him for it, and not to punish the whole of creation, which is guiltless. Let us try to find out where Sita has been taken. Let us search the three worlds and, if she cannot be found, then you can go about destroying the worlds, but not until then. O tiger among men! You bore the trials and tribulations of a banishment on the eve of your coronation without a single word. How can you give in to your emotions now? You are to set an example to others. If you give in to grief like this, how can an ordinary man control himself! Who is it who has never had any troubles? Even the history of our race shows that many of the kings had difficulties which they overcame with fortitude. No one can escape his karma. You should not allow sorrow to gain supremacy over your mind. You have always been a god to me. Now the god in you seems to be sleeping due to sorrow. Control your emotions and let your intellect rule your mind. Search for the one who has done you this grievous wrong and punish him. That is the duty of a *Kshatriya*."

Rama heard him out in silence and unstrung his bow and returned the arrow to its quiver, "You are right, O Lakshmana! You must tell me what to do. I will follow your advice. My mind refuses to function. You must think for both of us."

They went forward and soon came to the mighty, fallen figure of Jatayu. At first, they thought he must be the *rakshasa* but in getting closer they discovered that it was their dear friend Jatayu, who was hanging on to his life in the hope of seeing Rama before drawing his last breath.

Jatayu was dying and spitting blood. Making a tremendous effort, he said, "Rama, don't waste your time here. My life as well as your wife have been taken by the *rakshasa* king, Ravana. I tried to stop him and almost succeeded but he cut me with his sword, and sped away to the south with Sita in his arms. Go to his kingdom and you will surely find her."

Rama was overcome with sorrow to know that he was the unwitting cause of his friend's death. Jatayu had fought valiantly but had to succumb to Ravana's superior strength. Rama knelt on the ground beside Jatayu and hugged him and wept.

"O Lakshmana," he said, "we have lost Sita and now our poor friend is also dying. I'm sure there is no one in the whole world who is as unfortunate as I. If I were to touch the waters of the ocean, I'm sure they would dry up, due to my misfortune. Fate has pushed me into this deep pit of pain and I know not how to get out of it."

Rama sat beside the dying eagle, stroking him with his loving hands. Life was ebbing fast from his body.

Once more, Rama asked him, "Tell me if you can, how this has happened. Why has Ravana done this to me? I have not harmed him in any way. What prompted him to commit such a heinous act? What does he look like? Where does he live?"

Rama scarcely expected the dying bird to reply. He was speaking from the depths of his own sorrow, but the bird, seeing Rama's unhappiness made a tremendous effort and whispered, "Child, my life is fast ebbing away. All I can say is that he was carrying her away like a whirlwind, toward the south. But take heart, for the time that he abducted her is called *vijaya* and it is certain that anything lost during that time will be found again. Though he is a master of astronomy, Ravana seems to have misjudged the time. You will surely find Sita and kill Ravana, so please don't give in to grief. Now, I beg of you, hold me in your arms, for my last moment has come and I will surely find release from this bondage of *samsara* if I am held in your holy hands." He could speak no more and died in Rama's arms, with Rama's eyes looking tenderly into his and giving him salvation.

Rama was heartbroken and recalled to mind all the happy times they had spent with Jatayu. He told Lakshmana, "O Lakshmana! Jatayu was like a father to us. We must give him a fitting funeral. Collect some firewood. He died for my sake and I shall cremate him with my own hands."

He carried him tenderly in his arms to the banks of the river

Godavari. A spot was selected and covered with *darbha* grass. Lakshmana brought wood and made a pyre, on which Rama placed the bird with great love.

"O king of birds!" he said. "May you reach those heavenly regions which are reserved for those who have performed great austerities." So saying, Rama kindled the fire by rubbing a fire stick and lit the pyre himself. Then he made his offerings to the forefathers and recited the appropriate verses. After the cremation was over, the two princes purified themselves in the river and sadly proceeded on their way.

Thus ends the thirteenth chapter of the glorious Ramayana *of Sage Valmiki called "Rama Bereft"*

Hari Aum Tat Sat

FOURTEEN

THE UNHAPPY TREK

*Mahayoginé
Namaha!*

Homage to
the great yogi.

*I bow to Sri Ramachandra who wears a garland of white flowers
And is the repository of all good qualities.
His speech is sweet and he is the succor of the gods.
He pierced all seven palmyra trees with one arrow.*
—SOURCE UNKNOWN

THE FINAL MEETING WITH JATAYU seemed to have put hope in Rama's heart. At least now he knew where Sita had been taken. It was up to him to find her. There appeared to be some reason for trying. Lakshmana was greatly relieved at Rama's change in attitude. He had never seen his brother angry and it had frightened him. They walked quickly southward since Jatayu had been quite definite about the direction taken by Ravana, and it was a sad trek. Usually, Sita would walk between them and ask a thousand questions. There would be frequent stops to allow her to pluck flowers or watch a deer or bird.

Rama could not speak at all and Lakshmana walked silently beside him. Both were absorbed in their own unhappy thoughts. They penetrated deeper and deeper into the dense forest, inhabited by wolves and tigers. The darkness was deep and forbidding. They had to rest frequently on the way, since Lakshmana had to hack a path for them. This was not a place frequented by *rishis*. Soon they came to a cave. At the entrance stood a *rakshasi*. She was immense in size and fearful to look at. She approached Lakshmana and solicited him as Surpanekha had done earlier.

"My name is Ayomukhi," she said, "and I want you as my mate. Come with me."

Lakshmana had just about reached the end of his

patience. He was wracked by feelings of guilt about Sita, sorrow at Jatayu's death, and Rama's extraordinary behavior. Without bothering to exchange words with her, he simply lifted up his sword and sliced off her nose, ears and breasts. She roared with pain and rage and ran away. They walked on without a word.

Lakshmana sensed that there was some danger ahead and warned Rama to be alert. Just then, they heard a dreadful noise as if the whole forest was being felled. Soon they came upon an enormous figure of a *rakshasa* who appeared to have no head. His mouth was in his stomach. He was glaring ominously at them through his one eye, which was on his chest. His enormous tongue was lolling out of his cavernous mouth, as if licking his lips in anticipation of the approaching meal. He had arms as long as trees and there was no way that they could bypass him. Stretching his arms, he caught them both and pulled them to the mouth on his stomach.

Lakshmana was stricken with fear and said, "Brother, please save yourself and go and look for Sita, while this monster eats me up."

Rama told him not to despair. The creature was delighted at his prize and said, "It has been a long time since I've eaten human flesh. It's so much tastier than the flesh of animals. You will never be able to escape me."

Rama turned to Lakshmana and said, "Misfortune after misfortune has been heaped on us, and now it looks as if we are going to be eaten up by this monster. Fate is the one enemy whom no one can conquer."

Lakshmana said, "Brother, let us cut off the arms of this monster." Hearing this, the *rakshasa* tried to cram them into his mouth as fast as possible, but quick as a thought, Rama cut off his right arm and Lakshmana the left, and the monster fell to the ground with a horrendous noise, crushing some trees as he fell. He realized that these were not ordinary mortals and asked them who they were. They told him their lineage. Upon hearing this, Kabandha (that was his name), became very happy and said, "I became a *rakshasa* due to the curse of the *rishis*. I was once as handsome as the two of you, but I used to play pranks on the *rishis* by taking on different forms in order to frighten them. At last, one day I took on this monstrous form and they cursed me that I would remain like this for the rest of my life. When I begged them to release me from the curse, they said that

I would be released when Rama, the son of Dasaratha, came to the forest and cut off my arms. And now you have come. Rama, I beg of you to cremate me, and thus release me from this dreadful curse, so that I can regain my old form."

Rama said, "My wife has been abducted by a *rakshasa* called Ravana. Could you tell us anything about him?"

Kabandha said that he had lost his memory but he would regain it with his old form and then he would tell them everything they wanted to know. He asked them to dig a huge pit and throw him in and make a bonfire with his body. As the huge body was cremated, there rose the figure of a handsome man called Dhanu.

His memory returned and he said, "There is one person who can help you to get your wife back and his name is Sugriva. He is a monkey chieftain and is the brother of Vali. This Vali has driven him out of his kingdom and, at the moment Sugriva is living with four companions on another hill called Rishyamukha on the banks of the Lake Pampa. He is brave and powerful and he will be able to help you. Do not indulge in grief but proceed straightaway toward Pampa. Follow the path to the west. It will lead you to a park called Nandana and very soon you will reach the Lake Pampa. There, in that beautiful place, you will find some solace. A disciple of the old *rishi* Matanga is living there, waiting for you to come. She is very old and her name is Shabari. She is waiting to see you before leaving her body. This place is at the foot of the mountain called Rishyamukha, on which Sugriva lives. Go to him, O Rama, and you will succeed in your mission. Now please grant me leave to return to my celestial abode." So saying, the divine being disappeared from their sight.

The two princes felt very happy at this unexpected meeting and Kabandha's message of consolation. They decided to proceed straight to Shabari's *ashrama*.

After two days journey, they reached Lake Pampa. They made their way to Shabari's *ashrama*, situated alongside the lake. Shabari was a very old woman, bent and wrinkled with age. Her long matted grey hair fell almost to the ground She had been awaiting Rama's arrival for many years and she recognized him at a glance. Rama made kind inquiries about her welfare and about her austerities.

She bowed humbly before him and said, "My Lord, the fruit of my austerities is now standing before my eyes. The moment your glance fell on me, I was purified. I am now certain to attain salvation. The *rishis* whom I served for many years have all gone to their heavenly abode. They asked me to wait here for your arrival. All these years I have been waiting for you. Every day, I have been collecting fruits from this forest and preserving them for you."

She went and brought her cherished store of fruit. She had tasted each berry and kept only those which were the most delicious. It is considered to be very bad manners to offer another person, something which has been defiled by one's own mouth but, being a woman of a lower order, she was not aware of these rules. All she knew was that she should give only the best to her beloved Lord. Rama knew her heart and, much to Lakshmana's astonishment, he sat and ate all the fruits which the old woman offered to him. She made him sit down and squatting beside him she took the fruits one by one and placed them lovingly in his mouth while Lakshmana watched, fascinated. Rama smiled reassuringly at him and continued to eat the fruits with apparent relish. After this, she begged him to give her permission to depart to another world.

Rama said, "You are indeed a highly realized soul. May all your desires be granted. You will surely attain the world of the *rishis* whom you served so faithfully." Hearing these words from Rama, she was very happy. She sat in meditative pose and was consumed by the fire of her *tapas*.

After she shed her body, Rama and Lakshmana walked along the sides of the lake and they were amazed at the holiness of the spot. The vibrations left by the *rishis* were so powerful that tigers and lambs strolled about in harmony with each other. Rama found a lot of solace for the pain in his heart, but they had no time to waste and they hurried forward, impatient to reach the mountain of Rishyamukha and meet Sugriva.

Soon they reached the banks of another lake. Nature was lavish in her gifts to this place. Flowering trees and bushes abounded. The grassy banks were strewn with flowers, peacocks were dancing and birds singing melodiously. Rama was overcome with sorrow once again and he sat down dejected and asked Lakshmana to go on and meet Sugriva, for he could go no further. Lakshmana was surprised.

"What is the matter, brother?" he inquired.

"The beauty of this place makes me ache for Sita. I cannot live without her. How she would have loved it here! I can have no peace until I am reunited with her. Please go on and meet Sugriva on my behalf. I will sit here with the memories of my beloved wife."

"This is the vernal season, O Lakshmana. It makes me long for my beloved. My love for her has grown with every passing day. Look at the beauty of this lake, filled with lotuses. I used to love to pluck them for her and decorate her hair. My mind is pierced with the arrows of the god of love. I cannot concentrate on anything. I can only think of the princess of Videha. The wind which blows is filled with the perfume of flowers. It is scattering petals on my face, as she used to do sometimes, to tease me. It seems to be dancing to the tune of the cuckoos. Look at the branches of these trees—how they are entwined. They seem to be embracing each other. The perfume of sandalwood is being wafted all over my body. Sita used to love it. I am drowned in sorrow and only Sita can comfort me and she is far, far away. Look, Lakshmana, at those birds. They are all flying in pairs. Ah! My little dove. Where is she now? In this beautiful springtime, she must be equally smitten with the pangs of separation. O Lakshmana! I am on fire with desire for Sita. My whole body burns. I miss her large black eyes, her sweet voice, her caressing touch. How can I continue to live apart from her? She used to love the spring and she must be pining for me, as I am for her. Lakshmana, I am consumed with worry about her. I hope she will not kill herself. My life is in her keeping and hers in mine. We cannot exist without each other. Everything about this place makes me long for her and I am unable to bear this pain."

Lakshmana had thought that Rama had begun to get over his sorrow but now he realized that it was not so. He didn't know what to say. He had never realized the extent of his brother's feelings for Sita. He felt relieved that he had never felt such depth of passion for his own wife Urmila. He had been able to leave her without a pang. His whole life was bound up with his brother Rama and he was happy that he could be with him all the time. At last, in order to comfort Rama, he said, "I know brother, what a jewel Sita is and how impossible it would be to find another like her, but how can you let yourself be overwhelmed by this storm of feeling? Without a second thought, you threw away a kingdom and went to the forest, serene and unmoved. You have the courage of a lion. How can you give in to grief like this? It ill becomes you. Let us go on and find the one who stole Sita and punish him as he deserves to be punished. Moreover, don't you think that Sita will be waiting for you to go and rescue her? She will not expect you to sit here, bemoaning your loss. She will be expecting you to forge ahead to find out her whereabouts. Be firm and strong. The pain of separation becomes greater when you dwell on it. Abandon this grief and let us get started on our search for Sita. Wherever he has imprisoned her, in this world or the next, we will find her. Come, brother, shed this sorrow and become your own self—undaunted, firm and serene under all circumstances. Enthusiasm coupled with effort will get us anything we desire."

Rama found great comfort in these words of Lakshmana, and shaking off his despondency, he rallied himself and they proceeded to walk toward the mountain of Rishyamukha with firm steps. Rama's eyes looked longingly at the cascades, tumbling over themselves in delight, at the profusion of flowers and songbirds. But he set his lips in a firm line and refused to let his mind be swayed by thoughts of his beloved. The most important thing was to save her at all costs. Very soon, they reached the mountain and started climbing, looking around for anyone who resembled Sugriva.

Thus ends the fourteenth chapter of the glorious Ramayana of Sage Valmiki called "The Unhappy Trek."

Hari Aum Tat Sat

Rama asks:
*Where does the Lord dwell and how can I
reach Him?*

Vasistha replies:
*He who has been described as the Lord is
not very far. He is the intelligence dwelling
in the body. He is the universe though the
universe is not He. He is pure intelligence*

—THE YOGA VASISTHA

BOOK FOUR

*Saptatala-prab-
hetre Namaha!*

Homage to
the one who
pierced the
seven palmyra
trees.

KISHKINDA KANDA

THE BOOK OF KISHKINDA

FIFTEEN

HANUMAN

By thinking of Hanuman, we can gain intelligence, fortitude, fame, fearlessness, health, energy and cleverness in speech.
—SOURCE UNKNOWN

Sadahanu-madaasritaya Namaha!

Homage to the one, on whom Hanuman always depends.

SUGRIVA WAS SEATED ON ONE of the peaks of Rishyamukha with his four ministers, and anxiously watching the ascent of the two strangers. He had been beaten so badly by his brother Vali that he lived in constant dread of his spies. He had chosen a vantage point on one of the peaks, from where he could have a bird's-eye view of everything that went on within a distance of ten miles. As soon as he saw the two handsome young men at the foot of the hill, he was consumed with anxiety, for he feared that they had been sent by Vali to kill him. Hanuman was his chief minister and he tried his best to pacify his master and allay his fears, but Sugriva could not rest.

"They are dressed as anchorites, but look, Hanuman, they carry bows and arrows and I can see the flash of swords at their waist. I am sure they must have been sent by my brother Vali to kill me. I request you to go and meet them and find out their intentions. Speak to them sweetly and try to find out their real intention in having come to this lonely spot."

Hanuman was the son of the wind god Vayu. His strength was proverbial and he was astute as well. He could assume any form at will. He took on the form of a *brahmachari* (literally, one who is celibate and continent in thought, word and deed) and approached Rama and Lakshmana, accosting them with sweet words. This was indeed a momentous meeting. Next to Ganesha,

Hanuman is the most loved of all the demi-gods in the Hindu pantheon. He is known for his utter and selfless devotion to Rama. This was the first time that they were meeting and ever afterwards Hanuman was Rama's slave. It is one of the endearing qualities of Rama that no one could resist the charm of his personality, the intensity of his charisma.

Hanuman approached them and said, "Tell me who you are. You appear to be hermits but you are carrying weapons. How is it that you are wandering about on this lonely mountainside, when obviously you are meant to be living in palaces. I have been watching you for some time and I find that you seem to be constantly searching for something. Though you are both so handsome, there is a lurking shadow of sorrow on your faces. But first let me tell you who I am. I am Hanuman, the son of the wind god. I am one of the ministers of the *vanara* (monkey) king called Sugriva. He was thrown out of his kingdom by his brother Vali and is now living in exile on this mountain. He desires to make friends with you and has sent me to find out your motives. I am actually a monkey, but I can assume any form I wish."

Rama was thrilled when he heard the words of Hanuman. Turning to Lakshmana, he said, "Lakshmana, this Hanuman seems to be very sincere and well-versed in the *Vedas*. He has come with the very project which we had in mind—that is to make friends with Sugriva. Please talk to him and find out more details."

Lakshmana said, "We have come here with the express purpose of making friends with your master. We will be happy to do whatever you say."

Hanuman was pleased with this answer and asked them the reason for their having crossed the fearful forest of Dandaka and come to that lonely region and why they wanted to make friends with Sugriva.

Lakshmana told them their lineage, as was the custom, and also their reason for coming. "I am the younger brother of Rama, the eldest son of King Dasaratha of Ayodhya. Rama was banished to the forest for a period of fourteen years. For me, my only god is Rama and my only religion is complete obedience to his wishes, so I accompanied him. His wife Sita also came with him but she has been abducted by the *rakshasa* king Ravana. We have come to this place because we were told that your master, Sugriva, would be able to help us find her. It is indeed one of the quirks of fate that Rama, who is the refuge of all those in trouble, is now forced to seek the help of another to achieve his purpose."

Hanuman listened carefully to this story and said, "My master Sugriva has also had his fair share of problems. His wife was abducted by his brother and he is now forced to live the life of an exile on this lonely mountain-top. I will take you to him. I'm sure he will be able to help you. But these peaks are too steep for you to climb, so I will take you on my shoulders."

With these words, Hanuman took the brothers with ease on his back and brought them to Sugriva. Hanuman apprised Sugriva of the way he had met the brothers and why they had come there. He advised him to make friends with them and render all help. Sugriva was most relieved when he heard that they had not come from Vali, and did all that he could to make them welcome.

Offering his hand to Rama, he said, "Come, let us form a bond of friendship between us, which nothing can break."

Rama took his offered hand and embraced him happily. In the meantime, Hanuman had made a small fire and worshipped it with flowers. Rama and Sugriva went three times around the sacred fire and took an oath that they would remain friends forever. Rama swore to kill Vali and help Sugriva regain his kingdom, and Sugriva swore to help Rama regain his wife. Hanuman made a seat of twigs and the brothers sat on it. Then Sugriva narrated his tale of woe.

"My brother Vali captured my wife and threw me out of the kingdom. I escaped to this mountain, which is the only place he cannot come, since the *rishis* have put a curse on him. I pray you to help me get back my wife and my kingdom."

Rama was touched by his tale, which resembled his own, and promised to help him.

Sugriva continued, "My minister Hanuman has told me all about you and I promise that I will help you find your wife. One day not long ago, five of us were sitting on top of this peak when we saw a *rakshasa* sailing across the sky with a beautiful woman in his arms. She was crying out, 'O Rama! O Lakshmana!' I think it must have been your wife. When she saw us, she tied up something in a cloth, torn from her upper garment, and dropped it to us. We have kept the bundle safe. Here it is."

Rama turned pale when he saw the scrap of yellow cloth which he recognized to be Sita's. He opened it with trembling hands and almost fainted when he saw a few bits of her jewelery. He handed it over to Lakshmana, saying, "My grief, which I had somehow managed to overcome, has been fanned to flames again by the sight of these ornaments belonging to my beloved. Please inspect these and see if they are Sita's. My eyes are too blurred to see."

Lakshmana said, "Brother, I have never looked properly at her face, so I cannot recognize the necklaces. But these are her anklets. I know them well, since I fall at her feet every morning, to get her blessings."

Rama started to question Sugriva eagerly about everything he had seen on that day and what he knew about Ravana. Sugriva admitted sadly that he knew nothing about Ravana. All he had seen was a beautiful woman in great distress. From her cries he had guessed that she was being abducted. He assured Rama that they would soon rescue her.

"Be full of hope and courage. Please don't give way to your grief like this." Sugriva had a very affectionate nature and could not bear to see Rama's distress. "A friend considers the grief of his friend as his own, and I cannot bear to see your sorrow. Please rest assured that I will help you to recover your wife."

Then he recounted to Rama the full details of his own banishment.

"Vali is my eldest brother and was crowned king by my father. Kishkindha is the name of Vali's fortress. One day an *asura* (a kind of demonic being) called Dundubhi, in the shape of a buffalo, came and challenged Vali. Dundubhi was one of those who delighted in fights. He had challenged the ocean, who ignored him and swept over him with tidal waves, so that Dundubhi was forced to back off in a hurry. His next target was Himavan, the Lord of the Himalayas, who simply froze him with ice and sleet.

At last, Dundubhi came to Kishkinda and challenged Vali. After a good fight, Vali broke his neck and threw his carcass miles away, to this mountain. As it flew through the air, drops of blood fell on the altar of the *rishi* Matanga, who was practicing penance here and he cursed Vali that his head would break if he ever came here. That is why I have taken shelter at this place.

Mayavi was the son of Dundubhi. He came to Kishkinda to take revenge on Vali and challenged him to a fight. Vali and I came out and chased Mayavi, who ran off when he saw the two of us and hid in a cave. Vali followed him and told me to wait outside. I waited for a year and then, to my horror, I saw blood flowing out of the cave and heard the roars of the *asura*. I was sure that my dear brother was dead. I took a large stone and closed the mouth of the cave since I was afraid the *asura* would come out and kill me too. Sadly, I returned to Kishkinda and told my story. After due consideration, the ministers decided to crown me king.

One day, after a fairly long time, Vali returned. He was furious when he saw that I had been crowned. He spoke very harshly to me and accused me of having contrived a plot to oust him from his heritage. I spoke very sweetly to him and told him the whole story and begged him to take back his rightful inheritance. He would not listen to anything I had to say. He hounded me out of the kingdom and kept my wife Rumi for himself. For many years, I was a wandering mendicant. Eventually, I took refuge on this mountain, which is the one place to which Vali cannot come. O Rama! I can never forget the pain and humiliation which my brother has caused me." So saying, Sugriva burst into tears.

Rama comforted him and promised to kill Vali and get his kingdom back. Though he believed Rama, Sugriva had some doubts whether Rama could actually defeat Vali, for he knew his brother was very powerful.

Sugriva said, "Vali is as strong as a thousand elephants. Just for sport, he would pull down trees along the forest paths as he went along. He would snap off the peak of a mountain and fling it far away into the sea. Come, I will show you the huge skeleton of the *asura* Dundubhi, which is lying not far from here."

So saying, Sugriva took Rama to the skeleton. He also showed him seven huge palmyra trees, which Vali used to shake simultaneously as a joke, denuding them of their leaves.

Lakshmana was amused at this description of Vali's prowess. He realized that Sugriva doubted that Rama could defeat Vali.

He said to Sugriva, "I see that you have doubts about Rama's abilities. Tell me what he can do, to banish your doubts and restore your faith in him."

Sugriva hung his head in shame, for Lakshmana had correctly gauged his fears. "Please don't misunderstand me," he said. "My fear of Vali is so great that I find it difficult to accept that someone so slim and handsome as Rama can beat him. See those trees? Vali could pierce each tree with one arrow. Can Rama do that and will he able to lift up this skeleton of Dundubhi with one foot and fling it to a distance of a hundred lengths? If he can do these two tasks, my mind would be at rest."

Turning to Rama, he said, "Please don't think I'm trying to test you, or that I am trying to insult you by asking you to display your ability, but I don't want you to meet Vali until I'm sure that you can beat him."

Rama smiled reassuringly at him and said, "Your doubts are quite understandable. I'll try to convince you." Saying this, he walked up to the skeleton and lifting it with his foot, he flung it ten miles off. Sugriva was impressed but he still wavered.

"When Vali threw the body of Dundubhi, it was much heavier, covered as it was with flesh and blood. If you can pierce at least one of those trees with a single arrow, I will be convinced."

Rama smiled and, fixing an arrow on his bow, he shot it. The arrow sped like a golden streak and piercing all seven trees, it fell to the earth, along with the trees which were all split into two by Rama's arrow.

All five monkeys were jubilant when they saw this feat and jumped up and down with excitement. Sugriva's doubts had been relieved and he rushed to embrace Rama, begging his pardon for having doubted him.

"Let us go immediately to Kishkinda and kill Vali," he said with great excitement.

Rama agreed but he asked Sugriva to go first and challenge Vali to a duel. He promised to conceal himself and kill Vali when the opportunity arose.

Thus ends the fifthteenth chapter of the glorious Ramayana of Sage Valmiki *called "Hanuman."*

Hari Aum Tat Sat

Rama:
Holy one, please describe the Lord

Vasistha replies:
That intelligence in which the universe
of names and forms ceases,
is the Lord.
He is the emptiness in which the
universe appears to exist.
In Him there is no subject-object
relationship.
In Him consciousness stands still, like a
mountain.

— THE YOGA VASISTHA

SIXTEEN

THE KILLING
OF VALI

Valipramadanaya
Namaha!

Homage to the
who killed Vali.

I bow to Sri Ramachandra
Who is the abode of Lakshmi (goddess of wealth),
Who is God on earth,
Whose smile is as bright as the autumn moon.
Who is the light of the whole world and who destroyed Lanka.
—*RAMAYANA OF TULASIDAS*

THOUGH HE WAS QUAKING inside, Sugriva went up to the fortress gates and roared, summoning Vali to a duel. Vali couldn't believe his ears. Sugriva must have gone mad, he thought, or else he would never dare to do such a thing. Vali took it as a joke and began laughing uproariously. Sugriva bellowed again and Vali thought it was time that he taught him a lesson and with an angry cry he came out. As he charged out of the city gates, he looked like a mountain in motion and Sugriva's heart lurched with fear but he held his ground, confident that Rama would come to his aid. They came to blows on the open ground, just outside the city gates.

Rama and Lakshmana were hidden behind the bushes which surrounded the grounds. Rama carefully watched the pair but the brothers looked so much alike, that he wasn't sure which was Vali and which, Sugriva. The latter was no mean fighter but he was certainly not a match for Vali, who thrashed him to pulp within minutes. Rama was quite helpless and dared not shoot, for fear of hitting Sugriva. Poor Sugriva had no choice but to run for his life towards Rishyamukha. He was pursued by the enraged Vali, who threatened to kill him if he dared to make a nuisance of himself once again.

Rama, Lakshmana and Hanuman now approached the chastened Sugriva, who was licking his wounds. Naturally, he was most unhappy about the whole affair and said, "Why did you force me to challenge Vali if you did not wish to kill him? You could have told me so in the beginning and spared me this humiliating defeat."

Rama was full of remorse. Having pledged his word to Sugriva, he was bound to kill Vali and he told Sugriva the reason why he could not shoot.

"In size and form and even in the way of fighting, both of you were so much alike that I dared not shoot my arrow, for fear of killing you instead of your brother. What a tragic mistake that would have been! Never mind, take heart. Lakshmana will put a garland around your neck so that I am able to differentiate between the two of you. Please don't lose your courage. Go once again and challenge him, and this time, I assure you, that my arrow will find its mark."

All of them went once more to the thicket behind the arena. Rama, Lakshmana and Hanuman stood behind the shrubs, while thick-necked Sugriva bellowed his war cry and strode forth, once again like a lion, in front of the city gates. Vali was in his seraglio at that time. He couldn't believe his ears. His amorous mood gave way to one of violent loathing. He gave a roar of anger and decided to finish off his foolharded brother, once and for all. Sugriva had been a thorn in his side for many years, and it was time he made an end of him. That way he could keep his sister-in-law Ruma without any feeling of guilt. He knew the laws and he knew that he had done a despicable thing in consorting with the wife of his younger brother, who should have been treated like a daughter. He had somehow stifled his conscience all the while with various justifications but if Sugriva were dead, he would have a legitimate excuse for keeping her, for it was well within the dictates of moral law for a man to marry the widow of his dead brother, in order to protect her. Thinking along these lines, he was about to rush out of the gate, when his own wife, Tara, stopped him.

"My Lord," she said, "Please don't go to fight with your brother now. You have just thrashed him and sent him away. How can he dare to come again almost immediately, unless he is being helped by someone. Our son Angada told me something a while ago. His spies had found out that Rama and Lakshmana, the sons of

King Dasaratha, are here in this region and they have made friends with Sugriva and agreed to help him. I have heard that Rama is a most noble person and a great warrior. If he is helping your brother, you have no chance of victory. Remember that you have done Sugriva a great injustice by throwing him out of the kingdom for no fault of his own and appropriating his wife. Please go and make friends with him and agree to take him back and make him *yuvaraja* (prince regent). After all, you are the elder brother and it is for you to set an example. By doing this, you will make friends with Rama also. Please take my advice and do not make an enemy of Rama for I feel very frightened for you."

However, her plea fell on deaf ears. Vali's time was up and he was drawn to face his brother once again, feeling sure that this time he would kill him.

"How can I bear to make friends with that arrogant coward? This is the end. I will not brook his audacity anymore. As for Rama, I have heard that he is the soul of honor. He has no quarrel with me, so why should I fear him?"

He forgot that though Rama was the soul of honor, he was also the soul of dharma and he would never be able to bear such harsh treatment of a younger brother by an elder.

Tara embraced her husband and prayed for his safety. She returned to her chambers with slow and dragging steps. She had a premonition that she would never see him alive again.

Vali rushed out with a roar and the brothers locked themselves in a fierce combat. Sugriva fought with all his might, and for some time, the only sounds to be heard were grunts and groans. Rama was watching the fight closely. Perhaps he hoped that Sugriva would manage to defeat Vali by himself, but soon he saw that his friend was weakening and looking around desperately for help. Rama knew that the time had come for him to do what he did not want to do, but which was unavoidable if he wanted to keep his promise to his friend. He fixed the arrow to the bow and let it go with a tremendous twang. It flashed forward and hit its mark with deadly accuracy and the mighty Vali fell with a groan. He lay on the ground like a fallen god, drenched in blood, yet filled with splendor even in death. Rama and Lakshmana came out of the bushes and walked toward the fallen hero.

Vali watched them come and, when they were close enough he said, "I was fighting with my brother when suddenly an arrow hit me from somewhere and felled me, like a mighty tree. I had no quarrel with you, Rama, yet you deemed it right to kill me, while hiding behind the trees. Why did you do this? What have you gained by it? You are the son of an emperor and said to possess all great qualities. They say you are valiant, generous and righteous. You are famed for having observed the rules of dharma all your life. Why have you forgotten your own rules? When Sugriva challenged me a second time, my wife Tara warned me that he might have been helped by you, but I was not afraid of that, since I was sure that you would never stoop to anything unrighteous. You are the king of this land and we are only monkeys, living on this small piece of territory and fighting over trivial things. Why should you concern yourself with our squabbles? Rama, today you have killed me, although I am innocent. This act of yours will always be questioned. It is against all the rules of dharma. I know that you have lost your wife and Sugriva has promised to help you, but had you approached me first I could have aided you without any difficulty. I would have brought her back to you in a single day. I have already defeated Ravana once, long ago." So saying, Vali fell back, exhausted, to the ground. The monkey king was fast losing his strength.

Now the question is often asked why Rama did this. Why do all the ancient Hindu scriptures revel in such dilemmas? They could surely have avoided the whole problem, instead of putting their heroes in positions which are so controversial. We find the same thing in the *Mahabharata*. Arjuna was put in the difficult position of having to slay his own kin. The whole of the *Bhagavad Gita* is Lord Krishna's response to such problematic situations.

The fact is that, in life, we are often put in such perplexing situations. The way we face these situations depends on our character and view of life and the type of dharma which we follow. Here the question is often asked why Rama didn't go and challenge Vali himself. Valmiki has taken pains to show us that Rama was far superior to Vali in strength. So certainly it was not fear of defeat that stopped him. The reasons why he did not do so are many. Vali was actually a great soul and had he seen Rama face to face, he would certainly have desisted from fighting and done his best to become friends with him. This meant that Rama would not have been able to keep his promise to Sugriva, with whom he had already forged a pact of friendship in front of fire. It was a solemn covenant which could not be broken. Moreover, Vali had done the very thing for which he was going to punish Ravana. He had abducted Sugriva's wife. The punishment for one who abducted a brother's wife was death, and Rama, as the embodiment of dharma, had to mete out this punishment. Considering all these things, Rama did not go and challenge Vali to a fight, for he knew that Vali would immediately have surrendered to him and taken refuge at his feet, and Rama could never resist pardoning anyone who surrendered to him, as we shall see in the war with Ravana. This meant that he would never have been able to kill him, as he had promised Sugriva to do.

Rama waited patiently for Vali to have his say, for he knew that on the face of it, Vali had every right to berate him. After Vali had exhausted himself, Rama spoke with compassion in his eyes, though he put on a semblance of anger.

"O Vali! You speak of dharma and *adharma* as if you know all about them, but you fail to see your own misdemeanors. Your younger brother, who is full of good qualities, should have been treated as a son by you. Instead of that, you banished him from his kingdom and misappropriated his wife Ruma. According to the law of this land, anyone who looks on his daughter, his sister or the wife of his brother with lust should be punished, and the punishment is death. You have been sleeping with your brother's wife, when he is still alive, and this violates the eternal dharma. Why do you accuse me of transgressing the law, when I have only complied with the law? Sugriva is as dear to me as Lakshmana. I have sworn to be his friend and publicly gave him my word to restore his kingdom and his wife to him. How could I go back on that promise? I have only kept my word to him, nothing else, so why do you accuse me of *adharma*? You would have done the same if you had been in my position."

Vali considered Rama's words and realized that he spoke the truth. He bitterly regretted his cruelty to his younger brother, whom he should have treated as a son, as Rama said. He also knew that his action in having stolen his brother's wife was despicable. With flowing eyes and choked voice, Vali said,

"O Rama! You are right. I deserve to be punished. I am not

worried about myself. I should die for my crimes but I am worried about the future of my only son, Angada. Please consider him as your own son and look after him. Please don't let my beloved Tara be insulted by Sugriva. She was a very good wife to me. I realize now that I was fated to meet death at your hands and that is why I did not listen to her when she begged me not to go."

Rama spoke comfortingly to Vali and promised him that he would take very good care of Angada. "What Angada was to you, he will be to me and to Sugriva, so depart in peace." He stroked Vali's dying body with loving hands and Vali felt a great peace creeping into his soul at Rama's tender touch. He begged Rama to forgive him for his hasty words, spoken under delusion and anger. Then he lost consciousness.

Tara heard that her husband was killed and she rushed out of the fortress with her son. The other monkeys tried to stop her and said that she should flee from that place with Angada, in case Sugriva might want to harm them. She spoke scornfully to them.

"My beloved husband is lying dead and you expect me to protect myself! Of what use is life to me, after he has gone. I don't want the kingdom and I don't fear for my son. All I want is to go to him." She ran out of the fortress gates to the spot where Vali had fallen. She threw herself on his body and cried as if her heart would break. Angada followed suit. Sugriva felt sorely grieved at this scene. So did Rama and Lakshmana.

"I am Tara, my Lord," she said, "why don't you answer me? This hard ground is not a fitting bed for you. Come, let us go back to the palace where I have prepared a silken mattress for you. My heart must indeed be very hard or how could it go on beating, when you are lying dead? Why did you not listen to me when I begged you not to go? Angada, my dear child, take a last look at your valiant father. Who knows what your fate will be! Rama has kept his promise to his friend and dispatched your father to heaven. Sugriva, the kingdom is yours. Your enemy is killed and you will be reunited with your wife. All your desires will be fulfilled. I hope you will be happy." She beat her breast and wept bitterly. It was a most painful scene for everyone.

Hanuman went to her and tried to console her. "A man reaps the fruits of his actions, be they good or bad. The human body is like a bubble on the surface of the water. No one need mourn for another, since we are all to be pitied. Where is the cause for grief in a world where everything is transient? It is not right for you to think of giving up your life when you have a son to protect. Your son looks up to you and so do your subjects. Angada will surely be king. Let him now perform the obsequies for his father, which is the duty of a son. After that, he will crowned as *yuvaraja*. You are a wise lady and you know only too well that life and death are inevitable and this life is most impermanent. This is why we should always try to perform as many good acts as we can while alive. Your thoughts should now be only for your son."

Vali painfully opened his weary eyes and saw his brother and said, "Sugriva, forgive me for what I have done to you. We were not fated to share affection with each other. Accept this kingdom from me, as well as my son, my immense wealth and great fame. Listen to my last wishes. Here is my son Angada, dearer to me than my life. Treat him as your own. He will prove his valor in the war with Ravana. Don't forget your promise to Rama. Help him to find his wife. He was prepared to besmirch his own name for your sake, for the sake of a friend. So do all you can to help him. My wife Tara is a very wise woman. Take her advice in all matters of state. She is invariably right about these things. And finally, take this golden garland. It is divine and will lose its power once I die, so remove it before my life ebbs away. Take it. I have no further use for it."

When Sugriva heard these words of Vali, he started sobbing and all his pleasure at his victory vanished.

Vali called his son to his side, saying, "My child, remember your altered circumstances and obey Sugriva in everything. Accept happiness and sorrow as they come and do not be too moved by either."

By now his end was fast approaching and he fell back gasping. Within a few minutes he was dead. Tara was inconsolable. Sugriva too was filled with remorse. Approaching Rama, he said, "Rama, you kept your word and Vali is dead, but now I have lost interest in becoming king. The death of Vali, the sorrow of his queen and the helpless look in the eyes of his son have made me averse to stepping into my brother's shoes. I have had so many fights with him, in all of which he could have easily killed me at any moment, but he always gave me a thrashing and let me go. I should never have wished for his death. I am a sinner and not fit to rule. I will not break my promise to you. Hanuman will help you but all I want is to fall into the pyre with my brother and die."

Tara also approached Rama and said, "You have been separated from your wife and you know how painful it is. Don't you think that Vali feels the same pain as you do? Please do me one favor and use the same arrow on me, as you used on my husband, so that I can join him."

Rama was sorely distressed by these words and tried to comfort her.

"You are the wife of a hero and you should not give way to despair. The *Vedas* say that everything functions according to the will of Brahma. You cannot overrule the dictates of fate. It is the sole and powerful cause for all happenings. No one can escape its decrees. It is not partial to anyone. Vali has now reached the heavens, which he has well earned through his valor. Rouse yourself from this despondency and ask your son to perform the last rites for his father."

Lakshmana urged Sugriva to do what was necessary. A richly decorated palanquin was brought, on which Vali was placed and carried to the pyre, which Angada lighted. After performing all the rites, they bathed in the river and returned to the city of Kishkinda.

All the *vanaras* surrounded Rama and begged him to take charge of their affairs, since Sugriva was in a state of shock. Hanuman invited him to enter the city and attend the coronation.

Rama said, "According to the vow I made my father, I cannot enter a village or city until my fourteen years of exile are over. Let Sugriva be taken to the city and crowned." Turning to Sugriva, he said, "Go and take up the reins of government. Crown this young prince as *yuvaraja*."

Then turning to Lakshmana and the others, he continued, "This is the month of *shravana*, the first month of the rainy season. Lakshmana and I will spend the four months of the monsoons in some cave in the forest. When the month of *kartika* comes and the rains cease, you can think about fulfilling your promise to me."

Sugriva went into the city and was crowned. After that, he crowned Angada as heir apparent. He was reunited with his wife and spent the next four months reveling with her and the other women of Vali's harem.

Rama and Lakshmana went to the hill called Prasravana, where they found a comfortable and spacious cave which they decided to make their home for the duration of the rainy season.

Thus ends the sixteenth chapter of the glorious Ramayana *of Sage Valmiki called "The Killing of Vali."*

Hari Aum Tat Sat

One who keeps the name of Rama,
Which is the sole mantra to escape from the coils of the world,
In mind constantly,
Will have all power in the palm of his hands.

—Ramayana of Tulasidas

SEVENTEEN

SEARCH FOR SITA

O mind, sing about the compassionate Lord, Ramachandra,
The lotus-eyed, lotus-faced, lotus-footed one,
Who takes away the fear of the cruel world.
—RAMAYANA OF TULASIDAS

Saumyaya
Namaha!

Homage to
the ever
pleasant one.

T HE CAVE WAS LOCATED in a very beautiful spot, surrounded on all sides by lovely trees, with flowering creepers entwined on their trunks. Everywhere they looked, they saw only beauty and Rama was filled with nostalgia and longing for Sita, for she loved to see such things and would exclaim in such delight that he, in turn, would find joy in her innocent enthusiasm. He spent sleepless nights thinking of his love. Soon the monsoons set in with a vengeance. Indra let loose the floodgates of his waters and the rain fell in sheets, with thunder and lightning thrown in for special effects. Rama and Lakshmana could scarcely step out of the cave. The enforced confinement was galling to both of them. There was nothing to distract Rama's mind. All he could do was to sit and brood over Sita's fate. Once when he saw the watery moon rising over the mountain, he could not contain his grief any longer and broke down and sobbed like a child. Lakshmana comforted him as best as he could.

"Brother," he said, "you have often told me that one who loses his mental equilibrium will never be able to accomplish anything. All we need is a little bit of time. As soon as the monsoons are over, we will set out and find her. We will kill the *rakshasa* and rescue her. So please don't grieve."

Rama was touched by his tenderness. "My dear child, I know that your love for me is infinite and you

135

speak words of wisdom. I realize that sorrow is debilitating and I'll try and shake it off. It is hard to be patient when I think of how unhappy my darling is, but I will do my best."

Lakshmana confessed that the enforced inaction was getting on his nerves also. Somehow they managed to contain their impatience, and at last the four months dragged to a close and the skies became blue once again.

Hanuman was always conscious of where his duty lay and when the stipulated time was over, he went to Sugriva to remind him of his promise to Rama. After his years of exile, Sugriva found his new life of luxury intoxicating. Having been deprived of proper food and women for many years now, he could think of nothing else. He left all matters of state in the able hands of his ministers and spent time in the harem, with women and wine. Tara, being a philosophical woman, had decided to drown her sorrow at her husband's death in wine and make use of the comfort and security which Sugriva offered her. Besides, the *vanaras* as a tribe were not famous for their morals.

Hanuman approached Sugriva and reminded him gently of his duty. "My Lord, your wife and your kingdom have been restored to you by the kindness of Rama. Have you forgotten that you owe him a debt? The time has come for you to repay it. Please set aside your other interests and devote yourself to the matter at hand. Rama is too noble to remind you of your duty, so it is up to you to make all arrangements and inform him of them. Do not provoke Rama's anger. If you do, nothing can save you."

Sugriva roused himself from his inebriation and sent for Neela, who was one of his generals, and told him to get the whole army to assemble in Kishkinda. "They must be here within fifteen days from today," he said. "Ask Angada to be my representative and arrange everything." So saying, he retired once more to enjoy the pleasures of the harem.

At last, the rainy season was over. The long autumnal nights with the harvest moon hanging like a golden orb in the sky caused Rama to ache for his beloved. He was filled with despair.

Lakshmana, who had gone to collect fruits, returned and saw his brother in a hopeless state and cursed Sugriva for his tardiness.

"My beloved brother, it does not become you to give way to grief like this. Don't fritter away your energy dwelling on sorrow. I'm sure

Sugriva must have commenced his search for Sita. Nothing bad can happen to her, for she is like a flame, which will burn to ashes anyone who dares to touch it."

Rama agreed with Lakshmana. "Child, your words filled with wisdom are always a source of great comfort to me. I'm sorry to have given in to my sorrow again but this season, with its haunting beauty, brings poignantly to my mind thoughts of my lovely wife and I long for her with all my heart. She must also be suffering the pangs of separation just as I am. She used to love to hear the call of the cranes and would imitate them. However lovely the flowers are, they mean nothing to me when she is not here to appreciate them. How long is this torture going to last? These four months have seemed like four years to me. Still, Sugriva has not sent anyone to call us. I think he has forgotten his promise. Filled with lust, the king of the *vanaras* seems to have forgotten our very existence. Lakshmana, go and ask him if he wants to hear the twang of my bow. Remind him of the death of Vali and the debt he owes to me. The rains have ceased and he has not awakened from his dream of pleasure. Time is passing and I have waited long enough. Go soon, O Lakshmana! Tell him to honor the promise he made to me or be prepared to face my arrows."

Lakshmana was not a calm person by nature and he had been confined inside the cave for four months, which had not improved matters. Now, the sight of his brother's agitation made his blood boil. He strapped the quiver to his shoulder and took up his bow. "Rama, Sugriva does not deserve to be king. Drunk with power, he has forgotten the codes of decent behavior. I will dispatch him immediately to the abode of Yama and ask Angada to carry on with the search."

Rama's anger abated when he saw his brother's reaction and he advised Lakshmana not to repeat what he had just said in anger but to adopt a conciliatory attitude.

Lakshmana walked to Kishkinda with purposeful strides. The earth shook with the force of his angry steps. The entrance to the city was through a cave which was guarded by *vanaras*, so that no one could enter without permission. Seeing Lakshmana, they uprooted trees, in order to stop him from entering. When he saw this, Lakshmana became doubly angry and, when the *vanaras* saw his fury, they flew off in all directions. They ran to Sugriva and told him of Lakshmana's violent mood. The king was inebriated, and lost to the world in the arms of his brother's wife. The monkeys ran to Angada, who hurriedly came out of the gates to meet Lakshmana and try to pacify him. Lakshmana ordered him to call his uncle immediately. He could hear the sweet strains of music and revelry floating in the air and when he thought of the agony of his brother these past four months, his anger could not be controlled. Angada was scared out of his wits and ran to tell his uncle and mother of Lakshmana's arrival. Sugriva could hardly understand what was happening. In fact, he could hardly stand. Hanuman came to him and told him once again to go out and try to pacify Lakshmana, who was in a fury.

"Why should he be angry with me? What crime have I committed?" whined the tipsy king.

Hanuman assured him that Rama was not seriously angry with him. "You must admit that you have allowed time to elapse. You have lost track of the seasons in your ardor. Rama has been counting the days till we would go in search of his wife. Pained in heart and mind, he has sent Lakshmana to you. Please go and talk sweetly to him."

Sugriva did not dare to go and face him. He begged Tara to go and appease Lakshmana, since he knew that Lakshmana would not display his anger before a woman. Tara was also in a state of inebriation. Her gait was unsteady and her hair and clothes disheveled. Lakshmana took one look at her and realized the state she was in, and averted his eyes.

Tara went out and approached Lakshmana, saying seductively, "Why, O noble prince, are you so angry? Who has been foolish enough to kindle your wrath?"

Lakshmana replied, "Your husband seems to have forgotten all the rules of dharma. Wallowing in lust, he has forgotten the promises he made to my brother. If you wish to do him some good, go and tell him to rouse himself from this orgy and help Rama. Ingratitude leads to the destruction of the best of men. We have been betrayed by one whom we considered a friend."

Tara replied in a sweet and gentle tone. "O prince, please do not be angry with Sugriva. You know that *kama* is a powerful emotion. Even *rishis* have fallen to its lures. What can I say about a mere monkey, who is fickle by nature and who has been denied these

pleasures for many years? Please forgive him for his apparent
indifference, which has been caused by weakness. Actually, he has
already ordered the army to be mobilized and soon hundreds of
monkeys from all over the country will be assembled here, to start out
on their quest to find Sita. Please come inside and meet Sugriva."

She led him into the inner apartments. Sugriva said not a word and
stood with palms folded in front of him, while Lakshmana berated him.
Tara tried once more to intervene and make excuses for her husband.

"O prince," she said, "For Rama's sake, Sugriva will give up
everything, even me and his wife Rumi. He is devoted to Rama. His
army will be here at any moment. Please relax and rest assured that
everything will be done as you wish."

Lakshmana was a little calmed by this assurance. Sugriva,
seeing his anger had abated a little, now humbly begged his pardon.
Both of them went to see Rama and tried to convince him that
things were already underway.

Sugriva bowed before Rama and said, "You are like a god to
me. How can I ever forget what you have done for me? Please don't
think me ungrateful. Soon this entire hillside will be covered by
monkeys. I will dispatch them to all corners of the globe and
discover the whereabouts of Sita. Rest assured that you will soon be
re-united with her."

Within ten days, as he said, the whole hillside was covered with
monkeys. They came in the millions, lion-tailed, dark-faced, red-
bottomed, white-furred and golden-haired, ranging from all parts of
the country, from the Himalayas to the southern sea. All the world's
tree folk answered Sugriva's call and crowded round their king, to
await his commands. The bears also came, with their king Jambavan,
who was an old and shaggy black bear, noted for his wisdom and
respected by all the monkeys.

Sugriva summoned his general, Vinata, and asked him to go east
and scour the forests, hills and caves of that region, for any signs of
Sita and return within a month, on pain of death. Another troop was
dispatched to the west and another to the north. Turning to
Hanuman, he said, "You are exceptional. Please take a troop and go
south. You are sure to find a way to reach Sita."

Rama was delighted that Hanuman was being sent south. Taking
out his signet ring with the crest of the Ikshvaku dynasty, he handed it

over to Hanuman as a token, to reassure Sita that he was indeed
Rama's messenger. His last words to him were, "Hanuman, remember
I am depending entirely on you. Make every attempt to locate Sita. I
know that you will succeed."

The monkeys who had been sent to the north, east and west
returned within the stipulated month and sadly admitted that they
had found no traces of Sita. Sugriva told Rama that Sita must be
somewhere in the south, as he had seen her being carried in that
direction. He assured Rama that if anyone could achieve the
impossible, it was Hanuman, who was the son of the wind god.

Hanuman's party, which had gone south, made a thorough
search of all the forests and caves. The time given to them was
coming to an end and they were fast losing hope. They hadn't been
able to find any food or water for days. Suddenly they saw a cave in
front of which birds were flying. They decided to go in and search it.
It was dim and dark and they could hardly see anything. Hanuman
went first and Angada caught hold of his tail and followed. All the
rest came, each catching the tail of the one in front. Thus they
slipped and slithered down the slope of the cave and suddenly fell
into a garden which was so enchanting, that it could only be
described as celestial.

There, they saw many beautiful mansions and lovely ponds
looking like gems. At last they came upon a lady ascetic and
questioned her about the place. She said that the site had been
designed by the architect of the demons, who was called Mayan. He
was the master of illusions and she said that all the wonders they
were seeing were pure illusion. She was the guardian of the place
and her name was Swayamprabha. She naturally wanted to know all
about them. But first, she entertained them with a lavish feast of
fruits and honey. Hanuman told her the whole story of their quest
and asked her the way out of the cave. She said that normally those
who entered the cave by accident would never be able get out of it
by themselves, but with her yogic powers, she wafted them out. She
pointed out to them the sea on one side and the Malaya mountains
on the other and told them to choose their course.

The monkeys stood dejectedly on the seashore watching the
magnificence of the ocean. Their stipulated time was over, for they
had spent a long time in the enchanted garden. They dared not go

back empty handed, fearing the wrath of the king. Angada called a meeting of the *vanaras*.

He said, "The time allotted to us is over and we dare not return for we will be executed. It is best that we fast to death on this seashore. The king has no affection for me and will punish me severely. I would rather die here than return to face his wrath."

The monkeys said that they would prefer to return to the cave, where they could live in comfort and plenty, rather than sacrifice their lives. Angada was undecided when he heard this. Hanuman had no desire to go and live a life of pleasure in the cave, nor did he wish to starve to death.

"Let us go back and beg forgiveness from Sugriva," he said, "that is the honorable thing to do."

But Angada, who feared his uncle greatly, was not convinced of this. He decided that he would give up his life on the seashore. Those who wanted to join him could do so and the rest could go back. So saying, he lay down on the hot sands and prepared for death. The rest followed suit.

Thus ends the seventeenth chapter of the glorious Ramayana *of Sage Valmiki called "Search for Sita."*

Hari Aum Tat Sat

EIGHTEEN

WISE COUNSEL

Wherever the name of Rama is chanted,
There does Hanuman, the destroyer of the demons, reside,
With overflowing eyes and bowed head.
—SOURCE UNKNOWN

I N ONE OF THE CAVES NEARBY, there lived an old
eagle called Sampati, who was the brother of
Jatayu. He hadn't eaten for quite a while, since he
had lost the strength to look for food. Hearing the noise
made by the monkeys, he came out of his cave and
found them all lying on the shore, waiting for death.

"Today fortune has indeed favored me! I haven't
eaten for days and here are some delicious monkeys, all
laid out in neat rows, waiting for me to go and eat
them!" With these words, the bird started to hop toward
them, since he didn't have any wings. The monkeys
heard him say this to himself and became frightened.
They did not wish to be eaten alive by an eagle, even
though they were prepared to fast to death.

Angada started lamenting over their fate to
Hanuman. "Just look at what has happened to us! This
bird looks as if he is Yama himself, coming to make an
end of us. It is said that all birds and animals love
Rama. Even the old eagle Jatayu was prepared to give
up his life for his sake."

When Sampati heard the name of his brother he
called out, "Who are you? What do you know of my
brother Jatayu? How did he die? Tell me everything."

At first, the monkeys were suspicious but soon
they started to talk and gave him all their news.
Sampati's eyes filled with tears when he heard of the
fate of his younger brother and he wept bitterly.

Angada now asked him how he knew Jatayu.

Sampati said, "Jatayu was my younger brother. When we were young, we had a competition and flew straight at the sun. When it started to get really hot, I protected Jatayu with my wings, so that he escaped, I fell to the ground with burned wings. I have not seen him since."

Then Angada told him the story of Rama and why they had come there and asked him if he knew anything about Ravana.

Sampati said, "I saw Sita being carried away by that wicked *rakshasa*. He held her in a fierce grip while she did her best to wriggle out of his grasp. She was crying out piteously for Rama and Lakshmana. I will tell you where Ravana lives."

A flash of hope dawned in the hearts of all the monkeys when they heard this and they crowded round the old bird and begged him to tell them all he knew.

He continued, "Ravana is the son of Vishravas and his capital is the city of Lanka. It is on an island and Sita is a prisoner in his palace. With my eagle's keen vision, I can see all the way to Lanka. If any of you is capable of crossing the sea, you will be able to see her, as I can see her." As he said this, a miracle occurred and the old eagle sprouted his wings back. He had been blessed that his wings would grow again when he heard the story of Rama and he flew straight up into the sky, like a young bird.

The monkeys now clustered on the shore and thought of plans to cross the ocean. They felt quite helpless but Angada encouraged them to think of some plan and asked them if any one of them could jump that far. There was great excitement in the group when he said this and, in quick succession, one said that he could jump ten miles, another twenty, another thirty, and so on. Angada himself said he could jump all the way to Lanka but feared that he might not be able to make it back.

Now Jambavan, the old bear who was part of their group, went up to Hanuman, who was sitting apart, lost in thought.

"O Hanuman," he said, "why are you sitting like this, in a reverie? Don't you know that you are the son of the wind god and equal in strength to Rama or Lakshmana or Sugriva?" He then told him his life story.

"There was once a celestial nymph called Punjikasthala, who was cursed to be born on earth, as the daughter of a monkey chief. Her name was Anjana and she was famed for her beauty. She was married to a monkey called Kesari. She was able to take a human form when she wished. One day she happened to be roaming on the hills surrounding Kishkinda in her human form when the wind god Vayu happened to be passing by. He saw the beautiful girl and fell in love with her. With one gust, he lifted her garments and seeing the beauty of her limbs, he ravished her on the hillside.

"When she protested, he replied, 'Fear not, O charming girl, you will be blessed with a son, who will be a truly glorious being. He will be as powerful as I, and full of extraordinary courage, strength, energy and intelligence.' Anjana was mollified when she heard these words. She gave birth to a beautiful baby monkey on the same day. You had white fur, a red face and tawny, golden eyes. Since your mother was the wife of another monkey, she left you inside a cave and returned to Kishkinda.

"In the morning, you were very hungry. When the sun came up, looking like a golden mango, you took a flying leap at the golden orb and tried to catch it. Your father Vayu tried to protect you from getting burned. It was the time of the eclipse, when the planet *Rahu* comes to eat the sun. You now jumped at *Rahu* and tried to catch him. *Rahu* went and complained to Indra, who came on his elephant, to find out who the new troublemaker was. Seeing the little monkey, Indra hurled his thunderbolt at him, so that you fell on the mountain side and hurt the left side of your chin very badly. From that time, you have been known as Hanuman, the one with a broken chin. Your father was furious and refused to blow in the world anymore, so Brahma placated him and conferred a boon on you, that you would be invincible in battle. Indra too was sorry at what he had done to you and gave you another boon, that death would come to you only when you wished for it. Then you were taken by your father to Mount Kailasa, the abode of Lord Shiva, who taught you many things, including the knowledge of how to change your form at will. Shiva's bull Nandi taught you all the arts, so that you became an accomplished scholar, proficient in the *Vedas*. But he also endowed you with great humility so that you can never remember your strength, unless someone reminds you of it. Then, at Sugriva's request, you returned to Kishkinda and became his friend. We are all on the brink of despair and only you can save us. Know your own strength and leap to this city of Ravana and save us from this predicament."

When he heard these words of Jambavan, Hanuman suddenly realized his own strength and, drawing himself up to his full height he started growing and growing until his head seemed to hit the sky. The other monkeys watched, fascinated by this miracle.

From his enormous height, he spoke to them, "Vayu is very powerful. He pervades the whole universe. I am the son of that Vayu and there is nothing that I am not capable of doing. I will cross the sea in a matter of moments, see Rama's queen and bring her back if possible."

In his exuberance, he jumped from peak to peak, crushing mountains as easily as if they were small as pebbles. The monkeys watched open-mouthed at this display of power. Climbing to the top of the mountain, he concentrated his mind on Rama and took a flying leap into the air and, before the astonished gaze of the monkeys, he sailed across the sky.

Thus ends the eighteenth chapter of the glorious Ramayana *of Sage Valmiki called "Wise Counsel"*

Hari Aum Tat Sat

Rama:
How can we realize this Lord?

Vasistha replies:

The Lord can be realized only when one is firmly established in the unreality of the universe. It is as unreal as the blueness of the sky.
Dualism presupposes unity, as non-dualism suggests duality.
God can be realized only when the creation is known to be unreal.

—THE YOGA VASISTHA

BOOK FIVE

Sundaraya Namaha!

Homage to the handsome one.

SUNDARA KANDA

THE BOOK OF BEAUTY

NINETEEN

LEAP TO LANKA

Jagadgurave
Namaha!

Homage to
the preceptor
of the world.

*I bow to the messenger of Rama, who is swift as thought,
as fast as the wind
Who has conquered his senses and is of mighty intellect,
The son of the wind god, first amongst monkeys.*
—POPULAR VERSE

H ANUMAN STOOD ON THE MOUNTAIN and saluted the gods presiding over the quarters. He repeated the glorious mantra "Rama, Rama, Rama" and concentrated on Rama. Then he shook himself and roared like thunder. He swung his tail into the sky until it looked like a hooded serpent. Placing his hands on the rock, he sucked in his belly and folded his legs. Thrusting his neck far out, he held his breath and concentrating his mind on Rama and repeating the Rama mantra, he took a flying leap. He was absolutely confident of his ability to jump over the ocean and find Sita. Because of the force with which he jumped, trees were uprooted and some even sped after him, scattering their flowers on the sea. Hanuman coursed through the air like a thundercloud.

Varuna, the god of the waters, wanted to help him and asked the mountain, called Mainaka, to rise up from the waters and give him a resting place. Hanuman saw the mountain rising and thought it was an impediment in his path. He tried to push it aside but the mountain took on the form of a lady and told him that she had been sent to give him a resting place. Hanuman was pleased but refused her offer, since he was in a desperate hurry. The watching gods wanted to test his determination and sent Surasa, the mother of the serpents, to block his path. She came in the form of a huge *rakshasi*, who tried to gobble him up.

She said, "No one can pass without entering my mouth." So Hanuman started growing in size and she enlarged her mouth to suit his stature. Then suddenly, he became small as a thumb and entered her mouth and came out again.

"Now that I have done what you told me to do, let me pass," he said.

She was pleased and allowed him to proceed. Then there was another sea-monster who tried to catch him by his shadow but Hanuman swooped down and killed her and continued with his journey. Soon he saw signs of land and realized that he was close to his destination.

He thought that he would be the cynosure of all eyes if he went into Lanka in this huge form, so he changed himself into a small, insignificant-looking monkey and stood on the peak overlooking Lanka, in order to survey the land. He saw a magnificent city built on a hill, surrounded by a moat. It was so well guarded that it would be almost impossible to enter. The mansions were glittering in the evening light and the hill was covered with trees and flowering bushes. He could see the clean white roads, bordered by green, luscious-looking grass. Situated as it was on top of the hill, Lanka looked as if it were floating on air, for there were clouds surrounding it.

Hanuman nimbly jumped from rock to rock as he made his way to the northern gate, which was guarded by fierce-looking *rakshasas*. He felt that it would be an impossible task for an army to enter Lanka. First of all, how would Rama, accompanied by a horde of monkeys, cross the sea which he had just sailed over? Even if they succeeded in crossing, how would they assail this bastion which looked so impregnable? The sentries would be able to see anyone as soon as they landed on the shore. "Even my father, the god of wind, would not be able to enter this city undetected," he thought to himself. He decided that he himself would go and discover the whereabouts of Sita, for that was his immediate task. He waited till darkness had set in and then shrunk his body even further, to the size of a small cat, and went near the gate. He saw seven- and eight-story palaces with pillars, gleaming with pearls and coral. Precious stones were studded in the walls and the perfume of incense was rising from the hearths. He waited till a pale moon floated across the sky accompanied by her attendants, the stars. He was so small that he could easily have slipped through the bars of the gate but, as he tried to do so, he was accosted by the *rakshasi* who was the guardian of the gate.

"Who are you?" she demanded. "You look like a monkey. Why have you come here? Tell the truth or forfeit your life. No one can enter Lanka without my permission."

Hanuman spoke humbly, "Tell me, O lady, who you are. Why are you standing in this frightening pose?"

She said gruffly, "My name is Lankini and I'm here to obey the orders of the king. I have been ordered to kill anyone who enters without reason and I'm going to kill you, unless you tell me the purpose of your visit."

Unruffled by this apparition, Hanuman said, "Madam, I have heard about the beauty of Lanka and I've come here to see it for myself. I just want to see its glories and then I'll go away. I have not come here to stay."

She was not impressed by his sweet words and said, "You are a stupid little monkey. You will have to fight with me if you wish to enter." So saying, she gave him a slap on his face.

Without saying a word, Hanuman boxed her back with his left hand. Even though he didn't use all his strength, she fell down with a thud. She was astonished to be knocked down by a small cat-like monkey.

She said, "I had a boon from Brahma that I would be invincible. But he also warned me that I would be vanquished by a monkey. When such a thing happened, he told me that it was a foreboding of disaster for the *rakshasas*. I see now that the time has come for Ravana to be vanquished. I suppose that you have come in search of Sita. You are at liberty to enter the city and do what you wish." Then Lankini vanished from the city forever.

Having gotten rid of its presiding deity, Hanuman entered the fabulous city of Lanka and stared spellbound. Wherever he looked, he saw nothing but beauty. There was music everywhere, the tinkle of anklets on women's feet, the rustle of silks and satins, perfume of jasmine and sandalwood, and palaces, gleaming in the silvery sheen of the moon. The army was parading the streets but he was so small that no one noticed him. At one point, he saw the wonderous aerial chariot of Ravana's, which he had stolen from his brother, Kubera. It was called Pushpaka, or the flower chariot. *Pushpa* means flower, and the chariot was covered with flowers and many wonderful ornaments. He jumped onto the platform surrounding it and gazed fascinated.

At last, he reached a palace which was even more magnificent than the rest. "This must be Ravana's," he thought. He slipped in through the doorway, which was exquisitely carved and inlaid with gems and pearls. The seats, couches and beds were all of gold, set with gems. The rooms glowed with the shine emanating from all the gold and jewels. All the wealth of Kubera seemed to be here.

The scene was one of revelry and rioting. Hundreds of voluptuous females sprawled about in various states of abandonment. Some lay on the carpets with disheveled hair and scattered jewelry, some were dancing and some drinking. The red dots on their foreheads were often smeared by their lover's hands, their girdles were loosened, clothes crushed and garlands trampled. Pearls gleamed in the moonlight between their heavy breasts and gold pendants hung from their ears. Some ladies were caressing their lovers, who were very inebriated. Others were rubbing sandal paste on their perspiring bodies, some sprawled naked, some were welcoming their lovers with eager kisses, while a few virtuous ones were ensconced in their husbands' arms. They were all enchanting to look at, elegantly clad, fragrant with flowers, with curved eyes and long lashes and sidelong glances, guaranteed to entice all men.

All the most beautiful women from all over had been captured and brought to Lanka by Ravana. He had travelled through the length and breadth of all the worlds in his aerial vehicle, grabbing virgin daughters of the *nagas, gandharvas, daityas, danavas* and *rishis*.[1] All of them had cried and struggled when they were captured and sworn to kill themselves, but in the end they had succumbed to his charms for his expertise in the art of lovemaking was proverbial. He had been cursed by their parents over and over again and by those whom he had brought here forcibly. Seeing all these glamorous beauties, Hanuman began to feel sorry for Ravana. Instead of being contented with all these women, he was deliberately courting death by capturing Sita. Most of the women were obviously under the influence of wine. Hanuman's eyes roved over all of them and he knew for sure that none of these abandoned

---

[1] *nagas, gandharvas, daityas, danavas and rishis*—Nagas are a kind of snake people. Gandharvas are celestial muscians. Daityas and Danavas are two different demonic races. Rishis are sages.

women could be Sita, however beautiful they might be. He had created a picture of Sita as Rama had described her and he was sure that the description did not fit any of these women.

Suddenly, on top of a magnificent dais, Hanuman saw a cot made of crystal, ivory, sandalwood and gold. It was unbelievably beautiful and he stood for a while admiring it. The white umbrella of royalty was above it. Creeping up closer, he found Ravana sleeping on it. He was a magnificent figure of a man with huge, powerful arms and broad chest covered with white silk. Close by was a woman, sleeping on a separate cot, wearing necklaces of pearls and gems. Her beauty was such that she didn't need ornaments. Her skin was golden in hue and she had an elegance, which made him think that he had found Sita. Then he realized that Sita would never be able to sleep like this, without Rama beside her. She would not be clad in silks and jewels. She would not be found in Ravana's harem. Of this he was sure.

He wandered about from room to room of the palace without finding Sita. He felt embarrassed at the thought that he was being forced to look at all these voluptuous females in seductive poses, but then he realized that, though he was moving among such extraordinary beauties, his mind was unaffected and untouched by them. Unlike all other *vanaras*, Hanuman was a *brahmachari*, said to be eternally continent, and had never entered the marital state. He searched every inch of space in the palace and then scoured the gardens and arbors. He was feeling more and more distressed as the night wore on. Sita was nowhere to be found. He began to think that perhaps she had killed herself, or been eaten by the *rakshasas*. He knew that he couldn't return without some information about her— either her demise or her whereabouts.

"If he hears that she is dead, Rama will give up his life," he said to himself. He was sure of that. He knew he could not return without some news. "Better for me to go and take to a life of *sannyasa* than return without any news."

Suddenly, he spied another grove filled with *ashoka* trees, which he had overlooked. It was the only place he hadn't searched so far. He jumped to the top of the wall surrounding the grove and looked down. It was obviously a favorite haunt of the demon king, for it was very well tended. Rare trees and flowers were growing in abundance. There were several beautiful ponds with banks covered with white sand. The steps leading to them were exquisitely carved. The night was passing and he still had not discovered Sita. The birds were beginning to wake and fly up into clouds, chirping angrily, disturbed by Hanuman's jumps. He decided to hide himself in the foliage of a big tree which overlooked a splendid platform, in the hope that Sita might come there.

Thus ends the nineteenth chapter of the glorious Ramayana *of Sage Valmiki called "Leap to Lanka"*

Hari Aum Tat Sat

TWENTY

THE ASHOKA GROVE

*Sharvaya
Namaha!*

Homage
to Vishnu.

I worship the messenger of Rama,
Who removes all problems
And confers auspiciousness,
Who has tawny eyes and
Shines with the splendor of a thousand suns and moons,
Who is extolled by the whole host of gods, starting with Indra.
Who was the foremost amongst the monkeys
who searched for Sita,
Who made the island of Lanka tremble with fear
And thus delighted Sugriva.
—Source Unknown

RAMA HAD TOLD HANUMAN that Sita was extremely fond of flowers and trees and Hanuman hoped that she might come to that enchanting grove for a walk. The garden seemed to be made for her, with its flowering shrubs and waterfalls and ponds. Looking around in the light of the setting moon, he saw a small temple with white pillars. The steps were of coral and the surface covered with gold. It gleamed in the moonlight. As he peered closer, he suddenly saw her and he knew unmistakably that this was Sita—the beloved of Rama. She looked like the crescent moon, thin and wan. It was obvious that she had been fasting for a long while. Her beauty was like a flame hidden by smoke. She was draped in a crumpled piece of yellow silk. She had no ornaments. Tears were flowing from her lovely eyes. Sorrow seemed to be her constant companion. Her long black hair was tied in a simple braid, which fell to her thighs. She was surrounded by ugly looking *rakshasis*— horrendous monsters, some with one eye or one ear

157

and some without ears and some with noses on their foreheads, some hairy and some bald, some hunchbacked and some with faces resembling goats, foxes, camels or horses. In the midst of these monsters, she looked like a frightened deer surrounded by fierce hounds. She had never known sorrow before and now it was all she knew. Her eyes mirrored the depths of her despair.

Hanuman thought to himself, "This indeed is Sita. Neither the lack of ornaments nor the fact that she is clothed in rags and is frail and emaciated can hide the fact that she is a raving beauty. She is as beautiful as Rama described her—exquisite eyebrows, graceful, rounded breasts, lips as red as the *bimba* berry, peacock blue throat, slender waist, lotus petal eyes—all these can be seen through her screen of sorrow."

She sat on the bare ground, like a female ascetic, bound in a net of grief, the picture of shattered hope. The ornaments which Rama had described were hanging on the branches of the tree. Though parted cruelly from her husband, her mind was full of him alone. Her lips were constantly murmuring "Rama, Rama." This was indeed the woman for whom Rama was pining. Hanuman could see that she belonged only to Rama—body, mind and soul.

"She is meant only for Rama and he for her. Their love for each other is so great that it is only because of it that they have managed to remain alive." Hanuman prostrated mentally to Rama and told him, "Lord, I have found her."

Hanuman was overcome with sorrow at the sight of the princess of Videha, separated so viciously from the one she loved. "Fate is indeed all powerful," he thought to himself, "or else why should this innocent lady have to suffer like this? She was protected by no less than her illustrious husband and Lakshmana. Her husband killed thousands of *rakshasas* at Janasthana for her sake, because Surpanekha was threatening her, and now she is the captive of Ravana, surrounded by these dreadful women, with no privacy even to weep. She cannot even see this beautiful garden. Her eyes are with her heart and her heart is with Rama."

The night was almost gone. With the break of day, he could hear the chanting of the *Vedas* being recited by the bards to wake up the demon king. Drums were booming and lutes playing to welcome the dawn. Ravana woke up and his first thought was for Sita. He had never met with such resistance from any woman in all his life and he certainly had a lot of experience with females of every type. Her resolution had only served to whet his appetite. It was a challenge to him and he was determined to make the citadel fall, at all costs. He was sure that no woman could resist him for long and that it could only be a matter of time before she succumbed like so many others.

He strode toward the grove of *ashoka* trees. One hundred beautiful ladies, holding *chowrie* (yak tail) fans and golden lamps, followed him. They were madly in love with Ravana and though they were still sleepy with the wine they had imbibed the previous night, they were curious to get a glimpse of Sita and to find out what her approach to Ravana would be. Hanuman watched him carefully from the top of the tree. He had only seen Ravana asleep. Now he looked even more magnificent.

Hearing the tread of his feet as he approached, Sita trembled in terror and grief. She loathed the very sight of him but she tried to put up a brave front. She sat on the bare ground, looking like the fallen branch of a flowering tree. Crossing her arms, she tried to cover her scantily clad body with her two hands and thus avoid his piercing, lusty looks.

Looking at her pitiable efforts to cover herself, he said, "Why do you try to hide your beauty from my eyes? Wherever my eyes fall, I see nothing but your beauty. I'm sure there is no one in all the three worlds as exquisite as you. Honor my love and accept me as your husband. You think my action is unrighteous. In the code of the *rakshasas*, it is quite acceptable to take another man's wife for one's own. Do you think I cannot force you to be mine! It is only my intense love for you that stops me from doing this. I want you to come to me of your own accord. Why are you torturing yourself like this? Your lovely hair is matted with neglect, your silk garment soiled and dirty, and you are emaciated. Come, rise, dress yourself in lovely silks and satins. Wear jewels and perfumes. This ground is not a fitting couch for your flaming beauty. My seductive Sita, why don't you listen to me and accept my attentions? Youth and beauty are short-lived. Do not waste both in unnecessary sorrow. Come, shed your grief and accept my love. I will make you the happiest woman in the world, my chief queen. I cannot bear to take my eyes off your tantalizing form. Night and day, I am haunted by your face. Can't you see that I'm crazy with love for you? After having met you, I cannot bear to look at my other wives. Your dress is in rags and you have no ornaments, yet you continue to fascinate me. You have seen me and my glory. What has Rama got to compare with this? He is only a mendicant, clad in bark, with not even a kingdom to call his own. Take it from me that you will never see him again!"

From the moment he entered the garden, Sita had cast her eyes down and sat with averted face throughout his passionate declaration of love. Though she was terrified of Ravana and tortured by his sensual talk, she clutched at the remnants of her tattered pride and spoke. Without raising her eyes, she picked up a straw from the ground and placed it before her and spoke to it, as if addressing Ravana, no doubt with the idea of impressing on him the fact that she cared not two straws for him, however grand his opinion of himself might be.

"I am the wife of Rama and it is against all the laws of dharma for you to lust after me. Give up these sinful thoughts and go back to your own wives. Be satisfied with them. I'm not the one for you." Turning her back on Ravana, she continued, "Why are you bent on destroying your race? An entire kingdom can perish if its ruler becomes the slave of his passions. Lanka is doomed. Do you think you can tempt me with gold and riches? Rama is to me what sunlight is to the sun. Restore me to him and earn my gratitude, if that will suffice, but never hope to earn my love, for that is irrevocably given to Rama. Before long, he and Lakshmana will arrive and shoot their deadly arrows at you which will suck your life's blood. So beware!"

Ravana retorted, "You are different from any other woman I have ever known. Most women respond to compliments and gifts but the more I offer you, the more you reject me. It is lucky for you that my love controls my anger or else you would have been killed long ago. Don't think you can escape so easily. You have only two more months left of the twelve I promised you. After that, either you share my bed or become my breakfast! Bed or breakfast! The choice is yours." So saying, he glared at her. His angry eyes sparked with green and blue flames and pierced through the thin piece of silk in which she was clad. She trembled with rage and fear and spoke bitter words of condemnation to him.

"How dare you talk to me like this! I have warned you. Your

death is imminent. You call yourself a hero because you defeated the gods. Yet you stole me from my husband when he was not there and took me away by force. Is that the action of a hero?"

A few of the women who had followed Ravana felt sorry for Sita but none dared say anything. Some took the opportunity to ingratiate themselves in Ravana's favor and entwined their soft arms round his neck, offering themselves in lieu of Sita. But he shook them off angrily and told the *rakshasis* who were guarding her to make sure that she changed her mind fast, either by persuasion or by coercion. With this ultimatum, he strode off, making the ground tremble with the force of his strides.

As soon as he left, the guards started shouting and abusing Sita. "What a stupid woman you are, to refuse to be the wife of this king of kings! At his command, the trees scatter flowers and clouds release rain. The sun and moon would stop shining if he did not wish it. Why don't you agree to his wishes and become his wife?"

Another said, "You are very lovely. I have an irresistible desire to feast on your luscious breasts and berry-like lips and delicious liver and spleen. Come, let us have an orgy. Bring the wine and we will chop her into little bits and eat her."

All the pent-up feelings which she had repressed before Ravana now broke lose and Sita burst into heartrending sobs. She cried as if her heart would break. Leaning on the trunk of the tree on which Hanuman sat, she cried out, "O Rama! Rama! Where are you? Why don't you come? I realize now, that death will not approach a person till the appointed time has come, or else how can I continue to live, in the midst of these cruel *rakshasis*, in the palace of this lecherous man, parted from my beloved Rama?"

Hanuman could not bear to see her grief but dared not come down. Then one of the *rakshasis* called Trijarta, who was wiser than the rest, told the others to shut up and stop tormenting Sita, for she had seen a dream in which Rama and Sita were dressed in white and riding victoriously on an elephant, while Ravana was defeated and dressed in black, with shaven head.

Sita, in the meantime, had shed so many tears that she had none left. Heartbroken and lonely, she felt she had reached the end of her endurance and determined to end her life. As she was leaning on the trunk of the tree, her left eye and shoulder started to throb, which was a good omen for ladies. She was surprised. Was there some truth in what the woman was saying? Was her Rama coming for her?

Hanuman was wondering how he could approach her without frightening her. Surrounded as she was with these hostile creatures, she was sure to mistrust everyone. "If I jump down in front of her, she will surely scream and alert the *rakshasis* and thus foil my plan." Then he hit upon a bright idea. Since her mind was always full of Rama, he would start by extolling him and then perhaps she would trust him. Without revealing himself, he spoke from his hiding place in the tree on which she was leaning.

Suddenly, Sita heard these sweet words coming from above. "There was once a king called Dasaratha, who was famous for his prowess. He had four sons, of whom Rama was the eldest. He is the noblest of all men. He went to the Dandaka forest with his wife and brother. One day when the brothers were away, Ravana entered the hermitage and stole his wife Sita. Rama was heartbroken and wandered all over the country, looking for her. At last, he made friends with the monkey king, who promised to help him find her. The monkeys were sent in all directions to search for her. I am one of them and I have come here because I have found the person who has been described to me by Rama as being graceful, charming and beautiful." So saying he fell silent.

Sita was filled with wonder and hope when she heard this. Brushing her tangled hair aside, she looked up at the tree and tried to find out who was responsible for bringing this ray of hope into her despondent heart. The thick foliage hid him from her sight. Her eyes roved in all directions but she could not find him. The *rakshasis* had given up their efforts to persuade her. Some had gone to tell Ravana and the rest were snoring under the trees.

Hanuman jumped lightly down to a branch, from which he could be seen, and at last her anxious eyes spied him—the messenger of Rama, the harbinger of hope and happiness. She saw a small monkey, clinging to the branch of the tree. He was small and cute, with white fur and red face and his eyes were the color of liquid gold. He was seated humbly on the branch and looked harmless. Still, she had her doubts. She had been cheated and tormented so many times in the past few months that she was always suspicious of everything and everyone, in case it was some new ploy of Ravana's. Then she decided that it was all a figment of her imagination and started to call agitatedly again for Rama and Lakshmana. Hanuman guessed what was going on in her mind and decided that it was high time for him to appear. He jumped down lightly from the branch and prostrated before her. He held his folded palms above his head, in a gesture of worship, and began talking in a soft tone.

"O fair lady, tell me who you are. I see you wearing soiled garments but you look as if you are a princess. Like dewdrops on a lotus petal, tears seem to be clinging to your eyes. Why are you alone here and what is the cause of your sorrow? If by some great good fortune you are that Sita, wife of the noble Rama, who was forcibly brought here by Ravana, then please listen to me carefully. I feel that you are indeed Rama's queen. Your beauty has no parallel. Tell me truthfully, are you not Sita?"

Sita was elated when she heard these words and cried out, "Yes, indeed, I am the daughter-in-law of the great Dasaratha and wife of the noble Rama. My father is the king of Videha and I am called Sita. I accompanied my husband to the forest and was kidnapped by Ravana and brought here. He has given me two more months to succumb to his passion. If Rama does not come before that, I will end my life."

Hanuman listened attentively to these words and then spoke, "My lady! I have been sent here by Rama. He is well, though he is also desperately unhappy at being parted from you. He grieves for you night and day and has sent me, as his messenger, to tell you that he will come for you, very soon, and kill Ravana and rescue you."

Sita was thrilled when she heard these words. She had been living in the darkness of despair for so many months that she had almost given up hope of rescue. These words put new heart into her and she said, "It is said that if a person lives in hope, happiness will come her way, sooner or later. I see now that this is true."

Hanuman came closer and once again, fear rose in her heart. She shrank into herself. She had been tricked so often, that fear was always lurking in her heart and she doubted everyone. Maybe this was a new trick of Ravana's to beguile her into believing him, by pretending to praise Rama. Her mouth went dry and her limbs grew weak and she sank to the ground, unable to cling to the branch. Again, Hanuman guessed a little of what was going on inside her mind. He prostrated full length before her and refused to look up.

Timidly, Sita cast puzzled glances at him and said, "O Ravana, you tricked me once before, in the garb of a *sannyasi*. Have you now come in the form of a monkey? If so, it is useless. Please don't torment me further."

Hanuman remained silent and Sita spoke again. "Perhaps you are indeed what you profess to be. Somehow, I feel drawn to you. Please tell me more about Rama and allay my fears." She was torn between doubt and hope and it was pitiful to see her.

Softly and sweetly, Hanuman began to speak of the one who was closest to her heart. "My lady! Please believe me. I have indeed been sent by your husband, the noble king of Ayodhya. In looks, he is a veritable god of love. In valor, he is a lion. He is a terror to his enemies but now he is in the depths of despair, at having lost you. I am the minister of the *vanara* king Sugriva, and my name is Hanuman. I have been searching for you all these days. I crossed the ocean and dared to enter the city to see you, and now my mission is over. All I have to do is go and give my message of hope to Rama, who is waiting anxiously for my return. Very soon you will see Rama and Lakshmana, entering the city of Lanka, with a large army, and you will be rescued."

At last, Sita was convinced that he was indeed a messenger from Rama. She asked him to tell her everything about Rama. What did he do after she was abducted, where did he go, how long would it be before he reached Lanka, and so on. She was thirsty for news of Rama and eagerly lapped up every scrap which Hanuman gave her. Hanuman was only too happy to speak of Rama, who was his god. He told her how they had picked up the jewels she had thrown for them while they sat on the peak of Rishyamukha and all the other incidents, ending with his finding her. At the end of the recital, he stood respectfully with folded palms before her. Sita's joy knew no bounds. She was now convinced that he had indeed come from Rama. Tears of happiness replaced the tears of sorrow, which had been flowing in torrents down her cheeks. She was speechless with delight.

Hanuman said respectfully, "My lady! Please give me leave to go now. I have told you all that you wanted to know. Rest assured that Rama will arrive shortly and rescue you. Here is his signet ring—the ring of the Raghu dynasty, which he has sent with me to reassure you of my identity." He went near her and handed over the ring which she knew and loved so well.

Taking the precious article in her cupped hands, she gazed and gazed at it, as if hungry for the hand which used to wear it. Tears coursed down her cheeks. With eyes filled with gratitude, she looked at Hanuman, who had brought new hope to her barren heart.

"O Hanuman!" she said, "You are indeed the noblest and bravest of all beings! How could you have crossed the ocean, which is a hundred miles wide, and dared to enter this citadel, which is guarded on all sides? You must surely possess some miraculous powers. You have also given me news of my beloved husband, who is dearer to me than my father or mother or anyone else in the world. Banished from his kingdom, he walked about all these years in the forest, with me by his side. We were so happy together, until this calamity overtook us. I hope he has not lost heart. Please tell him that I cling to life only in the hope of seeing him again."

"My lady! If Rama had known where you were, he would have come for you long ago. As it is, he lives in a cave and hardly eats or sleeps. He does not care for anything anymore and is always lost in thought. Even when he falls into a fitful sleep from exhaustion, he wakes up calling, 'Sita! Sita.' Whenever he sees something which is pleasing to you, he sighs and is inconsolable."

Sita was thrilled to hear that Rama's desire for her was as great as hers for him. At the same time, she was unhappy to know that he was neglecting his own health. "Your words bring both happiness and unhappiness to me, O Hanuman. When I think of his unhappiness, I become sorrowful too. Both extreme happiness and extreme sorrow are the result of one's actions in a past life. I wonder if he will be able to reach me in time. I have barely two more months to live. This is the tenth month of my captivity and I have been given one year by the *rakshasa* king, before he kills me."

Hanuman could not bear to think of going away and leaving Sita alone for another two months. "My lady!" he said, "No doubt Rama will come soon. But I can't bear to think of you being left alone here. Come with me and I will carry you across the ocean and take you to Rama this minute. Just give me the command."

Sita was both touched and amused by these words. "Dear little monkey," she said, "your good nature has made you suggest the impossible. How can a tiny creature like you carry me across the sea?"

Hanuman smiled and said, "My lady! Do not doubt my capacity. I can grow to any size." So saying, he began to expand his body, till it looked like a huge mountain. He was a gargantuan figure, with a body of flint.

"If necessary, I can carry off the whole of Lanka. Don't be frightened. Come with me and I'll take you to Rama and make him happy."

Sita's eyes were round with wonder and she said, "I see that I have underestimated your prowess. I'm sure that you can easily take me across the sea but we have to consider this proposition carefully. It is possible that your speed may make me feel giddy and I may fall into the sea. It is also possible that we will be spied by the *rakshasas*, who will pursue us and take me back, and then my fate will be worse than what it is now. You will also be placed in great danger and you will not be able to return to Rama. Moreover, if you rescued me, it would bring no credit to Rama. It is only proper and fitting that Rama himself should come and rescue me, after killing the *rakshasa*. Another point is that, I belong only to Rama, and the thought of touching another man willingly is abhorrent to me. Of course, it is a fact that Ravana held me when he brought me here, but at that time, I was helpless and had no choice. Hanuman, please go back and bring my husband and Lakshmana, as fast as you can. Then, and only then, will my sorrow come to an end."

Hanuman was pleased to hear these words of Sita and said, "My lady! It is fitting that a pure soul like you should speak like this. My suggestion was only because of my immense devotion to Rama and intense desire to make you happy. I will return immediately and give him all the news. Do you have any special message for him?"

Her eyes filled with memories and she said, "Hanuman, ask Rama if he remembers the hill of Chitrakuta, where he was relaxing on my lap on the banks of the Mandakini. A crow came to our spot and pecked at my breast with its sharp beak. I tried to shoo it off with a stone but it would not leave me alone. Just then, Rama woke up and saw my distress and teased me. He took me on his lap and comforted me and then he dozed off once again, his head on my lap. Then the crow came again and pecked at my breast so hard that drops of blood fell on Rama and he woke up. He was furious when he saw that I was hurt. Looking around for the culprit, his eyes lighted on the crow, whom he realized to be the son of Indra. Taking a blade of grass, he invoked a fatal mantra and sent it after the crow. The crow flew in panic to all the worlds, with the *astra* pursuing it like a ball of fire. At last, it returned to Rama and fell at his feet and begged his pardon. Though it deserved to die, Rama pardoned it, since it had surrendered, and let it go, but the blade of grass in which the mantra had been invoked could not go waste, so he took the crow's right eye, as punishment. O Hanuman! My Lord invoked the terrible *brahmastra* for killing a crow who had dared to harm me. Ask him why he is keeping silent now, when this wretch has kidnapped me?"

Hanuman assured her that Rama was not indifferent and would come, the moment he knew about her whereabouts.

Then Sita told him of another incident which was known only to her and Rama. "Ask him if he remembers the time when the red mark on my forehead was obliterated by his hand. He powdered a red stone and placed the dot on my cheek, instead of on my forehead, to tease me."

Sita then sent her blessings to Lakshmana also. She said, "If there is anyone who is capable of looking after my Lord when I am not there, it is Lakshmana, who loves him like his own father and me, like his mother. No one can withstand his anger. Tell them both to come soon, O Hanuman! I will not live a day longer than two months."

She unwrapped the end of her garment and carefully took out her precious hair ornament and gave it to Hanuman, saying, "Please give this to Rama. When he sees this and hears the story of the crow and the red dot, which is known only to the two of us, he will be convinced that you have indeed met me. O Hanuman, my life depends on you. Do you really have to return immediately? Your presence is like balm to my wounded spirit."

Then she was suddenly assailed by another doubt. "Are you sure Rama and the others will be able to cross the sea and come here?"

Hanuman assured her that everything was possible and told her not to worry. He comforted her as best as he could but she could not control the tears which were pouring down her cheeks, at the thought that the one friendly face she had seen in ten long months was now about to depart. But she knew that it was dangerous for him to be seen with her, so sadly she allowed him to leave.

Thus ends the twentieth chapter of the glorious Ramayana *of Sage Valmiki called "The Ashoka Grove."*

Hari Aum Tat Sat

Rama is the veritable garden of wish-fulfilling trees.
He beguiles the world and ends our miseries.
He alone is our Lord.

—SOURCE UNKNOWN

TWENTY-ONE

HANUMAN'S WRATH

He is known as the messenger of Rama,
The son of the wind god.
Marked by tawny red eyes.
He removed Sita's sorrow,
And conquered the ten-headed one.
And saved Lakshmana's life.
—SOURCE UNKNOWN

Mahabhujaya
Namaha!

Homage to the
long-armed one.

H ANUMAN WAS SO ANGRY at the way that Sita was being treated that he decided show his power to Ravana before he left. He wanted him to realize the might of the army he would have to face. He thought of a method to rouse the ire of the *rakshasa* king and decided that the best way would be to destroy this garden, which was obviously one of his favorites. He set about the destruction, in a most methodical manner. Like a raging tempest, he uprooted every tree and trampled it with his feet, the creepers were twisted, the temple smashed, the pools splattered with the copper-colored buds of the *ashoka* trees. Lakes were churned up and made muddy, the little hillocks were ground to powder and the beloved garden of Ravana was made into a desolate waste. Having done his dirty work, Hanuman climbed to the top of the archway to the garden and waited expectantly for things to happen. He didn't have long to wait. There was a great commotion in the garden itself. The birds were screeching in terror and the deer and the peacocks were crying out loudly.

The *rakshasis* who were in charge of Sita now woke up from their drunken stupor and demanded to know what was happening. They saw the monkey and wanted to know who he was. Sita said she knew nothing about

169

him. They saw a huge monkey sitting on the arch and ran to report to Ravana. "There's an enormous monkey who has laid waste the whole garden. The only place he has not destroyed is the tree under which Sita sits. He was seen talking to her but she denies knowing anything about him."

Ravana was furious when he heard of the fate of his precious garden. He sent some strong *rakshasas* to kill the monkey. Hanuman was delighted. He had been waiting for an opportunity to show his prowess. They surrounded him and tried to beat him. He grew in size and clapped his hands on his shoulders, in the manner of wrestlers, and said in a reverberating voice, "I am Hanuman, the servant of Lord Rama. Not a thousand Ravanas are capable of withstanding my powers. I will return only after devastating Lanka."

Pulling up a pillar on which the arch was supported, he struck and killed all the *rakshasas* who had come to subdue him. This was reported to Ravana, who found it very difficult to believe. He sent a young warrior called Jambumali, who was the son of his minister, with a large contingent of soldiers and Hanuman killed him at once, causing great confusion among the other troops.

Next Ravana sent another battalion with the sons of his other ministers and they were also killed. Streams of blood flowed down the main highway of Lanka leading to the palace, carrying with it the mangled bodies, legs and arms of *rakshasas*. Ravana was quite bewildered by this unexpected turn of events and decided to send his youngest son, Aksha Kumara, to subdue the monkey. Wearing armor of gold and looking like the morning sun, the young boy went forth in his chariot, sure of success. There was a terrible encounter between the two of them.

Hanuman was greatly impressed by the boy and did not feel like killing him, but he knew that, in war, there was no question of showing mercy. He killed the horses first and then smashed the chariot. The boy flew up into the air and Hanuman jumped up and caught him and dashed him to death on the ground. Ravana was sunk in gloom when he heard about the death of his dear son. He summoned his eldest son, Meghanatha, who was also known as Indrajit, after he had defeated Indra, the king of the gods, in battle. Ravana told Indrajit to go and punish the monkey, for he feared that there was something unusual about him and the army could not handle the situation. Indrajit was an invincible warrior and he set out with delight.

He hurled missile after missile at Hanuman, who evaded them with great dexterity. Indrajit was amazed at this monkey's powers and realized that it was impossible to kill him, so he decided to invoke a divine missile, which would paralyze him. The impact of this celestial *astra*, called the *nagapasa*, knocked out Hanuman and made him feel as if he were bound. He recovered immediately but he decided that it would be good to pretend to be unconscious, so that he would be taken into the presence of Ravana. He was tied up with stout hemp ropes and dragged before the demon king. The moment the gross ropes touched his body, the subtle effects of the *astra* were nullified. Indrajit saw this and knew that the effect of the *astra* must have dissipated but, to his surprise, the monkey allowed himself to be dragged to the court. Indrajit was puzzled but he went and reported the matter to his father.

Hanuman was kicked and pulled into the hall where Ravana was seated, surrounded by his retinue of ministers. Hanuman had to admit that he was indeed a magnificent personality. He was clad in the softest of white silks, which looked like billows of surf on the seashore. Many wonderful gems were around his neck and bracelets on his strong arms. His green eyes were gleaming with strange lights and looked piercingly at Hanuman. For a few minutes, Hanuman was dazzled by his charisma and could not help but gaze admiringly at him. He thought to himself that if Ravana had only been a righteous person, he could easily have been the king of gods, so glorious was his magnetism.

Ravana looked deep into the tawny eyes of the monkey and some unknown fear assailed him. He remembered an incident long ago, when Shiva, his favorite deity, had failed to comply with his demands. This had infuriated him so much that, in his arrogance, he had put one finger under the mountain of Kailasa, the abode of Shiva, and tilted it, perilously. Parvati had been frightened and Shiva, to comfort her and to quell Ravana's pride, had simply pressed the mountain down with his big toe and crushed Ravana's finger. Ravana is supposed to have placated Shiva by composing the fantastic hymn known as the "Shiva Thandava stotra." However, Shiva's bull-vehicle, Nandi, had cursed Ravana that he would suffer defeat, when Nandi himself came in the form of a monkey. For a moment, Ravana thought that this was the time foretold by Nandi and then he dismissed the incident as of no consequence and asked his minister to question the monkey about his purpose in coming to Lanka.

"O monkey! Have no fear. Answer truthfully and no harm will come to you. It is obvious that you are no ordinary simian but one who has come in disguise, sent by one of the gods. If you lie, you will be killed!" said the minister. Hanuman did not deign to reply to him.

Turning to Ravana he said, "I am not an emissary of the gods, neither am I in disguise. I am a monkey by birth and I destroyed the garden because I wanted to meet you face to face. O king! I have come here as a messenger of Sri Rama, whose wife Sita has been abducted by you. No one who has wronged Rama will escape death. Decide to act according to dharma and then perhaps you will be allowed to go free. Your life has been blessed by many gods and is filled with glorious things. Why should all this glory come to an end, because of a woman? You are wise and you should know the dictates of dharma. Is it correct to abduct another man's wife, against her wishes? There is no power in all the three worlds which can withstand the might of Rama. Let dharma and self-interest guide you. Restore Sita to her rightful husband. I have seen her and she is in the grip of grief. My valor alone is enough to destroy the whole of Lanka. What then if Rama comes? Sita is like the noose of death, which you have placed securely round your neck. Rama's anger is deadly. Your duty is to protect your subjects, kinsmen, children, wives and wealth. Think well about what I have said and then act."

Ravana's anger was mounting with every word uttered by Hanuman. He could hardly contain himself till the end of the talk and roared to the guards to kill the precocious monkey.

Ravana's wise brother Vibhishana now intervened and said, "My Lord, please consider well before you put this monkey to death. I admit that he has done a lot of damage but remember, he is a messenger and it is against all rules of etiquette to execute a messenger."

Ravana was in no mood to listen to such wise counsel and again ordered that Hanuman should be killed immediately.

Again, Vibhishana said, "He is here only to convey a message sent by the enemy and is himself guiltless. The rules are very clear on this point, that a messenger should not be put to death. You can torture him, shave off his hair or whip him, but you cannot kill him or else there will be a blot on your fair name. Attempts should be made to attack the princes who have sent him. Only a small portion of your army need be sent to kill those two human beings, but don't kill this monkey."

At last, Ravana was convinced and said, "Vibhishana, you may be right that a messenger shouldn't be killed but I have to punish this monkey somehow, for the mischief he has done. The tail is a monkey's dearest treasure, so let his tail be lighted and let him be dragged through the streets of Lanka, and thus provide a joyous spectacle to the citizens."

The *rakshasas* were delighted at the order. All the while he was being dragged to the court, they had been shouting fiendishly, "Kill him! Roast him! Eat him!", and now they fell on his tail with glee and started to wrap it round with cloth dipped in oil, but the more they tied, the longer grew the tail, so that they had to bring bales and bales of cloth from all the shops in Lanka, and still it was not enough. Hanuman's tail was encircling the city of Lanka ten times. The confused demons ran around in circles, trying to wrap cloth round the tail, and still the tail grew and grew.

At last, Hanuman took pity on them and allowed them to finish their job. After having wrapped the immense tail with cloth, they dipped it in oil and set fire to it. It was a colossal tail and it made a great conflagration. Everyone ran out of their houses to watch the spectacle. Hanuman was mad. He slashed his tail at the *rakshasas* and they fell in heaps but then he allowed them to bind him tightly and drag him through the streets of Lanka, which he had seen only during the night. He thought it would be a good idea to know the layout of the city, since the knowledge might come in handy when he returned with the army.

This news was brought to Sita by some of the *rakshasis*, who were greatly elated. Poor Sita started weeping again. Hope had just started to creep into her heart when this savior had come, but now it looked as if it was all in vain. She prayed with all her heart to Agni, the Lord of Fire, and begged him not to hurt Hanuman. The fire god's response was prompt and the fire became cool on his skin, while Hanuman's father, the god of wind, blew softly around his son, thus cooling him. Hanuman was astonished at this miracle.

Now that he had succeeded in talking to the king of the *rakshasas* and seeing the whole of Lanka, Hanuman decided that it was enough. He was no mean monkey, to be reviled and persecuted by these stupid *rakshasas*. In a minute he broke free by flexing his body. Giving a bloodcurdling roar, he sprang up on top of the city gates and, picking up a pillar as easily as if it were a piece of wood, he knocked the guards down. He considered what further havoc he could cause before leaving for Kishkinda.

"Ah!" he thought, "This fire, which has been used to punish me, has been denied its food, so I will give it some sustenance." He took an enormous leap into the heart of the city and jumped from mansion to mansion, setting fire to each with his flaming tail. The pearl- and gem-encrusted palaces and houses started to crackle and crumble. At last, he landed on Ravana's palace and set it ablaze. The exuberance of the people gave place to panic. Screams and cries rent the air as the terrified citizens ran in every direction in their effort to extinguish the flames and escape from the conflagration. The whole of Lanka was like a flaming torch. It was an awesome spectacle.

At last, his anger abated and his conscience suddenly pricked him. "What have I done!" he thought. "In a fit of anger, is it possible that I have even destroyed the very person I have come to save? How could I have become such a slave to my anger. People commit crimes easily while in the throes of anger. An angry man may kill even those who are to be respected. The truly great man is he who can control his wrath. If I have killed Sita, it means I have killed my master also."

Then he reflected awhile and thought, "No, this cannot be. If the fire could not harm me, surely, it could not have harmed her. The radiance of her purity will safeguard her. The strength of her austerity and her devotion to her husband will protect her." As he was thus ruminating, he saw some astral beings, winging their way toward him. They were talking amongst themselves and commenting on the fact that in the whole of Lanka, the only person who was unaffected by the conflagration was Sita. Hanuman was thrilled to hear this and he leaped towards the grove where she was sitting, in order to take his leave. Sita was overjoyed to see him and gave him her blessings and told him to hurry back.

Hanuman was eager to get back to Rama. He turned around to

have a last look at the city. The fabulous city of Lanka, which had appeared like a gleaming pearl in the moonlight the previous evening, now lay in shambles at his feet. He felt a twinge of regret but decided that Ravana deserved it. He then returned to the top of the hill and took a flying leap. He saw the sea surging beneath him as he turned his face north and sped on his way. He passed with ease through the crimson-tinted clouds and coursed through the sky like an arrow. The *vanara* host, who were eagerly awaiting his arrival, were thrilled by his war cry as he landed in their midst. They broke into joyous shouts as he approached. He told them all the news—how he had found Sita in the *ashoka* grove, how he had set fire to Lanka, and all the rest of the story. As they heard the details, the excited monkeys danced about and jumped up and down in the air. The crown prince Angada boastfully declared that they should return to Lanka and he himself would quell Ravana's army and they could return with Sita. But Hanuman said that Sita was expecting her Lord to come and rescue her, so they should head for Kishkinda straightaway.

Their enthusiasm lent wings to their feet and the monkeys made the return back to Kishkinda in half the time. When they reached the outskirts of the city, they saw the garden called Madhuvana, which was full of fruit, filled with intoxicating honey. The monkeys begged Jambavan and Hanuman for permission to enter this garden and taste the wine. As a special treat, they were given leave and the whole crowd rushed in and enjoyed themselves to their hearts' content. They were so drunk that they could hardly walk. Some were singing and others dancing. Sugriva's uncle was the guardian of the grove and he tried his best to prevent them, but they paid no heed to him. The whole garden was filled with intoxicated monkeys, reeling about in different stages of inebriation. The guard ran to report the matter to the king but Sugriva, contrary to his expectations, told him not to worry about them. He was sure that they had come back with good news or else they would not have had the courage to ravish the king's favorite garden. He told the guard to bring the monkeys to him immediately. He was with Rama and Lakshmana at the time, in their retreat on top of Prasravana Hill, and they were all thrilled by his words and waited anxiously for Hanuman's arrival.

The monkey host arrived with a great clamor. Each one of them strutted in as if he had personally achieved the impossible. Hanuman and Angada now came forward and Hanuman bent low before Rama and said, "Seen have I Sita." He phrased his sentence in this way because he knew that Rama's heart was filled with expectation and that until he heard the word "seen," he would be in agony. Hanuman wanted to spare him even this one moment of pain if he could, and thus said, "Seen have I Sita." Rama's happiness cannot be imagined. To hear that his beloved was alive and well, even though unhappy, was the greatest news he could hear. He hugged Hanuman and gave him all his blessings.

The monkeys vied with each other in their attempt to tell the narrative, which they had heard from Hanuman. Rama looked lovingly at them and then said, "I would like to know more about Sita. What did she say? Did she send any message for me?" At this, the monkeys turned sheepishly to Hanuman and begged him to continue the story.

Hanuman bowed low to Rama and told him the whole story of his conquest of Lanka and his meeting with the lovely, lonely princess of Videha, who was eating her heart out for her beloved husband. He narrated the stories of the crow and the red dot. He did not leave out even a single word spoken by the bereft queen. Rama listened with tears coursing down his cheeks. Hanuman told him how happy Sita was to receive Rama's ring and then he presented the hair ornament which she had given to him for Rama. Rama took it in his hands and pressed it to his chest. A flood of memories swept over him and he said, "This was given to Janaki by her father Janaka and she wore it for our wedding. How beautiful she looked!" And he fell into a deep reverie thinking of his lovely, young bride.

Turning to Lakshmana he said, "How ironic that I can see her jewel but not the wearer of the jewel! If she says she will live for a month more, then her life will be longer than mine. I cannot live for a moment more without seeing her. Take me to her, O Hanuman!" Thus he lamented.

Hanuman and Lakshmana tried their best to console him. At last he managed to attain a measure of composure and praised Hanuman for his fantastic effort.

"You have accomplished that which no one else could have done.

I am only sorry that I am unable to reward you in a fitting manner. I can only embrace you as a token of my gratitude." With these words, Rama enfolded his servant Hanuman in his firm clasp and pressed him to his bosom, while everyone looked on with delight.

Thus ends the twenty-first chapter of the glorious Ramayana *of Sage Valmiki called "Hanuman's Wrath"*

Hari Aum Tat Sat

BOOK SIX

Setukrite Namaha!

Homage to the one who built the bridge.

YUDDHA KANDA

THE BOOK OF BATTLE

TWENTY-TWO

MARCH OF
THE MONKEYS

*Dhanurdharaya
Namaha!*

Homage to the
one who carries
the bow.

*O! Heroic Hanuman! Who brought the medicinal herb
And crossed the ocean with ease,
Please reside in my mind and enable me to
Carry out all actions with equal success.*
—DEVOTIONAL VERSE

NOW THAT SITA HAD BEEN found, Rama's next worry was how best they could invade the island and rescue her. Sugriva told him not to worry about these minor details since his army was ready to obey his slightest command.

"My dear friend," said Sugriva, "this is not the time for sorrow. Please think of a way by which we can bridge the ocean and my *vanara* army will do the rest. We are all here to help you. Remember, there is no one in the whole world who can face you, once you enter the battlefield with bow in hand. So now, replace your sorrow with anger and then we can destroy the enemy in no time."

Rama listened to Sugriva. He replied, "If you can't think of a way to bridge the ocean, the fire of my austerity will dry it up and make a path for the monkeys to cross. But first of all, tell me about the city. How it is fortified, what the strength of its army is, how the gateways are guarded and so on. Then, we can plan our attack."

Hanuman bowed low to Rama and recounted every detail of the city and its barricades, which he had been astute enough to scout.

He concluded, "Lanka is an exquisite city, built on a hill. It is surrounded by a golden wall studded with gems.

Down below is a moat filled with crocodiles. It has four massive gates with iron bars. Four drawbridges are there, one in front of each gate, all fiercely guarded by the *rakshasas*. Ravana has fire-spewing machines and catapults, which are capable of hurling enormous rocks great distances. He is always alert. It is almost impossible to enter, but do not fear, I'm sure we can do it."

Rama was pleased with this account and said, "I am sure we can destroy Lanka. The sun has reached its zenith and is entering the constellation called *abhijit*. Any activity started at this time is sure of victory. Sugriva! Give orders to march immediately! The time is propitious. Let Neela take a section of the army and advance along a way which has fruits and roots. Let him be on his guard against the *rakshasas*, who might try to poison the water tanks, and torment us in many ways. They are sure to do this, when they hear of our march. Let Hanuman carry me on his shoulder and Angada carry Lakshmana, so that we can move faster. Let the army be divided into sections, each led by one mighty warrior."

Sugriva did as commanded and the army lost no time in advancing. There was great excitement amidst the monkeys, who leapt from tree to tree, shouting and waving their tails in glee. They bounded and hopped and swung from branch to branch, plucking trees and waving banners of flowering creepers, sparring and playing pranks on each other and feasting on fruits and honey. They were all in high spirits. Mile after mile they covered, effortlessly, the *vanara* horde, camping beside lakes and traversing hills and forests, until they reached the southern ocean.

Rama ascended the hill called Mahendra, from which Hanuman had jumped, and surveyed the broad expanse of water below him. Coming down, he decided to camp in the forest below the hill and plan their campaign. Thousands and thousands of monkeys arrived and camped on the shore. In fact, they appeared like another sea. They stared fascinated at the storm-lashed waves of the ocean and wondered how they could cross it.

Rama sat apart with Lakshmana. "O Lakshmana! My heart is heavy when I see this ocean. It is said that time assuages all grief, but it is not so with me. Every moment that I spend apart from my beloved increases my sorrow. Moreover, time is running short. She has sent word that she will not be able to live for longer than two months, out of which one month is already over. What shall we do?"

Feeling the wind on his face, he said, "O gentle breeze, please blow over my beloved's face and then return and caress me, while her touch is still warm upon you. She must have called for me, time and time again, as she was being carried away over this ocean. I am tormented by the thought of her helplessness. Now that I know where she is, I'm on fire to see her. I long for her smile, her gentle glances, her caressing voice. She has always been slim and now with this continuous fasting, she must be weak and emaciated. I am aching for the day when I can kill that fiend and clasp her to my bosom."

In the meantime in Lanka, Ravana had called a council of ministers to discuss the events of that catastrophic day, when Lanka had been burned. He was quite chagrined to find that a mere monkey could have destroyed, in a few hours, a city which had been built up with years of effort. His spies had informed him about the approach of the monkey contingent. He felt sure that Rama would succeed in crossing the sea. He thought it prudent to ask the opinion of the wise men of his assembly. Unfortunately, he was surrounded by sycophants and toadies. All they knew was to bolster up his already bloated ego.

"Your Majesty," they said, "you have defeated the gods and even Lord Shiva Himself. There is no one in the whole of the three worlds who doesn't tremble at the very mention of your name. Why should you fear Rama? His army is only composed of monkeys and bears. How can it be compared to your army? Your son, Indrajit, has conquered the heavens. He can easily defeat this monkey army of Rama's, single-handed, without the help of the army." These words of comfort by all his ablest men, made Ravana very confident and happy. The only one who spoke against his wishes was his own brother Vibhishana.

"We should never underestimate an enemy. How has Rama offended you? You are the one who stole his wife and are keeping her here, against her will. Lusting after another man's wife will lead to unhappiness and infamy. Sita will be the cause of untold misery for you and for your subjects. Take my advice and return Sita to Rama. He is a dangerous opponent. If you do not act immediately, great danger will befall us. I have dared to advise you, because you are my brother and I have great love for you. We would all like to live in peace and harmony, so please take my advice."

Ravana did not say a word and dismissed the council. Next morning, Vibhishana went to his brother's chamber and bowed before him. He was a gentle and noble soul, unlike his ferocious brother. Again he tried to reason with Ravana and make him realize the effects of his foolishness. He spoke to him of the bad omen which were to be seen in the whole city, all boding ill for their clan.

Blinded by his lust for Sita, Ravana was in no mood to listen to these well-intentioned words and replied harshly, "We have nothing to fear from anybody! Even if Rama comes with all the gods in attendance, he will not be able to defeat me. You may go, O Vibhishana! I do not need the advice of cowards."

Vibhishana left sadly. Though he had not listened to his brother, Ravana was a little worried. He called a council of war once again. All his ministers came, including Vibhishana.

Ravana spoke. "I have called all of you today in order to ask your advice. I was waiting for my brother Kumbhakarna to wake up and give his opinion and now he has also come. You all know that I have a great attraction for Sita but she refuses to look at me. Rama had sent his emissary who came here and set fire to this city. Now I hear that Rama has encamped on the opposite shore of the sea. I would like the opinion of the wise people, assembled here, as to what our next step should be. The princes of Kosala should be killed and the *vanara* army vanquished. How should we set about this?"

His brother Kumbhakarna, who was noted for his passion for sleep and who had known nothing of Ravana's doings, now bestirred himself from his fog and said in a thunderous voice, "We should have been consulted before, you chose to abduct Sita and bring her here. At that time, you listened only to your own lustful desires. Now that you are in trouble, why do you bother to consult us? The abduction of Sita is an act which has become like food mixed with poison. I'm surprised that Rama did not come earlier! You have started a chain of events without consulting any of us. Now it is up to you to see that no harm befalls us. Of course, I will fight with Rama and kill him and then perhaps Sita will be yours, but remember I do not approve of this at all."

Ravana was silent. He did not care for the frank manner in which his brother spoke. Another minister then spoke in a conciliatory way to him, pointing out that he had no cause for fear.

Then he asked Ravana why he had not taken Sita by force, if he was so anxious to have her.

Ravana said, "I'll tell you the reason. Once long ago, I ravished an *apsara* (heavenly nymph), called Rambha. She became like a wilted lily and went and complained to her husband Nalakubera. He was very angry with me and cursed me.

'Ravana, if ever you rape another woman, your head will burst into a thousand fragments!' This is the only reason why I don't dare take Sita by force. Rama does not know this, neither does Sita. However I'll make short work of Rama. How can a mere human being, helped by a pack of monkeys ever hope to beat the might of the *rakshasa* king?" With these words, he laughed uproariously, shaking with mirth. The rest of the court, except for his brothers joined him, and the whole court dissolved into laughter at this ridiculous picture of the great Ravana being defeated by some monkeys and bears. But Ravana had forgotten the boon he had received from Brahma. He had asked for immunity from death from all types of heavenly and demonic beings and it had been granted to him. In his arrogance, he had not considered human beings and monkeys as worthy opponents and now they were the very ones who were advancing purposefully towards him.

Once again, Vibhishana tried to convince Ravana. "Can't you see that Sita is like a serpent around your neck. Your warriors are not powerful enough to withstand the might of Rama. Neither you nor Kumbhakarna will be able to face him in battle." Turning to the other ministers, he said, "It is the duty of a minister to advise a king wisely and save him from the consequences of his own folly, if possible. Why are you all determined to bring about his downfall and the destruction of our race? You are only hurrying him toward his death."

Indrajit, Ravana's eldest son, now spoke with impatience. "Father! I am amazed at these words coming from your brother. These are the words of a coward. You name will be in dust if you listen to him. His nature is quite different from yours. Do not listen, if you don't want to be the laughing stock of all people. I have made my name as a formidable warrior. I have made Indra's valorous elephant bite the dust. Why do you think my valour will be diminished at the sight of these two human beings?"

Vibhishana listened to his nephew's talk without rancor. "My boy, I'm afraid you are not able to distinguish between right and

186 • The Song of Rama

wrong. You are not aware of the path of dharma and that is why you speak such words." Turning to Ravana, he said, "My Lord, listen to me. Take with you the rarest gems you have. Take also Sita and go to Rama and give her back to him. Then, once and for all, you can shed this burden from your shoulders. I entreat you to do as I say."

Spurred by fate, Ravana bitterly reproached his well-meaning brother, "I can now understand the truth of the words which people say. One can live amicably with an enemy and even with a serpent, but not with one who pretends to be your friend, yet is always on the lookout for a chance to harm you. 'Fire and weapons I do not fear, the dangerous ones are the near and dear.' Bees fly away after sucking the last drop of honey from a flower, so the unworthy give up a relationship which has ceased to be profitable. If anyone else had spoken to me like this, I would have choked the life out of him, then and there, but because you are my brother, I will spare you—but I curse you. You are a shame on our race."

Vibhishana stood up, together with three of his friends, and said, "O king! I tried to save you from your own folly. Whatever I said was meant only for your good. It is always easy to find people who will try to please you with honeyed words, but there are very few who will dare to tell a king the unalloyed truth to his face. You are older than me, so I ask your forgiveness. But I cannot stay here any longer. You can be rid of the thorn in your side. I wanted to help you, but when death is approaching, a man will close his ears to the words of well-wishers." So saying, Vibhishana departed to the other shore, to Rama's camp, along with his four friends.

It is said that the three brothers—Ravana, Kumbhakarna and Vibhishana—typified the three types of *gunas* or modes of nature— *sattva*, *rajas* and *tamas*. Vibhishana was the example of *sattva*, or the quality of harmony and goodness; Ravana, of *rajas*, or the quality of activity and passion; and Kumbhakarna, of *tamas*, or the quality of inertia, sloth and stupor; hence, his extreme partiality for sleep.

Thus ends the twenty-second chapter of the glorious Ramayana of Sage Valmiki called "March of the Monkeys."

Hari Aum Tat Sat

Rama:
What are the characteristics of a jivan mukta?
(liberated one)

Vasistha replies:
He who experiences the whole world as emptiness.
He who, though awake,
enjoys the calmness of deep sleep.
He who is unaffected by pleasure and pain.
He who is unattached in action and inaction.
He who is free from volition and egoism.
No one is afraid of him He is in dread of none.
Such a one is the jivan mukta.

—*THE YOGA VASISTHA*

TWENTY-THREE

CAUSEWAY TO LANKA

Worship the blissful Raghunandana,
The full moon of the land of Kosala, son of Dasaratha,
The succor of the distressed,
Annihilator of the demons.
—SOURCE UNKNOWN

Vibhishana
Prathistathre
Namaha!

Homage to
the one who
installed
Vibhishana
as king.

AFTER LEAVING HIS BROTHER, Vibhishana went to the opposite shore and approached Rama's camp. The monkeys who were guarding the entrance saw him and his four companions, poised in the air. He was decked with jewels and held a massive mace in his hand. Sugriva came out and observed him and told the monkeys to prepare for a fight. Seeing this, Vibhishana spoke loudly from the sky. "I am Vibhishana, the younger brother of Ravana. I tried my best to advise him to return Sita to Rama but he insulted me and sent me out. I have abandoned everything I possess, including my family, and have come to take refuge at Rama's feet, for I have heard that he is merciful and friendly to all creatures. Please announce my arrival to him."

Sugriva ran back and reported to Rama. "These *rakshasas* are wily creatures. They should never be trusted. He says he is Ravana's brother but he may be a spy. He may win your confidence and then betray you. Like an owl, which waits for the opportune moment and then destroys the whole clan of crows, he will join us and wait for the right time and then annihilate us."

Rama gave careful attention to what he said and then asked everybody else to give their views. All of them were of the opinion that Vibhishana was not to be trusted.

At last, Hanuman spoke, "I saw this man in Lanka when he spoke against Ravana's wishes to kill me. In fact, it is because of him that Ravana desisted from putting me to death. Neither his mien nor his behavior was suspicious in any way. I think he must have tried to advise Ravana to give up his plan and the latter must have refused. That must be the reason why he decided to leave. The *shastras* (scriptures) say that it is not correct to stay with one who is steeped in *adharma*. Moreover, someone who comes as a spy would not announce himself, as he has done."

Rama, the compassionate one, was pleased with Hanuman's words, for they were only an echo of his own thoughts. "Whosoever approaches me with a heart filled with love, I will accept with equal love. I will not abandon one who has taken refuge in me, even though he may be filled with faults. This is my decision."

Sugriva, the prudent, again tried to dissuade Rama to give up the idea of accepting a *rakshasa* as an ally, for his experience told him that they were not to be trusted.

With a slight smile, Rama said, "A righteous man can be born even in the clan of the *rakshasas*. Evidently, he found it impossible to stay any longer with his vicious brother and thus, he has come to me. I shall accept him."

Sugriva said, "My Lord! You are too noble. I'm sure he is a spy. It would be safer to kill him."

Rama smiled and said, "It is of no importance to me whether he is good or bad. The code of dharma says that one who has taken refuge should never be abandoned. My principle in life is to give succor to anyone who comes and declares that he wants to join me. His character is immaterial. Even if Ravana himself came and fell at my feet I would not refuse him, although he has wronged me woefully. Go and bring Vibhishana."

Sugriva was amazed at these words. He bowed low to Rama and went to do his bidding. Vibhishana was thrilled to hear that he had been accepted. He strode into Rama's presence and fell at his feet, clasping them with his hands. He then rose up and said, "My Lord, I am Vibhishana, the half brother of Ravana. I have been grossly treated by him and I have left everything I possess in Lanka and taken refuge at your feet. Now you are my everything. My life and welfare is in your hands. I have surrendered my joys and sorrows and my very life at your blessed feet. Please accept me as your devoted slave."

Rama was touched by his devotion and gave him permission to stay. He smiled tenderly at him and bade him welcome. Afterwards, he asked him about Ravana's strength and weaknesses.

Vibhishana said, "Brahma has granted the ten-headed Ravana a special boon. He is invulnerable against all creatures, including gods, birds, snakes and celestial beings. My brother, the huge Kumbhakarna, is an exceptional warrior. The commander of the forces, Prahasta is an indomitable soldier. Ravana's son Indrajit is invincible. His armor cannot be pierced. And Agni, the god of fire, has granted him many magic boons, by which he can make himself invisible at will. The army consists of scores of *rakshasas*, who subsist on meat and blood, and who can change form at will. As for Ravana, he has defeated even the gods in battle."

Rama listened carefully to this account and then said with a smile, "Fear not, O Vibhishana! I will kill all of them and install you as king of Lanka. Though he may run to all the worlds, Ravana will not be able to escape the fury of my arrows. Until I achieve this objective, I will not enter Ayodhya. I swear this, in the name of my three brothers."

Vibhishana fell at his feet and said, "I swear in the name of dharma that I will assist you in all ways, to the best of my ability, in carrying out your resolve. But the one thing I will not do is to kill my own people."

Rama said, "Lakshmana! Bring water from the ocean. I will myself perform the coronation of Vibhishana, here and now." Rama took the water brought by Lakshmana and performed the *abhisheka*, or ceremonial bath, by pouring the consecrated water over the head of the prospective king, amidst great joy and applause from the *vanaras*.

Now both Sugriva and Hanuman asked their new-found ally to suggest a means by which they could cross the ocean. Vibhishana suggested that the lord of the ocean would surely comply with the wishes of Rama if he asked him. "This sea owes its very existence and name to the Sagara brothers, who were the ancestors of Rama. He will surely remember this and help Rama in his task."

In the meantime, Ravana sent one of his men to try and win Sugriva over to his side. The monkeys caught him and beat him up mercilessly. He ran to Rama, begging him to intervene and stop his people from killing him. Rama told the *vanaras* to stop harassing him and let him go. The man rose into the sky, praising Rama. "Noble Rama! You are indeed a hero among men. Please tell me what I should say to Ravana."

Sugriva replied scornfully, "Tell your great master that Sugriva can never become his friend. You are the enemy of Rama and you deserve nothing but death at my hands."

Rama decided to fast to death if the lord of the ocean did not comply with his request. So he lay on a mat of *darbha* in front of the ocean and meditated. Three days and three nights passed without any response from the lord of the ocean. At the end of this time, Rama lost his patience and said to Lakshmana, "As I told you before, O Lakshmana, people mistake my good nature for weakness. Some individuals can only be subdued by force and the lord of the ocean seems to be one of them. Bring my bow and arrows and I will dry him up with just one shot. I will drain him of his waters, so that nothing remains but an expanse of sand, and my army will easily cross over to Ravana's domain."

So saying, he started to discharge arrow after arrow from his mighty bow. The waters rose in upheaval. The waves were as tall as mountains. The earth trembled and quivered in agony. The sky became pitch black and meteors flashed across the heavens, even as thunder roared and lightning flashed. The ocean throbbed and moaned. Lakshmana caught hold of Rama's hand and begged him to desist. Out of the ocean, Samudra, lord of the sea, rose up, trembling with fear. The darkness caused by Rama's anger lifted, due to the radiance of the jewels round Sagara's neck. Long necklaces of pearls gleamed on his chest. His hair was covered with seaweed and water was pouring down his long grey hair and beard. He rose up on the crest of a wave, with folded palms kept above his head, and slowly came to the shore and approached Rama and stood humbly in front of him.

"O Lord," he said, "you are known to be the abode of kindness and mercy. I did not appear before you earlier because I cannot go against my nature, as you know only too well. Earth, water, fire and wind are all ruled by the laws of nature. I am by nature deep, wide and unfathomable. I cannot change that. But I can give you a plan by which you can cross easily. There is a monkey called Nala in your army who is the son of Vishvakarma, the architect of the gods. He is an expert in building bridges. Let him build a bridge and I will see that it does not sink or fall apart while the army is crossing. I can also promise you that my sharks and whales will not harm your army as they pass." Then Sagara melted into a wave, which came ashore to take him.

Rama called Nala, who immediately agreed to construct the bridge. Before starting the construction, Rama made a beautiful *linga* of Lord Shiva with the sand and worshipped it, asking Shiva to bless him with success in his endeavor. The place where Rama installed the *lingam* is known as Rameswaram, and it is a famous place of worship even to this day.

Directed by Nala, the monkeys scurried around, collecting material for the construction. They uprooted trees and brought huge boulders. Rocks as large as hills were carried on their willing shoulders. Hanuman also joined and repeated the magic mantra of Rama over every stone and boulder, and the work went on with great speed and enthusiasm. The bridge was a hundred leagues long and ten wide. One fifth was built the first day and construction was completed in five days.

Rama and Lakshmana sat on the shore and watched the work. It is said that a squirrel who wanted to help Rama used to wet his fur, roll in the sand and then go and shake off the dust on the bridge, since that was the only contribution he was capable of making. The monkeys made fun of him and shooed off or he would be trampled by their feet. He was frightened and sad and went and nestled close to Rama, who took him on his lap and comforted him by passing his three fingers down his back. It is said that, to this day, the squirrel bears the mark of Rama's fingers on his back. Rama calmed his fears and told him that his tiny efforts were as valuable to him as the gigantic achievements of the monkeys. The sand he had brought was as precious to him as the rocks of the *vanaras*. Thus, the little squirrel also found a place in Rama's heart.

At last, the causeway was completed. Even the gods came to survey it and from above, it looked like the parting in the hair of a woman, so elegant and beautiful was it. Rama was the first to set foot on it, then came Lakshmana and then Sugriva. The rest of the *vanara* horde followed, dancing and bounding with joy. Sometimes, they would jump into the sea and swim for a while and sometimes walk on the bridge. The noise made by the monkeys drowned out the sound of the waves. It was as if the sea held its breath while the army crossed. Finally, they set foot on enemy territory. Rama told Lakshmana and Sugriva to make preparations for camp. The sun had set and the moon had just risen, as the army settled down for the night. Rama was touched by the enthusiasm and devotion of the monkeys and their innocent love. The noises from the city wafted to them on the air. The monkeys were greatly excited and roared with joy.

Rama looked up at the city of Ravana, with its turrets of gold and silver and thought of his beloved Janaki, who was a prisoner of love. He stood gazing at Lanka for a long time, lost in thought. At last, he roused himself and went to talk to the commanders about their plan of action—who should be in charge of which battalion and other details.

Thus ends the twenty-third chapter of the glorious Ramayana *of Sage Valmiki called "Causeway to Lanka."*

Hari Aum Tat Sat

TWENTY-FOUR

THE SIEGE OF LANKA

I bow to Sri Ramachandra who is
A terror to the wicked and considerate to the good.
Friend of those in sorrow.
Lamp of the race of Manu, far from the darkness of tamas.
—SOURCE UNKNOWN

Dayasaraya Namaha!

Homage to epitome of kindness.

THE SPY WHOM RAVANA HAD sent returned and told him all the news. "This sea, which has never been crossed, has been crossed by Rama's army with ease and they have camped on the southern shore. You should either return Sita to him immediately or else prepare for a mighty battle."

Ravana was quite incensed at these words and shouted, "Let the entire world come and fight with me but I will not return Sita to Rama. Of course, it is true that I did not believe that they would be able to cross the sea, but apparently they have done so. I want you and another person to go into their camp disguised as monkeys and find out about their arrangements. Go immediately and return quickly."

The two *rakshasas* had hardly entered the encampment and started their investigations when Vibhishana spied them and penetrated their disguise and hauled them off to Rama. They fell at his feet, groveling for pardon. Rama smiled at them and said, "Have you finished your task? If not, ask Vibhishana to take you around the camp. I have nothing to hide. Go back and tell your master, 'You dared to take away my Sita from me because of your prowess. The time has come to put that bravado to the test. Tomorrow, when the sun comes up, Lanka will be destroyed by me and you will see the wrath of Rama!'" Then, turning to Vibhishana, he said,

"Release these poor creatures. What have they done? Let them go back and deliver my message."

The two culprits were vastly relieved and, having blessed Rama for his mercy, they hurried to Lanka and repeated Rama's message to Ravana. Ravana was furious and went up to the palace ramparts to survey the army. The whole of the southern shore and the groves beyond were swarming with monkeys and bears of every size, shape and color. He asked his spies to point out to him the chiefs of the various battalions and carefully scrutinized each of them. He then dismissed the two spies as being quite ineffective and traitors to boot, since they could do nothing but sing the praises of his enemy.

Next, he thought of another stratagem to torture Sita. He asked a magician called Vidyudjihva to make a realistic head of Rama with an arrow stuck in it, in order to frighten Sita. He marched to the grove where she was sitting, plunged in sorrow, her mind absorbed with thoughts of Rama, eyes cast down and filled with bitter drops.

Ravana arrested his stride a few feet away from her, in order to drink in her beauty, and then approached her. "It is high time you forgot that useless husband of yours, O Sita, for I'm sorry to tell you that he is no more. Evidently, your spiritual merits were not enough to save him. You boasted that your husband was invincible, but alas, he has been killed by me. He was camping on the shore with his army but, as he was sleeping, my general went and cut off his head. Vibhishana was captured and Lakshmana and the monkeys have fled for their lives. As for Hanuman, his jaw was smashed and he lies dead under a tree. The whole shore is drenched with the blood of dead monkeys." He gave her another of his piercing looks with his crystal green eyes and continued, "I see that you don't believe me. I anticipated that and so I have brought Rama's head to convince you."

He ordered one of the *rakshasis* to fetch the magician, who arrived promptly, with Rama's head stuck on a pole. This gruesome looking article was placed before Sita. Ravana threw a bow in front of her and said, "Here is the famous bow of Rama." Then, leaning forward, he whispered, as if meant for her ears alone, "Now, will you agree to be mine?"

Sita gave one look at the head and shrieked, "Oh my beloved Lord, have you deserted me? I am a despicable woman, for I am responsible for the death of my husband!" So saying she beat her breasts and wailed. Ravana watched with keen anticipation, hoping that in her sorrow, she would turn to him, but she did not even notice him.

Just then, news was brought to him that his presence was urgently needed in the council chamber. Fearing that something serious was afoot, Ravana left immediately. As soon as he had gone, both the magic head and the bow vanished, much to Sita's amazement. Just then, Vibhishana's wife, a *rakshasi* called Sarama, who was fond of Sita, came and told her about Ravana's foul plan to dupe her.

"Don't fear, Sita. Rama can never be killed. Your husband and brother are in good health and they are camped at the foot of the hill, ready to attack." Just as she was saying this, the trumpets and bugles blared, calling all *rakshasas* to assemble for the fight. Sarama revived Sita, who lay in a swoon on the ground and bade her to be of good cheer.

The sounds made by the approaching army of the *vanaras* was undermining the morale of the *rakshasa* army. Ravana laughed at their fears and said, "You are supposed to be great warriors and yet you have all become pale and frightened at the rumor that Rama is invincible."

Hearing this, one of the aged ministers said, "My child, a king should always have the welfare of his subjects at heart. Because of your infatuation for a woman, you are prepared to sacrifice the well-being of your people. Is that the correct attitude for a king? The whole cause of this hatred and ill feeling is Sita. Give her back to her lawful husband and save your country. Have you forgotten the boon given to you by Brahma? You asked for exemption from death from all beings, but you did not mention specifically either human beings or monkeys, and now, these are the very ones who are preparing to fight with you. I am afraid Sita will bring ruin on you and on our clan. Give her back and let us live in peace."

Ravana could never stand any criticism. Moreover, he was so infatuated with Sita that the very thought of giving her back was abhorrent to him. "This Rama, whom you all fear, is only a poor human being, who has been banished by his own father, and has now managed to get a few monkeys together and is daring to attack the might of Ravana, who has subdued even the king of gods! It is really laughable. After having taken so much trouble to bring Sita here, do you think I'll give her back to that mendicant? I will never give her up! I may break in two but I will never bend my heads before anyone or ask anyone's pardon."

With this ultimatum, he ordered all his generals to guard the city gates and to be prepared for a prolonged siege, if necessary.

In the meantime, Rama's army had come close enough to see the guards who had been stationed at the gates. Vibhishana's spies had reported all that they needed to know about the positions of the various forces. Hearing this, Rama decided which of his commanders should go to which gate. He himself, along with Lakshmana, decided to go to the north gate, which was being guarded by Ravana himself. By this time, night was falling and Rama, along with Lakshmana and a few others, went to the top of an adjacent hill from which they could get a magnificent view of the fabulous city in the pearly light of the rising moon.

They slept on the hill in the open and, when they woke up, the intoxicating fragrance of a thousand newly opened blooms was wafted to them from the doomed city. The birds started their melodious music to welcome the rising sun and Rama had his first glimpse of Ravana standing on the ramparts of his palace, with the white umbrella of royalty furled above his head. The gold on his garment of red silk glittered in the sun. Sugriva was standing beside Rama and when he saw Ravana in all his glory, he could not bear it, and on a sudden impulse, he leapt into the air and landed on the terrace beside the *rakshasa* king and sprang on him.

Ravana was taken aback but he guessed at once who he was and said, "O monkey chieftain! Very soon, you will lose that beautiful neck, which has given you your name!"

Ravana would have made short work of him but Sugriva realized his folly and evaded his grasp and jumped back to Rama's side. Rama chided him gently for his foolhardiness, though the watching monkeys were thrilled and cheered their leader.

Arming themselves with sticks, stones, rocks and trees, the *vanaras*, led by Rama, proceeded toward the city and took up the positions which had been decided for them. Rama was one who followed the rules of dharmic warfare, and he decided to send a messenger to Ravana to make a last bid for peace. Calling Angada, he ordered him to go and talk to Ravana.

"Tell him that I said, 'I have come to punish you for stealing my wife. But even at this last moment, I would like to give you a chance. If you agree to return Sita to me, I will stop the war. If not, it will be a fight to the finish and will end in the extermination of the *rakshasa* race.'"

Angada leaped into the sky and reached the conference hall where Ravana was closeted with his ministers. Boldly, he walked inside and gave his message. The infuriated Ravana ordered his ministers to capture the monkey and beat him to death. As they ran to do his bidding, Angada jumped on to the terrace, carrying the ministers with him. He then shook them off and returned to Rama. War was now inevitable. Ravana had been given his last and final chance. The army marched up to the bastions of the city. As Rama gazed at the city walls, his heart flew to Sita, who must have been anxiously waiting all these months for him to come and rescue her. This thought was enough to spur him to ferocious activity.

Thus ends the twenty-fourth chapter of the glorious Ramayana *of Sage Valmiki called "The Siege of Lanka."*

Hari Aum Tat Sat

TWENTY-FIVE

THE MIGHTY BATTLE

Divyastra dharine Namaha!

Homage to the possessor of divine weapons.

Rama is the savior of those who surrender,
Sita blesses all those who fall at her feet.
He has the color of rainclouds,
And she the color of gold.
—POPULAR VERSE

The *vanara* army now charged the eastern gate of Lanka, with bloodcurdling cries. They clambered up the walls and broke the ramparts. Very soon, they breached the other three walls. The whole place was alive with a mass of leaping and screaming *vanaras*, bent on destruction. The *rakshasa* army ably defended their stronghold and the first day's fight continued into the night, which was the time when the *rakshasas*, who were night wanderers, became more powerful.

Indrajit, Ravana's son, was one of their ablest warriors. The name given to him at birth was Meghanatha, but he came to be called Indrajit after he defeated Indra, the king of the gods. He was a master magician and a prince of illusions—Ravana's golden boy, who could take on any form at will. It is said that only his mother Mandodari knew his real form.

After having almost defeated Angada, he leaped into the air and disappeared into the clouds. From this vantage point where he couldn't be seen, he sent the deadly "*nagapasa*," or noose of the serpent, with which he bound the two brothers, who had already been badly wounded by him. Rama fell to the ground in a faint and Lakshmana followed suit. Enmeshed by the magic cords, lacerated all over their bodies with Indrajit's deadly arrows, they lay on their bed of suffering, drenched in blood, with hardly any signs of life, except for an occasional, feeble twitching. There was panic in the *vanara* army and they stared at the sky in the hope of being able to see Indrajit but none of them could see him except Vibhishana and he was also helpless against the snake noose. Indrajit was jubilant, for he was sure that he had killed the brothers. Having created havoc in the rest of the army, he returned to his father and gave him the happy news.

Sugriva was desperate when he saw Rama and Lakshmana in this state but Vibhishana comforted him, saying, "Take it from me that they are not dead. It is only a temporary faint. Let us chant some mantras and they will wake up. Now it is up to you to keep up the morale of the army until the brothers recover consciousness. You should not allow your affection to weaken you. Both of them will have to be guarded carefully until they come to themselves."

In the meantime, Indrajit entered the city covered with glory and gave the news to his father that he had killed his two enemies. Ravana was overjoyed and blessed his valiant son. That night, the whole of Lanka slept peacefully. In the morning, Ravana sent for the *rakshasis* who were looking after Sita and told them to tell her that her husband lay dead on the battlefield. Since she wouldn't be convinced by mere talk, he told them to take her in his aerial vehicle, called the Pushpaka, and let her survey the battlefield from the air and observe the body of her husband.

"Tell Sita to forget her husband and come to me, since now she has no other recourse but to accept my love and become my wife."

The *rakshasis* forced Sita to get into the vehicle and took her over the battlefield, where she saw for herself the devastation in the *vanara* army. In the midst of the sea of corpses, of dead and dying monkeys, she suddenly spied her beloved husband and his brother lying on a bed of arrows, their bodies bleeding and inert. She could no longer see clearly, due to the tears which were flowing in torrents from her eyes. For some time, the shock made her absolutely silent but then she started to moan and bewail her fate.

"How is it that my Rama who killed all the *rakshasas* at Janasthana, single-handedly, could not counteract the effects of these deadly arrows of the evil-minded son of Ravana? Our Guru Vasistha prophesied that my Rama would perform many *Ashvamedha yajnas* and win great fame as a king and that I would never be a widow and would be the mother of heroic sons. How is it that all these words have proved false? There is no one that we can trust. Fate is all powerful. Of what use are the lotus marks on my feet, which proclaim that I will be a queen? I have all the twelve auspicious signs, my body is symmetrical, my teeth even, my navel set deep in my stomach. My breasts are full and skin and hair soft. My complexion is pearly and my soles touch the ground when I walk, yet this calamity has overtaken me."

One of the *rakshasis* who was kinder than the rest and had befriended Sita before, now comforted her with these words, "My lady, please do not weep. Your Lord is not dead. Neither of them is dead. See how the *vanaras* are guarding their bodies. They appear to be waiting for them to recover. Take this opportunity and have a good look at the face of your beloved husband, from whom you have been parted for such a long time. There is a glow about their faces which would not have been there if they were dead. So forget this sorrow and take heart."

Sita was thrilled to hear this. She observed the two carefully and confirmed what was said by the kindly *rakshasi*. She raised her palms in prostration to Rama and then returned.

Slowly, after some time had passed, the *nagapasa* ceased to have effect and Rama came to. When he saw his brother lying apparently dead, he started lamenting and fainted again.

At this moment when all of them were sitting and crying around the fallen princes, Sugriva's court physician came and said, "Once long ago when the gods and demons were fighting, the gods were struck down in a similar fashion but their guru revived them with special herbs from the milky ocean. These herbs are known as *sanjeevakarani*, which is capable of reviving those who are fatally stricken, and *vishalyakarani*, which heals all wounds inflicted by weapons. Let Hanuman be sent to get them."

Hardly had he finished speaking when a tempestuous wind rose from the ocean, making the waves leap up into the sky. The force of the wind appeared to bend even the mountains. Trees were snapped like sticks and flung to the ground and animals ran in every direction. Suddenly Garuda, the king of birds, vehicle of Vishnu, cleaved his way through the tempestuous sky. The storm had been caused by the wind raised by his enormous wings. He was the bitter enemy of all snakes and, as soon as he appeared, the snake-noose which had bound the two brothers started loosening its deathly hold on them. As Garuda came nearer, they were released completely and Lakshmana stirred, as if from sleep. The wide-winged Garuda now came close to them and stroked their faces lovingly with his wings, and instantly their wounds vanished and lustre returned to their faces. Their splendor, majesty, intelligence and courage increased ten-fold. Garuda embraced them warmly. Rama said, "When you caressed me with your wings, I felt as if my father was touching me. Because of you, we have been saved from this deadly snake-noose. How wonderful you look! Pray tell me who you are?"

The bird said, "I am Garuda, the son of Vinata, and I am your constant companion. I am your vehicle and will always be hovering around you, even when you are not aware of it. I am the only one who could have saved you from this noose made of snakes, who have taken on the form of arrows, which Indrajit invoked by a special mantra. I am their ancient enemy and that is why they vanished as soon as they saw me. Rama, fear not, you and your brother are destined to destroy your enemies and have a glorious future. Your strength lies in your adherence to dharma and you will be victorious, even though your enemies are mightily treacherous. Now give me leave to go. Whenever you need me, just think of me, and I'll be there."

Witnessing the miraculous recovery of the brothers, the monkeys chattered and clattered with delight. They beat their tails and thumped their kettledrums and jumped up and down with joy.

Ravana heard these sounds and was puzzled. How can they be so joyous when Rama lies dead? he thought. He ordered his spies to go and find out the truth and was amazed when they returned with the news of Rama's miraculous recovery.

Now Ravana sent another horde, led by the terrible warrior called Dhumarksha, the fiery-eyed one, but he was killed by Hanuman. Next to be sent was Vajradamshtra, with fangs like sharpened diamonds, another invincible warrior, but he was killed by Vali's son Angada. Then came Akampana, who was also vanquished by Hanuman. Ravana was quite depressed at the death of three of his best warriors.

He called his commander-in-chief Prahastha and told him to go. "How is it that an army which can hardly be called an army at all has defeated three of my best warriors? They are only a bunch of wild, fickle-minded monkeys, who have never been trained in the art of warfare. They will never be able to face a well-disciplined army which marches ruthlessly under the guidance of a master general like you."

Prahastha was happy to see the confidence which was placed in him by his master and he advanced proudly to the front. He created havoc in the *vanara* forces until Neela confronted him and crushed his chariot and forced him to dismount. They fought face to face, until at last Neela took up a big boulder and crushed Prahastha's head. His frightened army abandoned their leader and fled back to the city.

Ravana could not believe that his favorite commander had been killed. He decided that it was time that he himself enter the arena. Rama saw the huge army advancing and asked Vibhishana who the leaders were, who were in the forefront of the troop.

Vibhishana said, "The chariot with the lion banner belongs to Indrajit and the one with the white umbrella holds Ravana, the lord of the *rakshasas*."

Rama watched them for a long moment and said, "Indeed, he is a glorious figure. Such radiance! Like the sun at noon. He seems to be endowed with all the qualities of a great hero. Yet when I think that he is the one who has stolen my Sita, I cannot help but pity him, for he is coming closer to his death."

Ravana arranged his army carefully and then plunged into battle. Sugriva had been itching to get his hands on the demon king and hurled rocks at him, which Ravana splintered with ease. At last, Sugriva fell in a faint from one of Ravana's arrows and the monkey horde fled in fear and ran to Rama. Rama stood up, ready to enter the fray, but Lakshmana stopped him, saying that it would be his pleasure to make an end of this wicked man.

Hanuman, in the meantime rushed at Ravana and said, "You have been granted many boons but none which will protect you from monkeys. Now allow my right hand to teach you a well deserved lesson."

Ravana was furious when he heard this. "I will give you the

opportunity of winning everlasting fame by hitting me, just once, and then I'll kill you."

Hanuman punched him on his chest and Ravana reeled under the blow. He admired Hanuman's strength but didn't wait for more. He turned his chariot toward Neela and did his best to wound him, but since Neela was the son of the fire god, he could not be killed. Ravana now directed his fury against the approaching Lakshmana. Then ensued a memorable fight between the two, which was watched by all the others. At last, Ravana was compelled to use the *shakti* weapon given to him by Brahma. He hurled it at Lakshmana, who fell down in a swoon. With a smile, Ravana came close and tried to lift him up but was unable to do so. He was amazed that he could not. He, who had once lifted the mountain of Kailasa, was now unable to lift Rama's brother. Hanuman came and struck Ravana down from his chariot and, before he could recover from the blow, carried Lakshmana back to Rama. As soon as he reached Rama, the *shakti* weapon left his side and returned to Ravana, and Lakshmana was his old self.

Ravana was bent on causing havoc to the *vanara* army and Rama decided that it was high time for him to enter the battle. Hanuman begged him to use his shoulder as a vehicle, since Ravana was fighting from a chariot and Rama from the ground. Rama agreed and went into battle on Hanuman's shoulder.

At last, the two protagonists came face to face. Neither could help admiring the other, but Rama said, "You think you are a hero, yet you have behaved as no hero would behave. You deserve nothing but death and I will see that you get it."

Without answering, Ravana took up his bow and aimed an arrow at Hanuman. It glanced off the mighty hero, like a mango leaf from its tree. Rama was furious when he saw the attack on Hanuman and he broke Ravana's chariot and wounded his horses and charioteer. Another arrow to Ravana's chest made him reel and still another knocked off his golden crown, which rolled in the dust. The king of *rakshasas* was now without his crown, his bow and his chariot. Denuded of his accoutrements, he appeared to have lost half his splendor.

Rama took pity on him and said, "You have acted in an unforgivable manner, yet I see that you are very tired, so I will refrain from killing you now. Go home and rest and return with another bow and chariot; then I'll show you what I'm capable of."

Ravana returned to Lanka, crestfallen and ashamed, filled with wrath against Rama and determined to kill him at all costs.

Thus ends the twenty-fifth chapter of the glorious Ramayana *of Sage Valmiki called "The Mighty Battle."*

Hari Aum Tat Sat

Rama:
Holy one, how can I attain that state?

Vasistha replies:

What is known as liberation, O Rama, is the Absolute itself.
That alone is.
That which is perceived here as "I," "you," etc.,
only seems to be.
Rama! In ornaments I see only gold In waves I see only water
In air I see only movement
In a mirage I see only heat waves
Similarly, in the world I see only Brahman

—*The Yoga Vasistha*

TWENTY-SIX

HANUMAN
TO THE RESCUE

Srimaté Namaha!

Homage to the
one who has a
clear intellect.

Meditate on Rama, who is the color of the blue lotus.
Whose eyes are like lotus petals.
Whose hair is in matted locks,
And who is accompanied by Sita and Lakshmana.
—DEVOTIONAL VERSE

RAVANA WAS COMPLETELY demoralized by this
scene. Far from appreciating Rama's generosity
in letting him go, he was filled with humiliation
and ideas of revenge. He began to recollect all those
painful incidents in his life, when he had insulted people
and been cursed by them. He aroused himself from
these mournful thoughts and ordered his brother
Kumbhakarna to be awakened from sleep.
Kumbhakarna had been summoned to the council nine
days ago and had gone back to sleep again.

"Go and wake him up," shouted Ravana, "or else
he will sleep for another six months. He will make
short work of the two Kosala princes."

Kumbhakarna's mouth was like a yawning cave
and his snores shook the rafters, making them rattle.
His breath reeked of alcohol and blood, for he had
eaten and drunk his fill nine days ago before falling
into a deep stupor. The *rakshasas* who went to wake
him up carried wagonloads of pork and buffalo meat
and buckets of blood and marrow and barrels of strong
wine. They covered his uncouth body with sandal paste
and perfume and garlands. Some made thunderous
noises, calculated to waken the dead, while others
blew loudly on conchs, bugles and trumpets and still
others beat drums. Some used sticks and rods to prod

him awake but he slept on, blissfully snoring, despite all these torments. A few jumped up and down on top of his chest, but to no avail. Then they fell to biting his ears and tearing his hair and punching his stomach.

At last, the monster seemed to be showing some signs of animation and gave a great yawn, and those who had been tugging his beard fell into his cavernous mouth, and had to be fished out before he closed it. Furious at having been woken up when he had only slept for nine days, he shouted at them, and they fled in terror before he caught hold of them and started eating them. He looked around and saw the mountains of food and started loudly chomping his way through them.

At last, he was a bit appeased and the *rakshasas* crept back and informed him that he was urgently needed by his brother. Having licked the pots and eaten the buffaloes which drew the carts, Kumbhakarna dressed himself with care before going to the council hall to meet Ravana. The very earth shuddered as he stomped down the street, his gargantuan body occupying the entire width of the thoroughfare.

Ravana was delighted to see him and informed him of the critical events which had taken place in Lanka while he was in the throes of his blissful slumber.

Kumbhakarna laughed at Ravana's description of the *vanara* army and said, "My dear brother, I warned you of the consequences of your ardor for that woman just ten days ago at the council hall but you would not listen to me. The king who follows the rules of dharma and listens to the words of the wise will reap the rewards of his good deeds, but the one who discards these words and acts according to his own perverted understanding will have to bear the consequences of his actions. Both Vibhishana and I advised you once, but you would not listen. It is still not too late. Try to avert this crazy war and make friends with Rama. I hear that you have already lost your best generals and been publicly humiliated. Will you not stop till your head is cut off from its shoulders?"

Ravana's lips quivered with rage and his eyes became like shining hot coals shooting sparks of fire. He shouted at Kumbhakarna, "An elder brother should be honored like a father. How dare you try to advise me! What has happened, has happened.

I'm not prepared to go back on anything I have done. If ever you have held me in respect or love, then tell me what to do now. Try to correct the result of my past indiscretions instead of blaming me for them."

Kumbhakarna realized that his words were like a red cape to a bull, so he pacified him with sweet words. "Don't worry, brother. I will pulverize the whole lot of them. Just by walking in their midst, I will make mincemeat of those puny princes. Let me get my hands on them! I will tear them apart with my bare hands. I need no weapons. Cast off your worries, and go into your harem and have fun with your women. Once Rama is dead, Sita will be yours."

Ravana was delighted. He placed many precious necklaces around his monstrous neck and sent Kambhakarna off with his blessings.

Kumbhakarna donned his bronze armor and golden helmet. His belt was as large as the chain on the drawbridge. Having quaffed two thousand barrels of wine and a few thousand barrels of hot buffalo blood to give him strength, he entered the battlefield with great enthusiasm, flourishing his iron spear, which was spitting flames from its tip. In front of him walked the one carrying his black banner with the wheel of death on it. He was followed by a mob of excited, shouting *rakshasas*, brandishing tridents, javelins and clubs. He looked like a colossal black thunder-cloud as he strode out onto the battlefield and the monkeys fled in terror.

Vibhishana told Rama the story of Kumbhakarna and why he had been cursed to sleep for months. While he was still an infant, he was in the habit of devouring thousands of creatures of all types for his breakfast and an equal number for lunch and for dinner, with a few snacks thrown in at odd times. Finally all the creatures of the world ran to Brahma for help. Even Brahma was alarmed at the sight of Kumbhakarna and cursed him that he would sleep for the rest of his life. Ravana intervened for the sake of his brother and Brahma modified his curse, by saying that he would sleep for six months at a time and then wake up for a day so that his insatiable appetite could be appeased and then sleep again for another six months.

"He can easily make one mouthful of our entire army," said Vibhishana. "Had he not been cursed by Brahma, he would have eaten up all life on this earth long ago!"

Kumbhakarna stepped over the wall and advanced like a mountain on the move, his eyeballs rolling like chariot wheels. The monkeys fled in terror and Angada had to rally them by saying that he was only a machine which had been trained to fight and that they could easily conquer him. They started to rain rocks and boulders and trees on him, but all of it glanced off him, like feathers off a rock. The monkeys tried to jump on him and bite him, but he brushed them off like flies. In fact, he hardly noticed them and walked on, crushing thousands under his huge feet. Suddenly, he pounced on Sugriva and held him aloft like a wriggling snake. Sugriva clawed viciously at his ears and bit off his nose and ripped his thighs with his nails and Kumbhakarna swore and dashed him to the ground. Sugriva bounded off to Rama.

Now Lakshmana challenged him and Kumbhakarna applauded his valor, but he brushed him aside, saying, "I'm eager to meet your brother Rama, so let me pass."

Lakshmana refused to let him pass and rained arrows on him till his mace fell from his hands, but still he continued to move forward. Finally, he came face to face with Rama and gave out a bloodcurdling roar, at which all the monkeys fell down senseless. Taking up a huge boulder, he hurled it at Rama, who stopped it with seven arrows. Lakshmana told Rama to make short work of him, before he caused further damage. Rama stood in front of him and said, "Brave *rakshasa*! I'm Rama, son of Dasaratha, for whom you have been searching. Take a good look at me, for soon your eyes will not be able to see at all."

Kumbhakarna laughed and said, "I'm not Viradha or Kabandha. I cannot be killed by you."

Rama was quite unruffled and, invoking the wind god, he sent an arrow which cut off one arm of the giant. With his other arm, Kumbhakarna pulled out a tree and threw it at Rama. Then Rama cut off his other arm. But still the monster kept advancing, shouting imprecations. With two more arrows, Rama cut off his legs and finally, with the fifth arrow, which had a razor head, the huge neck of the monster was sliced through and the diademed head fell to the ground with a reverberating thud. The whole earth shuddered with the impact. Far off in Lanka, Ravana heard the fearful noise and a shaft of pure terror shot through his heart. The mountainous head rolled down the hillside and dropped into the ocean in a whirlpool of blood, making the waters rise up in huge gory waves. Kumbhakarna, the terror of the world, the sole hope of Ravana, now lay dead in a lake of blood.

When Ravana heard about his beloved brother's death, he fainted away. When he recovered, he sat with his head in his hands and bemoaned his loss. He just couldn't understand how a mighty hero like his brother could have been killed by a mere man. Seeing their father's despair, his younger sons tried to cheer him up and insisted on going, in a gang, to the battlefront to try their luck.

Ravana embraced them and allowed them to go. Though the princes were all valiant, one by one they were all killed and the news was taken to Ravana. The heroes, who had set out so enthusiastically in the morning, now lay like felled trees on the battlefield. Ravana could not bear it. He just didn't know what he should do. He began to wonder if there was any truth in what he had heard about Rama—that he was Narayana Himself, who had taken on a human birth in order to kill him.

As he sat, sunk in gloom with his head in his hands, his golden boy, Indrajit, son of his favorite wife Mandodari, now came to him and tried to lift his spirits. "My beloved father," he said, "why should you worry when I am here to help you? I will go this very minute and punish your enemies. Before the sun sets, Sita will be yours."

Ravana looked at his golden boy. His skin and hair were gold and there were golden flecks in his eyes. His armor and helmet were both of gold, as well as his shoes and belt. He was as beautiful as his mother and Ravana was delighted to hear his promise. "Go, my son," he said, "and may you return victorious."

Indrajit bowed low before his father and got into his chariot of illusions and set out immediately, followed by a mighty army. Before reaching the front, he got down and kindled a fire and, pouring oblations into it, he worshiped Agni, the god of fire, his favorite god. After the ceremony was over, he disappeared into the sky and began raining arrows over the *vanara* hordes, who began to fall by the thousands.

The whole field was strewn with dead and dying monkeys. Most of the time, they could not see where he was, since he was an expert in the art of illusory warfare. How could they fight with an invisible enemy? Through the dark clouds of illusion, they could hear the sound of his chariot and the twang of his bow. Sometimes they could see the flash of his golden armor and the streak of his golden spear, but of him they could see nothing. One by one, all the great *vanara* heroes except for Hanuman and Jambavan, were killed. Again, even Rama and Lakshmana succumbed this time to Indrajit's fatal arrows.

Indrajit went back, well pleased with his day's work. After a long time, Vibhishana regained consciousness and painfully dragged himself to Jambavan and asked him what they should do now. Jambavan was badly wounded, but his first question was about Hanuman.

When he heard that Hanuman was fine, he said, "Now there is nothing to worry about." Calling Hanuman, he said, "O Hanuman, you are the only one who can save the lives of the Kosala brothers, as well as the lives of all the *vanaras*. Go immediately to the golden peak on the mountain called Himavan, which is rich in herbs, and bring back the four magic herbs. The one called *Mritasanjivi* will bring the dead back to life, and *Vishalyakarani* will heal all wounds and the other two will reset fractured bones and give a glow to the skin."

Hanuman grew in size and flew off into the sky with his face turned to the north. Flying smoothly, he soon reached the peak spoken of by Jambavan, but search as he might, he did not find the herbs which he was looking for. It appeared as if they were playing a game of their own and hiding from his eyes. Hanuman was quite fed up and decided to take the entire mountain. He uprooted it and sailed across the sky with the peak in his hands and soon reached Lanka. But there was no place to put it down, so he flew close to the battlefield below.

The air was suffused with the intoxicating perfume of the magic herbs and Rama and Lakshmana woke up after inhaling the fragrance. The rest of the monkeys who had succumbed to Indrajit's magic weapons also woke up after inhaling the fragrance of the medicinal herbs. All of them appeared to be in better condition now than they were before they fell. Hanuman returned the peak to its original place in the Himalayas and returned to Rama.

One might wonder how it was that the none of the *rakshasas* revived. This was because Ravana had commanded that all the dead *rakshasas* be thrown into the sea so that no one could count their number and thus taint his reputation. That night, the excited monkeys set fire to Lanka for the second time. The citizens started to cry and wail in panic. The noise woke up Ravana. He had been sleeping peacefully after hearing of Rama's death from his son. He couldn't believe that the monkeys were carrying on the war without Rama. When he heard from his spies the news of the princes' recovery, he became most disturbed.

He summoned the two sons of Kumbhakarna, known as Kumbha and Nikumbha, and asked them to go to battle to avenge their father's death. They were both fierce fighters and they marched in triumph to the battlefield. Even though the young *vanaras* fought bravely, they were defeated and even Angada fell in a faint. The news was taken to Rama and Sugriva decided to go to the front.

He accosted Kumbha. "I'm full of admiration for the way in which you handle the bow. I see you are a combination of your father and uncle—the dexterity of one, with the solidity of the other. I don't feel like killing you, since you are surely a jewel among your race but I have no option, since we are on opposite sides, so let us fight to the finish."

Though Kumbha was pleased with Sugriva's admiration, he didn't like the insinuation that Sugriva was superior to himself. He rushed at him with a roar and the two of them started wrestling with each other till the earth trembled and the leaves fell off the trees. At last, with a powerful blow, Sugriva knocked him to the ground and killed him. Witnessing the death of his valiant brother, Nikumbha rushed at the monkeys and killed them by the hundreds.

Seeing their plight, Hanuman came to the rescue and punched him on his chest. Nikumbha flung a huge iron pestle at Hanuman. Everyone expected him to fall but they were astonished to see that the pestle shattered into a million fragments on Hanuman's adamantine torso. After grappling for a while, Hanuman threw him on the ground and sat on his chest till he suffocated to death.

The *vanaras* sent up a roar of jubilation. The *rakshasas* marveled that their enormous strength and modern weapons counted for nothing in the face of these long-tailed tree folk, armed only with sticks and stones! Not one of them was capable of wielding a sword or using a bow, and yet they seemed to be gaining the upper hand.

Ravana was at a loss. He went to the secret grove where his son, Indrajit, was performing his magic rituals and begged him to kill Rama.

"O Father!" he said, "for your sake, I killed him once, but it appears as if the whole of nature is supporting him, or else how could he still be alive? Remember Father, that in your youth, you ruled the world, supported by dharma, but now your rule is supported by *adharma* alone. The very gods tremble at the mention of your name and the curses of the saints whom you have killed have taken on the form of this battle, which will be the end of you. You have made the whole of creation suffer by your inequities. Rama is the image of dharma so nature supports him. However, I shall do your bidding. I shall defeat the Kosala brothers as I promised to do."

As usual, Indrajit performed the fire ceremony and invoked the aid of Agni before setting out. The top of his chariot glistened with gold turrets and his banner also was tipped in gold. The chariot could appear and disappear at will. He appeared suddenly in the middle of the battlefield and started raining arrows in every direction. Then he disappeared into the sky and started a merciless onslaught of the two princes. They retaliated by sending their arrows upwards. He produced a thick fog which covered the whole field like a miasma, so that no one could see him but could only hear the twang of his bow and catch the gleam of his golden armor.

Rama's body was hurt in many places by his lethal arrows. Indrajit was gyrating around and around the sky at high speed, harassing the brothers, who could only shoot at random to where they thought he might be. Seeing the plight of the *vanaras*, Lakshmana was ready to send the *brahmastra*, but Rama stopped him and said, "This *brahmastra* will cause untold destruction and should be used only in the case of dire necessity. This is not the time for it. I will invoke some stronger mantras and make an end of him."

Indrajit could read Rama's mind and he decided to leave the field and return with a new strategy. Using his magic powers, he created a figure identical to Sita and brought it to the battlefield in his chariot. Hanuman recognized the same soiled, yellow garment which Sita had been wearing when he saw her, but it could not dim the radiance of her ethereal beauty. She was sitting forlorn and unhappy, as if she did not care what was happening to her.

Hanuman could not tear his gaze away from her grief-stricken face. He didn't know what was happening. He leaped towards Indrajit and began to belabor him. Indrajit grabbed hold of Sita's long tresses and started to threatened her with his sword, while she called loudly for Rama. Hanuman could not bear to see the princess of Videha being so treated. He hurled insults at Indrajit, who replied in kind. At last, Indrajit told Hanuman to watch carefully, for he was going to make an end of the woman who was the prime cause of all this destruction and of his father's infatuation. Taking up his sword, he slashed Sita across the chest and killed her. Not knowing that this was only a Sita created by his magic, Hanuman wept and decided to end the battle, since there seemed to be no further point in continuing it.

Hearing this news, Rama fainted and Lakshmana took him in his arms and tried to comfort him, as if he were a baby.

"O brother!" he said, "you have always followed the path of dharma and now see what has happened to us! If dharma could make us victorious, Ravana should have been killed long ago and you should never have been made to undergo such suffering. Dear brother, this is the time for action. I will avenge all the sufferings which have been meted out to you."

As he was saying this, Vibhishana came and wanted to know what had caused Rama to faint. When he heard that Sita had been killed in front of Hanuman's eyes, he said, "How can you believe such a thing? Don't you know the extent of Ravana's infatuation for her? Do you think it is possible that he would allow his son to kill her! How often have I asked him to give her up and seek peace but he has never listened. How can you imagine even for a moment that his son would have dared to kill a woman who was so dear to his father! I feel quite sure that the whole thing was a trick played by Indrajit, who is a master magician. He plotted the whole thing so that he could go and perform the *yajna* which will make him invincible. Even now, while we are sitting here and lamenting, he must be busy with the *yajna*. Without wasting any time, let us go to the spot where he is performing the ceremony and stop him from its successful completion. Let Lakshmana come with me. There is no time to be lost. If he is allowed to complete the ritual, he will be invincible. As it is, he has the weapon of Brahma with him, by which he will be able to kill quite a few of us. Brahma has warned him that only the one who is able to disrupt his *yajna* would be able to kill him."

Rama told Lakshmana to go at once and put an end to Indrajit's *yajna*.

Thus ends the twenty-sixth chapter of the glorious Ramayana *of Sage Valmiki called "Hanuman to the Rescue."*

Hari Aum Tat Sat

Vasistha says:
When the notion of the self is destroyed by withdrawing the fuel of ideas from the mind, That which is left is the Infinite.
In it, knowledge, knower and known exist as One.

—THE YOGA VASISTHA

TWENTY-SEVEN

THE INVISIBLE OPPONENT

Ananthaguna
Gambhiraya
Namaha!

Homage to
the one with
endless great
qualities.

Holding the bow in his hand,
The ever full, Unborn, incarnated,
In play, in order to save the world.
—SOURCE UNKNOWN

L AKSHMANA ARMED HIMSELF and took the blessings of Rama before proceeding. Vibhishana and Jambavan, with his army of bears, joined him.

"Come hurry!" said Vibhishana, "I'll take you to the magic grove where Indrajit is performing the ceremony. The god of fire will give him his magic chariot, yoked to tigers, which will make him invulnerable. Only *rakshasas* can see his hideout."

Vibhishana took Lakshmana to the secret grove where Indrajit was conducting his ritual. He touched Lakshmana, who was then able to see Indrajit, kneeling before an altar in the grove, invoking the aid of his favorite god Agni. He was pouring ghee into the fire with a wooden ladle and muttering incantations. His back was turned to them. The black sacrificial goat was tied to a stake and bleating piteously. Wearing a crimson robe and disheveled locks, he beat the earth with his javelin and out came thousands of serpents, coiling themselves around his arrows which were piled near the altar. His ax then fell on the neck of the goat and severed it neatly, so that it fell in a pool of blood. He held the ladle high above his head, ready for the final invocation. As the flames leaped higher and higher, the tawny figures of the tigers could be seen, snarling and growling, waiting for their cue to leap out of the flames to draw the invincible chariot. Vibhishana nudged Lakshmana and he sent an arrow straight at the upraised ladle and split it in two, just as it was descending for the final offering.

The *nagas* hissed and slithered back to the nether world whence they had come. Indrajit whirled around with an imprecation and snarled, "You traitor! You have betrayed me. You call yourself my uncle and yet you have disclosed my secrets. Otherwise, he could never have found out my place of worship. You have eaten the salt of my father and yet you have defected to the enemy! Shame on you! It is better to be a slave in one's own country than a friend of the enemy, licking his boots. One who abandons his own people and adopts the ways of his enemy is a traitor. I should kill you first, before killing Lakshmana."

Vibhishana retorted, "You are the wicked son of my wicked brother and I will have nothing to do with either of you. All these years, my brother has reveled in sinful acts. His anger and arrogance are proverbial. All these years, I have put up with it because there was nothing I could do. Though I was born in the clan of the *rakshasas*, my instincts were always those of a human. If I have abandoned you all now, it is because I am fed up with living a life of sin and wish to take up a noble path. You are a foolish, impulsive boy, bursting with pride, but beware! Both you and your father are doomed, and so is this fabulous city of Lanka!"

By now, Jambavan and his army of bears had began to harass Indrajit's army. The commotion created was so great that Indrajit was forced to put an end to the verbal combat with his uncle and come out through the secret tunnel into the open forest. The demon prince was furious at having to end his ritual to become invulnerable. He came out looking like the god of death. Hanuman barred his progress with a tree in his hand.

Vibhishana told Lakshmana to go to Hanuman's aid and attack the grandson of Mayan, the master magician. Lakshmana twanged his bowstring and the enraged Indrajit rushed towards him. Clad in silver from head to toe, with silver helmet and silver sword and arrows, Indrajit took up his bow and stood up in his chariot, facing Lakshmana. Hanuman immediately lifted Lakshmana onto his shoulders.

"Have you forgotten our last encounter, O Lakshmana?" he

roared, "When I made you and your brother lie flat on the ground? This time, I will not let you go so easily but will dispatch you quickly to the city of Yama!"

The two mighty protagonists faced each other for a fight to the finish. Arrow followed arrow with unerring accuracy. Lakshmana penetrated Indrajit's armor and Indrajit retaliated by smashing Lakshmana's armor. They were oblivious to the rest of the world. Their brilliant arrows, charged with incantations, flew like meteors across the sky, colliding in midair with earth-shattering explosions, each negating the other. Beasts and birds flew wildly in all directions and the very air seemed to hold its breath in fear.

Vibhishana joined in the fray but refrained from fighting with his nephew. Lakshmana sent four steel-tipped arrows that instantly felled the four beautiful, caparisoned horses. As the chariot started to swerve violently, another crescent-shaped arrow neatly severed the charioteer's head from his shoulders. For a minute, Indrajit faltered, then undaunted, he took up his bow and scattered thousands of arrows at Lakshmana's forces. The monkeys quickly took shelter behind Lakshmana.

As it became dark, Indrajit ran back to the city and returned with another chariot. Lakshmana was wonderstruck at the swiftness with which he returned. Lakshmana smashed this chariot also. Lifting his sword high above his head, Indrajit whirled it round and round, so that the blade seemed ablaze, but just as he was about to release it, Lakshmana shattered it with a hundred arrows.

The battle raged on furiously. At last, Lakshmana took out the arrow given to him by the Sage Agastya and charged it with the power of Indra and prayed to the weapon, "If Rama, the son of Dasaratha, is truly a *dharmatman*, if it is true that he has ever been truthful, has ever been loyal and is absolutely unrivaled, then let this arrow kill Indrajit, the son of Ravana." So saying, he let fly the mantra-charged arrow at Indrajit. It flew like a streak of lightning, straight to its target and, before Indrajit could counter it with one of his own, it neatly severed his handsome head so that it fell to the ground like a golden lotus. Like the bright sun setting behind the hills lay the head of Ravana's glorious son. The *vanara* army set up a roar of victory, which could be heard by Rama and Sugriva in the camp. The *rakshasa* army fled to the city, leaving their weapons behind.

Vibhishana, Hanuman and Jambavan were thrilled at Lakshmana's feat. He was carried triumphantly back on Hanuman's shoulders to the camp, where Rama welcomed him with joy. He took him on his lap and embraced him. He called the physician to come and attend to his wounds, which were many. The whole camp rejoiced and Rama hoped that, hearing of his son's death, Ravana himself would come the next day and fight with him.

When Ravana heard of the death of the beloved son of Mandodari, he fainted. Indrajit, who had once captured Indra, the king of gods, and brought him in chains to his father, now lay dead, killed by an arrow which had been charged with the power of Indra himself. Reviving from his swoon, he began to lament over his son. "My son! My beloved son!" he moaned, "there was no one like you in the whole world. You could defeat every enemy you encountered, yet you have been killed by that puny human being. How is it possible? Without you, this entire earth seems to be an empty place. Life has lost its charm for me, now that you are dead, my dearest child. Where have you gone, leaving me and your mother and your beloved wife? O Indrajit, why did you have to die?"

He forgot that he was the sole cause for the destruction of all his sons. His sorrow turned to anger, as it normally did with him, and he decided to really kill Sita, not as a trick, as his son had done, for she was the cause of all this. He forgot the fact that he had no one to blame but himself. It was his cruel and unjust act which had brought calamity on his whole race, as prophesied by Vibhishana.

Tears like liquid fire rolled down his cheeks. Picking up his sword, he rushed out of the palace, determined to kill Sita, who was still devoted to Rama. His ministers and wives rushed after him. They had seen him angry many times before, but that was nothing compared to what they saw now. Like a malefic comet approaching Venus, he flew at Sita with upraised sword.

She saw him coming, sword in hand, and realized that this time he was not approaching with words of love but with the sword of hate and meant to kill her, as easily as he had professed to love her. How easily swayed are the minds of the wicked! One day, they profess love and the next day, love changes to hate.

Sita was ready to die, since she was convinced that Rama had died. Luckily for her, one of Ravana's ministers, who was saner than the rest, approached him and said, "My Lord! How can you contemplate such a sinful deed? It was bad enough that you abducted her! How can you think of killing her now when she is helpless and at your mercy? Leave this poor, defenseless woman alone and turn your fury against her husband and brother, who are the ones who killed your son. Today is the fourteenth day of the dark lunar fortnight. Tomorrow is the night of the new moon, most auspicious for night rangers like us. That is the time for you to march against Rama and, after having killed him, you can return victoriously and claim Sita as your own."

Luckily for Sita, Ravana seemed to find this advice palatable. He checked his stride and stood for a moment, lost in thought. Then without saying a word to anyone, he turned around and marched to his assembly hall.

The next day, he sent his crack regiment of carefully chosen men famed for their valor to the battlefield, with orders that they should not return until the Kosala brothers were dead. Armed with all the best weapons of the time, the ill-fated army set out at break of day. The two factions met with a terrible clash and blood flowed like a river. Rama tackled them singlehanded as he had done the army at Janasthana. The army could not be seen due to the shower of arrows which engulfed them. At last, Rama took up the weapon called the *gandharva*, which created a kind of illusion by which many hundreds of Ramas could be seen on all sides. Within the period of an hour, he had ruined Ravana's crack regiment.

There was a loud wail in the whole of Lanka, sent up by the wives of the deceased. They blamed Surpanekha for being the sole cause of all their troubles. Every house in Lanka was sunk in sorrow. Those houses from which, at one time, only the sound of music and revelry could be heard, were now shuddering with the sounds of moans and sobs. As Ravana approached his bedroom, the fascinating Mandodari, daughter of Mayan, the maker of illusions, approached him and softly wound her arms round his neck. "My Lord," she said, "do you have to go to battle tomorrow? Can you not change your mind?"

Gently, he pushed her away from him and said, "My faithful one, you know I have to go, but please believe in me. I will not let you down."

"You have never let me down, my Lord," she said, "from the day you married me, you have given me nothing but delight. How can I forget!"

For the last time, Ravana climbed up to the ramparts of his castle and sang the *Sama Veda* hymns in which he was an expert, and by singing which he had once pleased Maheswara (Shiva), the Lord of the world. The whole of nature seemed to be providing an accompaniment for his chants, with the sighing of the wind, the lashing of the waves and the eerie creaking of the trees, as they swayed to and fro in tune with the rhythm of his song. Rama heard it down below and watched fascinated as Ravana's mighty figure, silhouetted against the sky, swayed and danced to his own music.

Eventually, with the approach of midnight, *amavasya*, the night of the new moon, the wind dropped, the waves calmed down and Ravana came down for his final battle.

For the first time, there was a tinge of fear in Ravana's voice as he ordered the last of his generals to get ready for the battle, for he had decided to go himself and avenge the death of all his loved ones. His divine chariot with the golden banner, equipped with all the latest weapons and drawn by eight swift horses, gleaming with jewels, was brought to the gate and Ravana leaped into it like a tiger and took the reins himself. The demon warriors cheered and clapped as he thundered down the street. He chose to take the fifth gate, the gate of illusion, and rose up like a black swan into the sky.

Thus ends the twenty-seventh chapter of the glorious Ramayana *of Sage Valmiki called "The Invisible Opponent."*

Hari Aum Tat Sat

TWENTY-EIGHT

THE END OF RAVANA

*Dasagreevashiro-
haraya Namaha!*

Homage to the
one who cut the
heads of Ravana.

*I surrender to Sri Rama, the Lord of the Raghus,
With lotus-petal eyes,
Handsomest in the whole world,
Yet a terror on the battlefield.
The compassionate one, filled with kindness.*
—RAMAYANA OF TULASIDAS

THE VANARAS WERE WATCHING all the four gates, but Ravana came through the illusory gate in the sky and landed in their midst with a thud. As he emerged, it is said that the sun lost its lustre and the birds started to scream discordantly. Clouds rained drops of blood and horses tripped and fell. Ravana's face lost its customary glow and his voice became horse. His left arm and eye started to throb. All these omen were indicative of death.

He did not heed any of them and drove at a fast pace through the ranks of monkeys, accompanied by those who remained of his loyal ministers. He forged into the thick of the *vanara* army and fought like one demented. None of the *vanaras* was able to face the onslaught of his fury. Sugriva fought a duel with Ravana's general Virupaksha. At last, with a blow from his open palm, Sugriva killed him. Like a lake drying up as summer advances, the forces on both sides were decreasing, as more and more of them fell. Slowly, it dawned on Ravana that fate seemed to be siding with Rama or else how could this have happened to him—he who was considered invincible in all the three worlds? It was unbelievable that his valiant general Virupaksha could have been killed by a single blow from a monkey's paw. Ravana sent Mahodara to take his place, but

Sugriva took up a fallen sword and chopped off his head as easily as cutting a ripe fruit from a tree. The third and last of his great warriors was Mahaparshva. Angada the boy prince killed him.

Seeing the death of his three dear commanders, Ravana ordered his charioteer to take him immediately to where Rama was. Once again, he came in front of Rama. He preferred to forget their first encounter, when Rama had treated him so chivalrously. He saw Rama leaning against his famous bow, the Kodanda, with Lakshmana beside him, and the thought crossed his mind that he looked like Narayana Himself, with Indra by his side.

He passed by Lakshmana and came face to face with Rama. Rama was happy to encounter him, for he had been waiting for him all these days. It was a glorious meeting. It is said that even the gods came to watch. Both were well versed in the art of warfare. The rest of the army stopped all their individual fights and came to watch this magnificent duel. The earth and sky lit up with the brilliance of their arrows, charged with various types of incantations. In one way, it was an unfair duel since Rama was on foot and Ravana in a chariot, but Rama was not perturbed.

Now Lakshmana entered the fray, for he had been itching to fight with Ravana. He could never forget the piteous face of his dear sister-in-law, as he had last seen her when she had begged him to go after Rama. He felled Ravana's splendid banner, which had been fluttering in the breeze, with a single arrow; then he brought his charioteer down and broke Ravana's bow. Vibhishana rushed up and killed the horses. Ravana was furious. He jumped down from the chariot and sent the famous *shakti* weapon at his brother. Lakshmana intervened and saved Vibhishana. Ravana decided that it was high time he put an end to this puny brother of Rama's. His green eyes sparking with copper fire and roaring with anger, Ravana hurled another javelin, made by Mayan, endowed with magic powers. It sizzled through the air, making a horrendous noise. It flew like a awesome meteor to its target and Rama quickly chanted a mantra in order to rob it of its strength. Though it lost its power to kill, it was still potent enough to knock Lakshmana senseless. Rama was most upset to see blood gushing out of his brother's wound, but he knew that this was not the time for weeping, so he continued to fight with Ravana. He shouted to Hanuman and Sugriva to come and get

Lakshmana, whom he had taken into his arms, unmindful of the fact that Ravana's arrows were piercing him all over his body.

After handing over his beloved brother to their tender ministrations, he concentrated all his energy on Ravana. Turning to his friends, he said, "It is obvious that this world cannot contain the two of us. Either he or I will have to die. You may all take vantage positions on the hill and watch, for this battle will be talked about as long as the worlds remain, as long as the earth stands above the sea and as long as living beings inhabit this planet!" All the pent-up fury which he had against Ravana, which he had been bottling up for eleven months, now rose to the front and he fought like a mad elephant.

The *rakshasas* were night wanderers and, with the approach of night, they became more powerful. But with the approach of day, Ravana perceptibly weakened. This encounter with Rama was even more fierce than the previous one and the spectators could only hear the twanging of bowstrings and could hardly see the warriors. The arrows of the demon king had the faces of fiends, lions, tigers and wolves, while Rama's arrows looked like firebrands, lightning and meteors. At last, stung and pierced by numerous gold-tipped arrows, Ravana left the field to rest and Rama could turn his attention to his brother, who lay unconscious. He begged Sugriva's court physician to do something for him.

"If my brother dies, I care not if I win or lose the war. I don't desire the kingdom or even my life. I seem to have lost the desire even to rescue Sita. A wife like her may perhaps be found, but I will never find another like Lakshmana, who was born with me and was like my own shadow and who has been my sole support and comfort during these dark days." So saying, Rama sobbed over the body of Lakshmana.

The physician said, "My Lord! Lakshmana's face has not lost its glow, which makes me believe that he is still alive. His skin does not have the darkness which is associated with death. His palms are still pink and soft. Moreover, he has all the auspicious signs of a long-lived man. So please don't grieve."

Turning to Hanuman he requested him to go once again to the Himalayas and bring back the magic herb known as *vishalyakarini*, which had the property of bringing a person back to consciousness. Before he could complete his sentence, Hanuman had winged his way to the north but, as usual, he could not recognize the medicinal herb in question so he lifted the whole mountain and carried it back, so that the physician could choose what he wanted. When he breathed in the healing fragrance of the herb, which the physician crushed and held to his nostrils, Lakshmana woke up, as if from sleep, with no loss of energy or sign of fatigue. Both Rama and Lakshmana were deeply grateful to Hanuman.

Shedding tears of joy, Rama clasped his beloved brother in his arms and said, "My dearest brother, if you had died, life would not have held any meaning for me. Neither Sita nor kingdom would have meant anything."

Lakshmana was embarrassed by his words and said, "Brother, please keep your oath to kill Ravana today. Please don't worry about me. Go and challenge him to a fight. Before the sun sets, you should kill him."

Rama knew that his brother spoke the truth but he went into a reverie and, for a moment, felt that perhaps he might not be able to defeat Ravana. Seeing Rama looking utterly exhausted and sitting in deep thought, the Sage Agastya came to him and gave him the great mantra known as the *Aditya bridaya,* which is a famous hymn to the sun god, said to have the power to overcome all obstacles.

"O prince of the Solar race—mighty armed Rama," he said, "listen to this ancient mantra, by which you will be able to vanquish all your foes in battle. The presiding deity of this hymn is the sun and if it is chanted fervently, it will result in the destruction of your enemies and bring you victory and unending bliss. It is guaranteed to destroy all sins and allay all anxiety. Worship the golden-orbed deity of the sun, therefore, with this hymn, for He represents the totality of all celestial beings."

The all-knowing sage knew that Rama was Narayana incarnate, but he also knew that he was still unaware of his divinity and so he initiated him into the secret mantra as a guru would initiate an ordinary mortal. By the sincere chanting of this holy hymn, not only will material obstacles be removed but all other obstacles in the path of the seeker of eternal truth. He advised Rama to look at the sun and repeat the mantra and he would surely be victorious in his battle. Hearing this, Rama was thrilled and, gazing intently at the rising sun, he repeated the hymn with all fervor and sincerity.

"O Lord of victory! Lord of the East! Lord of the West! O Thou Immeasurable One! O Thou resplendent One! Golden-limbed creator of the Universe! Witness of all things! I bow to you." After repeating the hymn three times, he went forth to challenge Ravana. Just at that moment, the sun came out in a burst of glory, as if he applauded Rama's decision and was urging him to hurry up with the deed at hand!

Rama shouted for Ravana to come out and the demon king came charging out, seated in another magnificent chariot. A fierce battle began between the two. The watching gods declared it to be an unequal fight since again Rama was on the ground and Ravana in a chariot. Indra dispatched his own charioteer Matali to go immediately and take his chariot to Rama. He sent his divine weapons and armor to aid him. As Rama watched, a brilliant silver chariot, with weapons shining like lanterns, yoked to ten silver-grey horses, landed gently in front of him.

Matali came down and bowed low before him and said, "O king of the solar race! I have come at the behest of the king of gods. Pray get in and let us start the fight."

Rama looked at Lakshmana and gave a smile of understanding. They both recognized the chariot as the one which had been parked outside the hermitage of Sharabhanga, when they had gone to pay homage to the sage. At their meeting with Agastya in the forest, he had told Rama that Indra would send a chariot for him when the need arose, though at that time, he had not known what the sage meant. Rama alighted from the divine cart and faced Ravana on an equal footing.

The charioteers wove the chariots in a series of skilful and bewildering maneuvers. Each used a number of deadly arrows charged with various potent mantras. The snake arrows of Ravana, which flew with unerring precision at Rama, spitting poison from their wide-open mouths, were foiled by Rama's eagle arrows. Eagles are the avowed enemies of snakes. The sky was covered with arrows flying in the air and colliding with each other, cancelling each other out with noise like thunder. The world trembled to witness the wrath of Rama. The sun lost its brilliance and the sea came in huge waves to watch this terrifying battle. The frown on Rama's face, so rarely seen, made even Ravana tremble in terror. Birds and beasts ran about crying. Valmiki says that just as the sea can be compared only to the sea and the sky to the sky, so the battle between Rama and Ravana can only be compared to the battle between Rama and Ravana.

At last, Ravana took an enormous javelin in his hands and decided to make an end to his opponent once and for all. The weapon was smoking and hissing at its edges, as if anxious to go and find its rest in Rama's chest. Ravana shouted to Rama that this would be the end of him and hurled the mighty javelin. Rama countered with a shower of arrows which should have burned up the javelin but the arrows fell down singed to ashes by the fury of Ravana's weapon. The sight incensed Rama and he took the *shakti* weapon which Indra had sent him and hurled it with all his force at the oncoming javelin. The javelin and the *shakti* collided in midair and the javelin broke into a thousand splinters and fell to the ground, its power exhausted.

Now Rama spoke, "You call yourself a hero, after abducting Sita when she was alone and unattended in the *ashrama*. What chance did she have against brute force? You are nothing but a thief and a molester of women and a coward. But beware, your head will provide food for hungry vultures and your blood will be lapped up by wolves before the day is over!"

Ravana was beginning to be unnerved by Rama's unflagging enthusiasm and his barrage of arrows. His charioteer, seeing the condition of his master, skillfully steered the chariot away from Rama. When Ravana came out of his temporary swoon, he swore at the charioteer and ordered him quickly back into the midst of the fray. "Ravana never turns his back on his enemies," he said. "He does not retreat until he has wiped out his foes!"

"My Lord," said the man, "it's the duty of a charioteer to protect his master. Our horses were tired and you were also fatigued and in a swoon. I saw nothing but evil omen, so I thought it best to bring you away from the situation."

Ravana was pleased by the devotion of the servant and presented him with his own bracelet. The charioteer whipped up the horses as commanded by his master and took him in front of Rama once again. Rama requested Matali to maneuver the chariot to a good position, and soon Ravana's vehicle was covered with the dust of Indra's cart.

The rest of the army stood like painted figures, spellbound by the scene. Ravana tried to bring down Indra's divine banner but failed, while Rama's arrow found its mark and brought down Ravana's pennant. Ravana was biting his lips and glaring with fury when he found that none of his arrows were hurting Rama. The latter, on the other hand, was smiling slightly as his arrows found a sure mark.

Finally, fitting an arrow resembling a venomous serpent to his bow, Rama sliced off the resplendent head of his opponent, adorned with its huge golden earrings. But to his astonishment, in front of his very eyes, there arose another head in the place of the previous one and then another and then another, as each one was cut off. Ravana's ten heads are meant to convey the idea of his inordinate ego. With just one head, all of us have egos which are impossible to control. Then think of the ego of a person with ten heads! When each ego head was cut off, another reared its haughty hood! It is the same with us. When our ego is put down in one place, we immediately find another reason to make ourselves feel important.

Rama was starting to feel worried, though his face remained calm and a continuous stream of arrows kept flying from his bow. Thus they struggled through that day and night without rest, until at last, Matali, Indra's charioteer, spoke to the prince of Kosala. "My Lord," he said, "remember who you are. Ravana's moment of death has come. Dispatch the *Brahmastra* and kill him. Do not aim at his head but at his chest."

When he looked at Ravana's heart, it is said that Rama saw Sita mirrored within and inside the heart of Sita, he saw himself enshrined. He was in a dilemma. What could he do? He waited for the split second when Ravana forgot Sita in his anger against Rama, and at that psychological moment, he whispered the incantation of Brahma and sent his golden-tipped arrow, given to him by Agastya, straight at Ravana's heart.

It was the most powerful weapon known to man or god and very few human beings were initiated into its mysteries, for its power was so great that no one who had not learned to control himself could use it. The arrow was made of the essence of all the elements. Flaming like the fire of universal destruction and as fatal as the end of Time, the arrow fled from Rama's bow like a streak of lightning and found its mark in Ravana's chest. Piercing through his body, it sank into the earth and then swerved and returned to Rama's quiver, like a meek servant. As soon as he was struck, the invincible bow of the king of demons dropped from his nerveless grasp, and his body, full of splendor, fell like a thunderbolt from the chariot.

A shower of flowers streamed from the sky and the sun came out from behind the clouds. Ravana's life was fast ebbing away. The mighty king of the *rakshasas* who had ruled the entire world with the power of his arms alone, now lay dead on the battlefield, prey to every passing vulture and jackal. He who had no equal in might and valor, who had terrified the whole world and thus earned the name "Ravana," who had pleased Lord Shiva Himself by his glorious chanting of the *Sama Veda*, had been killed by a mere mortal, as had been prophesied. Though he had been a great hero, because of his lust for a woman, he now lay dead. Even in death he had not lost his magnificence. Dazzling as a fallen sun, he was glorious even now.

The remnants of the night rangers fled in terror, pursued by the jubilant cries of the *vanaras*. Lakshmana, Sugriva and Vibhishana and all the others crowded around Rama and congratulated him. Vibhishana was suddenly struck with remorse and wept for his proud brother, who had come to such an end. Rama comforted him by saying that Ravana had indeed died a hero's death.

"This is the path pursued by the heroes of old," he said, "For a *Kshatriya*, there is a right way of living and a right way of dying and he has chosen the right way, on the battlefield. Vibhishana, all enmity ends with death. Now go and do whatever rites are to be performed for him, as per the rules, for there is no one else to do it for him but you."

News of Ravana's death had spread like wildfire to Lanka and out of his harem there poured out thousands of beautiful women who had been picked from all over the world, famed for their beauty, whom not even the sun had seen, for they had never been allowed to go out in the streets. They ran to the gory battlefield and threw themselves on his body and wept piteously.

"Our Lord had been granted immunity from death by Brahma and now he has been killed by a mortal. Why did you never listen to us? You abducted Sita, despite our advice. She has been the cause of the extermination of the entire race of *rakshasas*. Had she been restored to Rama, all this would never have happened. You spurned the words of Vibhishana. Fate is indeed all powerful. It was ordained that Ravana, the greatest of all monarchs, should be defeated by a mere mortal, helped by a pack of monkeys and bears!"

Mandodari, foremost queen of Ravana, mother of the brave Indrajit, now came running to the battlefield, her hair disheveled, her face wet with tears, lamenting over the body of her dead husband.

"How could such a calamity have overtaken you, my noble one? How is it possible for a mortal to have killed you! This Rama must be divine. The fact that single-handedly he defeated Khara and Dhushana must have convinced you that he was not an ordinary human being. When I heard that he had built a bridge across the sea, I knew that he was not an ordinary mortal. I know now who Rama is. He is Lord Narayana Himself—the Supreme Soul. He has assumed the garb of an ordinary man for the purpose of saving the world and the gods themselves have assumed the forms of these monkeys. My Lord! It is Narayana who has killed you, not a human being. Once upon a time you performed a lot of austerities, with your senses under perfect control, and now those senses, like untamed horses, have dragged you to your death.

"Sita is a noble lady, devoted to her husband. She should have been honored by you but instead, you chose to insult her. Her tears of shame and despair have killed you and not Rama's arrows. What does she have that I lack? In birth, I am equally high born, in beauty, she is in no way superior, yet blinded by lust, you chose to carve out your dreadful end. You brought death to yourself the day you brought Sita to Lanka. Sita will now be reunited with her Lord and will live happily, while I will be plunged into sorrow without you. Where has your smile gone, my Lord? Where is the look of love in your eyes when you gazed at me? How proud I was of my good fortune! I was the daughter of the architect of the *asuras* and my husband, the king of the *rakshasas,* and my son were the most valiant warriors in the whole world. How could I believe that death would rob me of my dearest treasures, in one fell stroke!" So lamenting, Mandodari fainted over the body of her husband and the other women had to carry her away. Again and again, she ran back to have a last look at her husband's beloved face, which she would never see again.

Rama told Vibhishana to set about the task of cremating Ravana. His body was placed on a pyre made of sandalwood and other fragrant woods and herbs and draped with the skins of black antelopes. Curd and ghee were poured on his shoulders and a wooden mortar inserted between his thighs. The corpse was draped with different costly cloths and roasted grain was sprinkled over it. With great reverence, Vibhishana touched the earthly remains of his brother with a flaming torch and set fire to it. He completed all the rites connected with the funeral and gave oblations to the departed soul. Then he went and saluted Rama and told him that everything had been done according to his wishes.

Rama prostrated to Indra's chariot and thanked Matali and sent the chariot back. He then asked Lakshmana and Sugriva to take Vibhishana to the city and crown him as emperor. He did not go himself, since his fourteen years were not over. Lakshmana took Vibhishana to the city of Lanka and placed him on the throne and gave him the ceremonial bath by pouring consecrated water over his head, thus proclaiming him emperor of Lanka.

Thus ends the twenty-eighth chapter of the glorious Ramayana *of Sage Valmiki called "The End of Ravana."*

Hari Aum Tat Sat

TWENTY-NINE

TRIAL BY FIRE

Again and again, I bow to Sri Rama,
The delight of the world,
The savior of those in distress,
And the bestower of all good fortune.
—SOURCE UNKNOWN

Paramatmane
Namaha!

Homage to the
Supreme Soul.

TURNING TO HANUMAN, RAMA, told him to go to the grove of *ashoka* trees where Sita was sitting and give her the happy tidings. It is to be noted that, despite his intense desire to see her, Rama did his duty to Ravana first, before rushing to Sita as he must have wanted to do. He performed the obsequies for his enemy, anointed Vibhishana as king, and then and only then, did he give in to his urgent desire to see his beloved.

When he entered the grove, Hanuman found Sita is the same sad pose as she had been when he first saw her—a picture of despair and sorrow, for no one had told her of the happenings on the battlefield.

He went and stood beside her with folded palms and said, "My lady! I have come with happy news. Rama has killed Ravana, and Vibhishana has been crowned king of Lanka. He has asked me to bring these happy tidings to you."

Sita was speechless with joy. Tears of happiness rolled from her eyes.

Hanuman spoke respectfully, "My lady, believe me, I have spent sleepless night thinking of your pathetic condition and now it is my luck that I have been chosen by our Lord to bring you this joyous news. I ask your permission to do one more thing. Let me kill all these *rakshasis* who have been harassing you for so long."

Sita smiled and said, "Dear Hanuman, they were only servants obeying their master. Why should you kill them? Everyone has to reap the fruits of their past actions. I must have done something in my past life to deserve this punishment. My rule is to show compassion and mercy to all, even if they are sinners. No one is infallible. To err is human. Go and tell my husband that I'm eagerly awaiting his arrival."

Hanuman bowed humbly and departed. He told Rama the whole story of his meeting with Sita and said that she was anxiously waiting for him. Rama's eyes filled with tears when he heard this but he remained sunk in thought for a while. At last, he sighed and told Vibhishana to ask Sita to have an auspicious bath and to clothe herself in beautiful garments and then come to him. Vibhishana conveyed this message, but Sita replied, "I want my Lord to see me as I am now."

Vibhishana answered that it was his duty to obey Rama's commands implicitly and that he could not take her to Rama in that condition. So Sita dressed herself in silks and jewels and came to Rama in the palanquin which had been sent for her. He was lost in thought, sitting with eyes fixed on the ground. The *vanaras* crowded around, eager to have a glimpse of the one for whose sake so much trouble had been taken and the whole race of demons annihilated. Vibhishana pushed them back and ordered them to go away, since Rama would want to see Sita alone and it was not correct for the common populace to view someone of the royal household.

Rama chided him and said, "A woman's protection should be her purity and chastity and not a wall or a curtain. Let them stay where they are and see her if they wish. Let them gaze as much as they want on the beauty of the princess of Videha. Moreover, it is only right that she should see me surrounded by those who fought for her."

Lakshmana was puzzled by Rama's strange behavior. He was sure that something was bothering him. Vibhishana went and led Sita to where Rama was waiting. Sita felt as if her legs would collapse and she shrank into herself. Covering her face with her upper cloth, she came near Rama and whispered breathlessly, "My Lord!" Tears choked her and she could not utter another word. Shyly, she looked up at him and her thirsty eyes drank in his beauty.

Rama averted his face and spoke in an unusually harsh tone. "I have accomplished what I set out to do. I have vindicated my honor and kept up the reputation of the fair house of the Ikshvaku clan. I have wiped out the insult which was offered to me and killed the one who abducted you. Hanuman, who leaped across the ocean and destroyed Lanka, has been rewarded; so has Vibhishana, who left his brother and took refuge in me."

Sita had been waiting for a year for this moment, when her beloved husband would come and rescue her and take her in his arms and comfort her and make her forget the trials which she had gone through. She couldn't understand why Rama, who had never spoken harshly to her at any time, was now using this tone of voice and why he was narrating all these incidents. She looked at him with her fawn-like eyes, which were slowly filling with tears, and Rama's heart was torn with sympathy and love, but he knew that he had to clear her name before the public.

"Don't think that I fought this war for your sake. I did it only to save my name and my honor. Having lived for eleven months in the city of Ravana, there is a great stain on your character. That lecherous wretch has feasted his eyes on you and carried you in his arms. Rumors are rife about you and I cannot take you back. You are now free to go where you wish, O Janaki. I can no longer bear to look at you. Your presence hurts my eyes, like blinding light to a feverish man. Now that I have done my duty and rescued you, I owe you nothing more. I belong to a noble house and it does not befit me to take you back. You have lived for nearly a year in the house of a notorious womanizer. Do you expect me to believe that he could refrain from ravishing you—you, who are so lovely and alluring?"

Hearing these cruel words coming from the mouth of her husband, from whom she had heard nothing but love, Sita swayed like a vine torn from its trellis. Tears streamed from her eyes and she looked like a wilting flower. To make matters worse, there was an interested and sympathetic audience to witness this painful scene. She had thought her heart had broken when she had been abducted by Ravana, but now she realized that it was nothing compared to this ordeal.

At last, she said in a faltering tone, "Why do you speak such harsh words to me? This is the talk of a common man to a woman of the streets and you are not a common man, neither am I such a woman. If you doubted me, why did you send Hanuman to search for me? Why did you not tell him that you had no further use for me? Why did you take the trouble of crossing the sea and fighting and killing Ravana? You risked your life and the life of all your friends by coming here. You could have saved yourself a lot of trouble and I could have given up my life then and there, and then I would not have had to hear these cruel words. If I had been touched by that sinner once, it was because I was too weak and helpless to protect myself. How can you blame me for that! Even after living with me for so many years, it looks as if you have never been able to understand me. My thoughts and love have never strayed from you, for even a moment. I might be called Janaki, the daughter of Janaka, but I am really Sita, the daughter of the earth. Did you ever consider my exalted birth before passing judgment? Does my love and chastity mean nothing to you? If that is so, why did you come?"

She turned to Lakshmana and said, "Lakshmana, make a pyre for me. It is the only cure for the grief which is burning me more than flames. I have been falsely accused and I don't want to live anymore. My husband has repudiated me in front of this big crowd of people and told me to go where I want. There is only one place that I can go and that is the heart of a fire."

Lakshmana looked angrily at Rama, who stood with his head cast down, like a painted statue. Rama did not make any protest when Lakshmana went reluctantly to make the pyre. Sita circumambulated Rama and went toward the blazing fire. Standing with folded palms before it, she said, "If it is true that my thoughts have been set on Rama and never swerved from truth, then let this fire, who is the witness to all minds, protect me. My husband thinks I am tainted. If I am innocent, so may the god of fire protect me. If I have never been unfaithful to Rama, in thought word or deed, let the god of fire protect me. If the earth and the sky and the four quarters and the gods believe that I am sinless, let the god of fire protect me."

So saying, she went around the fire once and then flung herself into the heart of the conflagration. All the *rakshasis* who had collected there set up a loud wail of protest. Wearing gold ornaments and yellow silk, Sita glowed like molten gold in the midst of the fire. Rama stood, as if carved of stone, with face turned to the ground. Though his heart was breaking, he did not do anything to save her, who was dearer to him than his own life. At that moment, the celestials came down and spoke to Rama.

"How is it possible for you to watch Sita immolate herself in the fire? Don't you know that you are Narayana, the primeval Being, and Sita is Lakshmi, your eternal consort? You are Vishnu and you were born to destroy Ravana. Now your task is accomplished and dharma is saved."

As soon as Brahma finished speaking, Agni, the god of fire, stepped forward from the blaze with Sita in his arms. She was dressed in red and even the flowers she wore in her lustrous tresses were unsinged.

"Here is your wife Sita, who is without blemish. She was never unfaithful in thought, word or glance. Believe me and accept this jewel among women."

Tears flowed unchecked down Rama's cheeks and he said, "I know that my wife is as pure and chaste as unsullied snow. I never doubted her even for a moment, but if she had not undergone this ordeal of fire, people would have spoken ill of her and of me. They would have said that Dasaratha's son, blinded by love for his wife, was willing to take her back even though she had lived so long in the house of another man. I knew full well that Sita would have been protected by her purity. Ravana could never have sullied her. Sita is to me what splendor is to the sun. As a good man cannot abandon a good name so also I can never abandon Sita. If I spoke harshly to her and watched unmoved when she entered the fire, it was only to clear her name before the eyes of all."

He went near Sita and looking deep into her lovely eyes, as he had been longing to do. When Sita turned her reproachful, tear-filled, lotus eyes at him, Rama chided her softly so that none could hear. "O daughter of the Earth! My beautiful Sita! How could you think even for a moment that I could have doubted you? Why do you think I trudged the length of this country if I was not crazy for a glimpse of your bewitching face? Why do you think I faced the wrath of the demon king and risked my life, if I didn't ache for you? My dearest love, I did it so that none could ever point an accusing finger at you." Hearing this impassioned declaration, Sita was pacified and looked at him with all her love pouring out her eyes. For a long moment they were lost to the world and gazed long and deep into each other's eyes, to the joy of all who were assembled there.

As they stood hand in hand, the gods brought Rama's father Dasaratha, so that Rama could see him and there was a happy reunion among the three of them. The celestials told Rama to return immediately to Ayodhya, for the fourteen years were drawing to a close and Bharata was waiting for his arrival with great eagerness.

Thus ends the twenty-nineth chapter of the glorious Ramayana of Sage Valmiki *called "Trial by Fire."*

Hari Aum Tat Sat

Vasistha says:
That mysterious power of Consciousness
produces this infinite variety of names and forms known as egotism.
The same consciousness, when it wants to experience itself,
becomes the knowable universe.
There is no real transformation,
for there is nothing other than Consciousness.

—*THE YOGA VASISTHA*

THIRTY

TRIUMPHAL RETURN

*Pattabhiramaya
Namaha!*

Homage to
the one who
was crowned.

Seated on the divine throne,
Wearing divine clothes and garlands,
With gracious glances,
They looked at each other.
—RAMAYANA OF VALMIKI

T HE NEXT MORNING VIBHISHANA came to Rama and said, "I have brought perfumed water for your coronation bath and sandal paste and silken clothes. Please accept them and make me happy."

Rama smiled and said, "You may offer all these precious things to Sugriva, for my thoughts are all with my dear brother Bharata. The way back to Ayodhya is long and hard. The fourteen years are coming to a close and Bharata has sworn that he will take his life if I don't arrive by the end of the stipulated time."

Vibhishana said, "My Lord, I'll help you to reach Ayodhya in a single day. My brother Ravana took the aerial vehicle, called Pushpaka, from his brother Kubera. It was his prized possession. Please accept my hospitality for a few more days and then you can return to Ayodhya in this flying chariot."

Rama was touched by his devotion and said, "Vibhishana, I'm well aware of your love for me but my heart yearns to return to Ayodhya and see my brothers and mothers and the people of Kosala, who must be anxiously awaiting my arrival. Please bring the Pushpaka immediately so that we can leave at once."

The fantastic, flower-bedecked chariot, drawn by swans, was brought, in readiness for their departure. Rama, Sita and Lakshmana climbed into the vehicle. Even though the Pushpaka, was as big as a palace,

Rama sat with Sita on his lap, much to her delight, with Lakshmana beside them.

Rama looked at Vibhishana, Sugriva, and all the other *vanaras* and said, "You have been my true friends. I don't know in what way I can repay you for the love and devotion you have poured on me. Sugriva, please return to Kishkinda with your army. My blessings will always be with you. Angada, my dear child, I can never forget your prowess and, as for you, O Hanuman! We owe our lives to you. Now please give me leave to return to my own city. I have been an exile for so long that my heart yearns to be back there."

Sugriva bowed low and said, "Lord, please give us leave to come with you to Ayodhya. We promise not to indulge in any act of destruction, as we monkeys are wont to do. After witnessing your coronation, we promise to return." All the others expressed the same desire.

Rama smiled at their eagerness to accompany him and their promise to behave themselves and said, "I'm delighted at the thought that I will enter my ancestral city accompanied by those who have helped me most. Sugriva, ask your people to get in."

Now Vibhishana also requested that he and his friends be allowed to join the party. Rama gladly gave his consent and the whole group got into the Pushpaka and still there was enough room for another army!

One of the most endearing things about Rama is his great love for all animals. Monkeys, bears and birds wander in and out of the pages of the narrative, as if it were the most natural thing in the world. Rama's love and regard for his animal and feathered friends shows another unique facet of his character.

The divine chariot could hold all of them and it rose into the air effortlessly. Celestial flowers rained from the sky as it lifted up. The *vanaras* shouted and whooped with joy, peering over the edge at the ground below, which was falling at an alarming rate.

Sita's face glowed with happiness and beauty as Rama pointed out sites of interest to her, through which they had wandered during their long and painful search. The vehicle landed on the other side of the bridge, so that Rama could worship at the shrine of Shiva which he had consecrated before he set out. At that time, he had made a vow to the three-eyed Lord that he would return and pay his obeisance, along with his wife Sita. After praying, Rama told Sita to have a good look at the wondrous bridge.

"There is the spot where the bridge was constructed. Now we come to Kishkinda, Sugriva's fortress."

Sita asked that the chariot be brought down so that they could take Tara and Ruma, Sugriva's wives, as well as the wives of the other monkey leaders.

So the chariot landed and the ladies joyfully joined the group. Later, Rama pointed out Rishyamukha, the place where he had met Hanuman for the first time. "There is Lake Pampa, filled with lotuses, where I was reminded of you so painfully and where we met the old lady called Shabari."

"O look, Sita," he said, "there is our *ashrama* at Panchavati, where you were so cruelly captured. We abandoned it soon after, for I could not bear to stay there without you." He remained silent for a few minutes reliving the painful scenes of that time and Sita buried her face on his shoulder and wept.

Later they passed Chitrakuta where they had spent so many happy days together and at last came to Bharadvaja's *ashrama*, where the Pushpaka landed. The sage asked Rama to stay for the day and go the next morning, so Rama told Hanuman, "I cannot refuse the request of the sage so please proceed to Nandigrama and give Bharata all the news. If his face shows his disappointment at my return and his desire to keep the kingdom, please return and tell me. I will not stand in his way. Even the best of men may be tempted by riches, some time or other."

Hanuman flew to Nandigrama, where Bharata was living. From above, he saw Bharata, with matted locks and long beard, clad in bark and emaciated, for he had never paid any attention to his body for fourteen years. He had undertaken to guard the kingdom till his brother returned and he seemed to be keeping alive only for that purpose. He looked like a *brahmarishi* (a sage who has realized the Supreme), sitting with eyes half closed in deep meditation. Hanuman assumed the guise of a human being and approached with all humility, for he realized that he was in the presence of a truly superior human being, one who had conquered his senses and had no desire for worldly possessions.

He said, "O Prince! I bring you tidings of your brother Rama, for whose sake you have donned this garb and for whose dear sake you have given up all thoughts of a happy, normal life. He has sent me in advance to tell you that he will be arriving here very soon, along with Lakshmana and Sita."

For fourteen years, Bharata had been waiting for this moment and when he got the news, he swooned with happiness for a few seconds. He embraced Hanuman and said, "I don't know who you are, but you have brought me the happiest news I could ever hear and so you are my best friend. Many, many years ago my beloved brother went away to the forest and all these years I have been waiting only for this moment. Tell me how I should reward you."

Hanuman's eyes filled with tears to see such devotion. He thought he was the one who loved Rama more than anyone else, but now it appeared that there were many who had the same adoration for him. Hanuman seated himself and gave Bharata all the details of Rama's life since he had left. At last, he said, "He has come to the *ashrama* of Sage Bharadvaja and will be reaching here tomorrow."

Bharata and Shatrugna made haste to prepare for Rama's arrival. The city of Ayodhya, which had been like a dead city all these years suddenly blossomed to life. Once again banners and streamers flew from the battlements. Musicians restrung their silent *veenas*. The trees burst into bloom and the streets were sprinkled with rosewater and fried rice and decorated with auspicious signs. Once more, the fountains started to play and the streams to run and sounds of laughter and rejoicing floated in the air. Citizens donned their best clothes, which had been locked away in their chests for fourteen years, and the whole city waited in anticipation for the arrival of her rightful Lord. The royal path leading from Nandigrama to the city was decorated with auspicious patterns, traced with colored powder and sprinkled with rosewater. Rama's sandals were kept on top of a caparisoned white elephant, with the white umbrella of sovereignty held above it. Bharata and Shatrugna followed, accompanied by thousands of citizens. Just then, the Pushpaka reached the sacred village of Nandigrama. It hovered for some time in the air so that Rama could point out the various landmarks to the excited *vanaras*.

"There is Ayodhya, the city of my fathers and citadel of the kings of the solar dynasty. There is the river Sarayu, which holds the land of Kosala in its embrace, and there is my dear brother Bharata, who is saluting me from below."

The vehicle landed gently and the brothers rushed toward each other. They had been parted for fourteen years and the reunion was tender and brought tears to the eyes of the *vanaras*. Bharata took the sandals, which had been the virtual rulers of the state, and placed them lovingly on his brother's holy feet and prostrated before him, saying, "I give you back the kingdom which was given to me to look after. It was a great burden on me but I have guarded it carefully. Today, my mother's name has been cleared and I have atoned for her sins. Please allow us to conduct the coronation which should have taken place fourteen years ago."

Rama agreed and all the brothers shaved off their matted locks and had a ceremonial bath and dressed themselves in clothes, befitting princes of the realm. Sita was dressed lovingly by Kausalya, Sumitra and Kaikeyi. Kausalya also kindly dressed the hair of the wives of the *vanaras*, who were highly delighted by this royal treatment.

Sumantra brought the chariot and Rama and the others ascended and proceeded to the city. The citizens went mad with joy at seeing Rama. Sugriva was invited to reside in Rama's own palace, along with his wives. He sent his people to the ocean and rivers to collect water in golden pots for the approaching coronation. The ministers requested Vasistha to take charge of the ceremony.

Vasistha made Rama sit on the jeweled throne of the Ikshvakus, with Sita at his side. All the great sages poured the consecrated waters brought from all the sacred rivers and seas of the land in golden pots over Rama's head, to the accompaniment of sacred Vedic chants. Shatrugna held the beautiful white umbrella over his head, while Sugriva and Vibhishana stood on either side and waved the royal yak-tail fans. There was joy and beauty everywhere. Rama gifted many cows and horses to deserving *Brahmins*. To Sugriva, he gave a golden necklace and decorated the strong arms of Angada with bracelets. He gave Sita the precious pearl necklace sent by Indra, as well as many other extraordinary gifts. He presented all the *vanaras* with many items. Only Hanuman was left out. Turning to Sita, he said, "Why don't you give a gift to one who has all the qualities which you think a great hero should have, like fidelity, truth, skill, courtesy, foresight and prowess, as well as a good intellect? Look round and present your necklace to such a one."

Sita took out the precious necklace of pearls which Rama had given her and, without a moment's hesitation, she gave it to Hanuman. He looked at it carefully and smelled it and bit it and scratched it and put it to his nose and his ears. Then he threw it off as being a worthless gift. Sita was amazed at this monkey-like behavior on the part of one whom she loved so much and who had done so much for her.

She asked him to explain this act of his and he replied, "To me, the only thing worthy of respect is the name of Rama. If something does not have it, I feel it is worthless. I looked at the necklace to see if his name was written anywhere, then I smelled it, to see if his perfume was in it and I bit it to see if it contained anything of his inside but there was nothing. This is only an ordinary pearl necklace and what use is such a thing to a monkey? My lady, I am, of course proud that you have chosen me as a fitting recipient for the honor of a gift from you, but please forgive me for not wearing it."

The audience was astounded by this statement and asked him, "Hanuman! What about your own body? Does it have anything of Rama?"

So Hanuman asked Sugriva to put his ear to Hanuman's chest and to his wonder, Sugriva heard the continuous chanting of Rama, Rama, in his heart. As if to put an end to all dispute, it is said that this great devotee of Rama split his chest open and, to the astonishment of all, there was Rama enshrined within. Rama embraced him warmly and placed his blessed hands on the wound, which healed miraculously at his touch.

The coronation was the glorious finale of the saga of Rama and Sita. There was no one in all of Ayodhya who had not been presented with some gift. Even the hunchback Manthara got a present. The whole day long, the people and the monkeys ate and drank to their hearts' content. That night, for the first time in fourteen years, Lakshmana slept in the arms of his dear wife Urmila.

The festivities lasted for a month. At the end of it, Sugriva and the others returned to Kishkinda and Vibhishana to Lanka. Hanuman, however, opted to stay on with Rama for he could not bear to be parted from him. Rama offered the position of *Yuvraj* to

Lakshmana, who refused the honor, so he crowned Bharata instead.

Ramarajya, or the rule of Rama, is famed over the whole world as being a glorious one. There was no disease or unhappiness and no one died an untimely death. Wild animals did not trouble the people and there was plenty for all. The land flourished and the people were happy, for they worshipped Rama as god incarnate. There was no avarice and no greed, for everyone had all that they could wish for.

Thus ends the thirtieth chapter of the glorious Ramayana *of Sage Valmiki called "Triumphal Return."*

Hari Aum Tat Sat

Vasistha says:
This Consciousness is not knowable.
When it wants to be known, it becomes the universe.
The mind, intellect and egoism are all vibrations of the one
Consciousness.

—THE YOGA VASISTHA

BOOK SEVEN

*Dharmakrite
Namaha!*

Homage to the
one who is the
foundation of
all righteousness.

UTTARA KANDA

THE AFTERMATH:
THE BEST BOOK

THIRTY-ONE

SITA ABANDONED

Satyavache
Namaha!

Homage
to the one
who spoke
only truth.

Hail to Raghava, scion of the race of Raghu,
Enemy of Ravana, the delight of the world,
King of kings, truth incarnate,
Son of Dasaratha, dark in color,
And peace-loving.
—DEVOTIONAL VERSE

It is in this book of the aftermath that Sage Valmiki recounts the whole previous history of Ravana, the king of the *rakshasas*. It is also in this book that the painful episode of Rama's repudiation of Sita is told. We may well wonder at the intentions of the sage in doing this. Maybe he wanted to compare the polaric differences in the towering personalities of the two men, both of whom loved Sita so passionately. One, the lusty, powerful *rakshasa*, Ravana, who was prepared to exterminate his entire race, his brothers, his friends and even his own sons, in order to quench his thirst for another man's wife. Next, the divine personality of Rama, who made the heart-rending decision to subdue his passion for his lawfully wedded wife and place his duty to his subjects first—who was prepared to sacrifice the one he loved most on the altar of the cosmic law of dharma, which proclaims that a king should put God first, his country next, and his own personal desires last. Ravana perished with the rest of his tribe while the land of Kosala, flourished under the rule of its saintly king.

❧

Thus did many years pass while Rama reigned with Sita by his side, supported by his beloved brothers and able ministers. There was an *ashoka* grove attached to their palace, which was even more beautiful than the one in

Lanka. Fragrant trees like the *champaka*, *kadamba*, *ashoka* and sandalwood were there and fruit trees like mango and pomegranate. After finishing his day's work, Rama would often walk in these fragrant gardens with his adorable queen.

One day while they were thus sitting in the garden and talking to each other, Rama noticed that his wife showed all signs of pregnancy. She was wearing a glistening red robe and her skin glowed with an ethereal beauty. Rama was delighted and taking both her hands in his, he led her gently to an arbor in the grove and seated her tenderly on a jeweled seat. He offered her the nectar of many flowers, untouched by bees, in a golden goblet. With his own hands, he raised the glass to her lips and made her sip the delightful concoction. He embraced his alluring wife with great love and said to her, "My darling one! I see that you are with child. This is the only thing which we lack in our lives. How radiant you look! I have no doubt that the child will be a wonderful infant. Tell me, my dearest love, how can I make you even happier? Is there some wish of yours which is still to be fulfilled? Ask for anything and it shall be yours."

Sita raised her lotus face to his and whispered, "My Lord, I consider myself to be the luckiest woman alive. What further wish can your wife have than to be beside you all the time?"

But Rama insisted, "My lovely one, I want to make you even happier than you are now, if that is possible. Tell me something which I can do for you. I'm longing to shower you with everything, for it is said that a pregnant woman should have all her whims humored."

Sita turned her beautiful eyes to him and said, "Do you remember the forest near Chitrakoota where we used to wander, hand in hand? Do you remember the sages and their wives and the peace of their hermitages? I have a great desire to go and visit them once again and eat the wild fruits and roots and drink the pure waters of the Ganga, and perhaps even stay there for a day or two."

Rama looked adoringly at his beloved wife. There was nothing he could deny her. If anything, his love for her had increased with the passing years. He had never felt the desire to take another consort, as kings used to do. In fact, the very idea was abhorrent to him. Sita was the most charming woman he had ever known and he desired none other.

Holding her hands in his, he looked deep into her eyes and said,

"O Vaidehi, my beloved wife, you shall certainly go there if that is what you wish. In fact, I will send you there tomorrow."

Having given his promise to the princess of Mithila, Rama left her and went to the outer courtyard to talk with his friends. In the course of their light banter, he turned to his friend Bhadra and asked, "Tell me, Bhadra, what do the people say about me and Sita and my brothers? Kings are always a focus of criticism for the common folk."

Bhadra folded his palms and said, "Sire, people speak only good about you. Sometimes they discuss the events of past years, when you achieved the impossible, by killing the demon king Ravana and rescuing the princess of Videha. Your exploits are recounted with great enthusiasm by everyone."

"What else do they say, Bhadra? Tell me all. Why do you avert your face? Is there something which you feel should not be reported to me? Have no fear. I want to know the good and the bad. No king can afford to ignore what people say of him, so tell me."

In a low, faltering tone, Bhadra said, "They also remark that though your action in having killed the *rakshasa* is to be applauded, your conduct with regard to your wife is shameful. 'How could the king have accepted a woman who had been kept on Ravana's lap and who had lived in his palace for so many months? How can the queen forget the indignities which she must have suffered? We will have to put up with similar insults. Our wives will be able to go as they please and we will be forced to condone them. As the king so the subjects!' This is what the people say, in their ignorance."

Rama's whole face changed when he heard this slanderous accusation against him and his immaculate wife. He couldn't speak a word. His friends tried to comfort him and said, "Your Majesty, it is the nature of common people to speak ill of the nobility. A king need not pay heed to such false accusations."

Rama hardly heard what they were saying. Taking leave of them in his usual courteous manner, he went to the garden and sat immersed in thought. He decided that it was his duty to check on this matter before coming to a decision. That evening, he wore the clothes of an ordinary citizen of Ayodhya and went incognito on a tour of the city. As luck would have it, as he passed the house of a washerman in one of the small streets of the city, he heard the sound of raised voices and went close to the door of the house and stood outside listening. The husband was berating his wife.

"I have heard reports of your indecent behavior. You have been seen talking to the nobleman who comes for a walk down this street. You may go back to your own home. I will not keep you here any longer. I belong to a respectable family and will not keep a loose woman as my wife. You are free to go where you please."

The poor woman pleaded that she was innocent and had only answered some questions the man had put to her. The washerman replied sternly "Do you think I'm Rama, to tolerate such behavior? He is the king and can do as he pleases. But, as for me, I will never keep a wife who has been seen with another man."

Rama stood riveted to the spot for a few seconds. He felt like a tree which had been struck by lightning. The tender buds and leaves of hope, which had sprouted in his heart after their return from Lanka, were scorched and the naked charred and blackened branches raised their arms, in mute appeal to the heavens. He felt as if his whole body were on fire. All the fresh, green leaves had fallen off and only the stark, bare branches remained. He managed somehow to stagger back to the palace and, going to a private chamber, he requested his brothers to come to him at once. They came immediately and were surprised at Rama's demeanor. He stood with his back to the door, looking out on the wintry garden. His face was pale and his eyes had a glazed look as he turned to face his brothers. His hands trembled slightly.

Lakshmana knelt before him and said, "Brother, what is it? Tell me. Where is the enemy? You know that you have but to command and I shall obey."

Rama spoke in a voice which was drained of all emotion. "Do you know what the citizens are saying about me and Sita?"

All of them hung their heads and Rama continued, "I see that all of you know and have hidden the truth from me all these years. O Lakshmana! You are witness to the fact that I refused to take her back after the war, until her purity was proven in the ordeal by fire. Yet these people now talk as if I had committed a heinous act. My heart is breaking and I am drowning in sorrow, yet my duty as a king is clear before me. The first duty of a king is to his subjects and not to himself. Sita is dearer to me than life itself but I have no choice but to abandon her, for the sake of my subjects. Lakshmana, take her away in the chariot with Sumantra, and leave her on the other side of the Ganga, near the Tamasa river, where we stayed a long time ago. Just this morning, she asked me to take her there. Let her have her wish. She will suspect nothing."

Lakshmana jumped to his feet and said, "Rama, you cannot do this to her! She is burnished gold, purified in fire. Please don't ask me to do this. I will do anything else you ask, but not this. Don't you know that she is carrying your child in her womb? How can you bear to do this? Can you not wait till the child is born?"

His face carved of stone, Rama said in a stern voice, "After the child is born, you will say, let her stay while she suckles the infant and then you'll say, let her stay till he is five years old, and thus it will go on and on and eventually, Rama would have betrayed his country for the sake of his own felicity." He continued in a hard, loud voice. "I don't want to hear another word from any of you. I want none of your advice. I am your king and I demand only your implicit obedience." For a few stunned moments, there was absolute silence, except for Rama's heavy breathing, due to his effort to suppress an emotion which threatened to overpower him.

At last, with an ashen and mask-like face, he said, "Go , Lakshmana! Leave her in a secluded spot on the banks of the Tamasa River, near the holy Ganga, close to some of the hermitages, and return immediately. Do not wait to talk to her. Don't try to explain anything. Let her think the worst of me or else she will die of a broken heart. Don't look at me so accusingly. Anyone who objects to my decision is my bitter enemy. Take her away this very instant, O Lakshmana! If I see her even once, I am doomed. I will be unable to carry out my own command. If I see her fawn-like gaze fixed on me with a beseeching look, I will be lost, and not all the slander in the world will enable me to let her go. So go now! Go, before my heart fails me—before emotion weakens my adamantine resolve. Why do you hesitate? It is I, the king of the country, who is commanding you." His brothers could not speak a word. Lakshmana cursed his luck for having been chosen to carry out this terrible command.

His eyes brimming with tears, Rama stumbled out of the room and went to an enclosed spot in the garden where he would not be able to see Sita.

He spent the night in the garden, keeping a lonely vigil with the stars. If he went to his room and took his beloved in his arms, he knew that he would never be able to let her go. Who knew what bitter thoughts passed through his mind but he was firm in his resolve. Dharma was his god and to dharma he was prepared to sacrifice his beloved queen and his unborn child. Sita slept alone that night. She wondered at her Lord's absence but then she thought it must be because he was held up with some official matters. Like a child, she was excited at the thought of the treat in store for her on the morrow. Some of the happiest moments of her life had been spent in the forest with her loving husband, and she was eagerly looking forward to spending at least another night in the hermitage with the loving wives of the sages. She had already tied up a small bundle of gifts for the ashramites and their wives and she was ready to go when Lakshmana arrived.

Without looking at her, he said in a voice drained of emotion. "The king, your husband, has commanded me to fulfill your desire to visit the Ganga and the hermitages of the sages. Are you ready to leave?"

Sita was delighted and happily accompanied him to the waiting chariot. He was a grim escort when they set out in the pearly mist of the morn. Neither Sumantra nor Lakshmana could speak a word or even look at her. Sita alone was full of cheer. She turned around for a last look at the sleeping town, not realizing that it was, indeed, her last look. Suddenly, her heart had misgivings. Everywhere she saw bad omen. Her right side and eye were twitching and all of a sudden, she felt weak.

In an agitated voice, she asked, "O son of Sumitra! Tell me, is all well with your brother? I haven't seen him this morning. Where was he in the night? I fear something inauspicious has happened."

In a choking voice, Lakshmana said, "The king, your husband, is quite well. He gave orders that you should have an undisturbed night, since you had to undertake a strenuous journey in the morning. He told me to wish you well." More than that he could not say.

By afternoon they reached the banks of the river Gomati and camped at one of the *ashramas*. The next morning, they went forward in the chariot and reached the banks of the holy river. Here Lakshmana could contain himself no longer and broke down and wept like a child.

"Why are you crying, Lakshmana?" asked Sita. "You are making me depressed. I have been longing to come here and now that you have brought me here, you make me sad by your weeping. Is it because you have been parted from Rama for two days? Then what about me? How much should I cry? I cannot endure life without him! Come, let us hurry and go to the *ashramas* and distribute our gifts and then we will return. I too am beginning to feel uneasy. I fear something is wrong with my Lord."

Wiping his eyes, Lakshmana brought a boat and escorted Sita to the opposite bank. He then fell at her feet and sobbed his heart out. Sita was really disturbed at the sight. "Tell me, Lakshmana, what is the matter? Has something happened to my dear husband? Why didn't he come? I was hoping he would come with me." Till the end, her one thought was for him who was her all. She never dreamed that the misfortune, which the omen foretold, was coming to her.

Eyes full of tears, Lakshmana looked pleadingly at her, "My noble queen! Forgive me for what I have to do. Rama has entrusted me with the ignoble task of abandoning you here. Better for me to have died rather than carry out this command of his!" So saying, he prostrated himself before her.

Sita bent down and gently lifted him up. "What is it, Lakshmana? What is the reason for my husband's sudden decision?" She could not believe that she was hearing right.

"Rumors are afloat everywhere, my lady, about you and him. I cannot tell you all. He forbade me to tell you anything. All I can say is that his heart broke when he heard the vile accusations against you. But he is the king. He is Dharma incarnate. The king's duty is always to safeguard the interests of his subjects. Forgive him and forgive me also, O gracious queen of Ayodhya! I can say no more. Night is fast approaching. How can I bear to leave you here, all alone, with none to protect you? Rama never left you, even for a minute, without asking me to guard you. The only time we both left you was when the wicked king of the demons came and abducted you. Now who is there to look after you? May your mother, the earth, give you all protection. May the sky be your canopy. May this holy river look after all your wants. My lady, remember, you are carrying the seed of the Iksvaku line in your womb. It is your duty to safeguard it at all times." Lakshmana was frightened that in her agony, Sita might do some harm to herself.

Sita looked like a frightened deer, listening to Lakshmana's words, and then said in a bewildered tone, "What sin have I committed, that for no reason of mine, my husband should repudiate me twice? Surely, I was born for sorrow. Grief alone seems to be my constant companion. Patiently, I have to look at her forlorn face. Leaving my all, I followed him to the forest, inhabited by wild animals and *rakshasas*. No woman would have done as I did, yet now he has abandoned me. Was it my fault that the *rakshasa* abducted me? When the sages ask me what crime I have committed that my husband should abandon me, what should I tell them, O Lakshmana? What wrong have I done? I cannot even take the easy path of ending my life in this holy river, for I will be guilty of breaking the noble line of the Ikshvaku race. Lakshmana, do not grieve. Leave me here and return to the king, my husband, and tell him that his wife wishes him well. A husband is a woman's god and I have always considered him as such. May he find eternal fame by following the dharma of a king. More important than my suffering is the fact that his honor should remain intact. Never will Sita be guilty of bringing dishonor to Rama. Farewell, Lakshmana. You have been more than a brother to me. I have deep regard for you. I hold nothing against you. The shades of night are falling and you must go quickly, lest my Lord become agitated."

Lakshmana fell at her feet once more. He could not speak a word. Slowly, he backed his way to the boat and was ferried to the other shore. He turned back for a last look and saw her lying on the ground, on the bosom of her mother, weeping as if her heart would break.

Sita lifted her head and saw the chariot receding in the distance. The plaintive cry of the peacock calling to its mate jarred her delicate nerves. The Ganga flowed smoothly on, as if to comfort her in her agony. She gazed, mesmerized by the glistening water and wondered what it would feel like to have the waves close over her head, like a balm, but then she felt the life within her move and she knew that she could not take the easy way out.

Thus ends the thirty-first chapter of the glorious Ramayana *of Sage Valmiki called "Sita Abandoned."*

Hari Aum Tat Sat

THE RULE OF RAMA

Vrathadaraya
Namaha!

Homage
to the one
who adhered
strictly to
his vows.

Hail to the nightingale, Valmiki,
Who sits on the poet's tree and
Coos the honey sweet words,
Rama, Rama, Rama!
—POPULAR SONG

LAKSHMANA RETURNED SORROWFULLY to Ayodhya, his mind filled with pictures of Sita. Where was she now? Had she gone to Valmiki's *ashrama*? He did not know and was tortured by doubts. When he entered his brother's chamber, he found Rama sitting bereft, with his head in his hands.

Lakshmana bowed low before him and said, "O king! I have carried out your orders and left your faultless wife on the other side of the Ganga. I hope you are satisfied. Why do you look so unhappy? Having made your decision, you should be happy and pleased that it has been successfully accomplished. You know full well that no relationship is permanent. What grows has to decay, what flowers has to fade and what rises, fall. Meeting and parting are both part of the game of life. We are born only to die. So why grieve?"

Still Rama said not a word.

The country rejoiced that the blot on the honorable name of its ruler had been removed, but for Rama, there was no joy in life anymore. Both he and Sita suffered the agonizing pangs of separation to the end of their lives, but the country flourished and the rule of Rama—*Ramarajya*—is remembered to this day as being exemplary, an era in which the very laws of nature bowed to the will of this saintly man who was prepared to sacrifice his own happiness for the sake of dharma. So the kingdom prospered, the rains fell on time and the earth yielded in plenty and the gods rejoiced. Contrary to the custom of the age, Rama never married again, though the pressure on him to do so was great. He led his lonely ascetic's life and never looked at another woman again.

Every day, Rama would sit in his council hall and ask Lakshmana to go outside the gates and see if there was anyone with a grievance. If there was, the person would be brought inside and his wrongs redressed.

One day, a dog was waiting outside. Rama called him in and asked him what he wanted. The dog replied that he had been hit on the head by a *Brahmin*. Rama asked the council to decide some punishment but the court said that a *Brahmin* could never be punished, so Rama asked the dog to decide on some way to redress his wrongs. The dog insisted that the *Brahmin* should be given an honorable position, as the spiritual head of a certain monastery.

When questioned about this strange punishment, the dog replied, "Your Majesty, in my previous birth I held that particular position and though I was honest and sincere, the post is so full of pitfalls that when I died, I was forced to take this birth, as a dog. Can you imagine the plight of that avaricious man, who has a uncontrollable temper as well!"

In the meantime, far away on the banks of the Tamasa where Lakshmana had abandoned her, Sita sat alone and helpless, with all the little presents she had brought for the forest dwellers scattered around her. She didn't know what she should do. Just then, some of the young *brahmacharis* from Valmiki's *ashrama* saw her pitiable plight and ran to tell the sage. Remembering his talk with Narada, Valmiki was immediately able to assess the situation. He returned with the boys and respectfully requested Sita to accompany him to his hermitage.

"Fear not! O noble wife of Rama, daughter of Janaka. I know that you are absolutely pure. Come with me to my *ashrama* and the wives of the other ascetics will care for you in your time of labor."
Sita followed him gratefully and lived a life of great austerity and *tapas* till the time came for the birth of her child.

She gave birth to twins. When the news was brought to the sage, he hurried to the labor room. His heart filled with joy when he saw the radiant babies, sons of Rama, looking like twin gods. He picked a handful of kusa grass, which is used in all rituals. With the tips of the grass, he stroked the first child and said, "He will be known as Kusha." With the ends, he stroked the second baby and said, "He will be known as Lava." He then performed all the appropriate rites connected with the birth of a baby and blessed them with all happiness and prosperity.

It was at this time that he began his immortal composition, known as the *Ramayana*. As soon as the children could learn to talk, he started to teach them to recite the poem. By the time they were twelve years old, he had finished the poem and they could sing it with ease, to the accompaniment of the tambura and a small mridanga.

In Ayodhya, at about the time when the babies were born, an old *Brahmin* arrived at the palace gate carrying the corpse of his son in his arms. He was hysterical with grief and wailed, "What crime have I committed in a previous life to be deprived of my only son in my old age? If innocent children die in a country, it is the king who is guilty. O Rama, if you do not give my child back, my wife and I will end our lives here, in front of your gate, and you will be guilty of having caused the death of *Brahmins*. What safety is there for children in your kingdom if they can be snatched away by death before they attain maturity? Crimes flourish and chaos prevails when a king is negligent in his duty."

Rama was stunned at this accusation from a new quarter. He summoned all his advisors and asked them to find out the reason for such an occurrence. Where had he failed?

The divine Sage Narada offered his advice. "Listen, O king, to the reason for the child's untimely death. Each age has its own laws and rules, by following which the whole land will prosper, and by failing which the whole cosmic order will be disrupted. In the golden age of *Satya Yuga*, only the *Brahmins* were allowed to practice austerities; in the next age of Treta, the *Kshatriyas* were also allowed to practice *tapas*. It was in this age that the next two castes were created. The *vaishyas* practiced trade and the *shudras* served the other three castes. In the Dwapara Yuga, *adharma* increased and *vaishyas* were also allowed to practice *tapas* but the *shudras* were still forbidden to do so. It is only in the age of Kali that *shudras* will be allowed to practice *tapas*. This is still the age of Dwapara and I fear that some *shudra* is practicing *tapas* somewhere in your kingdom. Unless he is stopped, calamities will continue to befall your country. It is your duty as a king to go and stop him from going against the dharma of his caste. It is only by following one's *svadharma*, or the duties of one's own caste, that one can achieve one's own salvation. One's own duty, though apparently inferior, is actually superior to the duty of another, however well practiced. It will bring nothing but infamy to oneself and calamity to the country. There is nothing inferior or superior as far as duty is concerned. The duty of the king and the duty of the subject are quite different but each has to follow his own *svadharma* and that is the law of the cosmos. That is the law of Nature, by following which a person will prosper. *Tapas*, in itself, is a noble thing but when a *shudra* practices it in this age, it will only bring ruin, on him and his country."

Rama accepted the advice of the sage and asked the *Brahmin* to embalm his child till he returned. Again, he called the Pushpaka chariot which he had sent back to Kailasa after his return from Lanka and toured the length and breadth of the country to discover the miscreant. At last, in the southern region, he saw a man hanging, head downwards from a tree, practicing rigorous *tapas*. Rama approached and asked him who he was and what he was doing. The ascetic replied that he was a *shudra* called Shambuka, who was practicing penance.

Without a word, Rama unsheathed his sword and cut off his head. For one who had abandoned his dear wife for the sake of his country, the killing of a *shudra* who had gone against the rules of his order was nothing. Rama begged the gods to grant the life of the *Brahmin's* son, and by the time he returned to the capital, the boy was restored to life and the country rejoicing. To Rama, the only thing that mattered was his duty to his country and to his subjects. For the greater good, the lesser had to be sacrificed.

Twelve years later, Rama decided to hold the horse sacrifice— the *ashvamedha yajna*. He called Lakshmana and asked him to summon all the sages. With folded palms, he addressed the sages and informed them of his decision. The sages were delighted but they told him that it would not be proper to conduct a *yajna* without his consort by his side. They urged him to marry again. Rama was adamant in his refusal. The cruel world had parted him from his beloved wife and he was determined never to take another. Eventually, he agreed to make a golden figure of Sita and keep it beside him while conducting the rituals.

Detailed preparations for the year-long sacrifice commenced. The place chosen was the Naimisha forest. A pure black horse, marked with all auspicious signs and richly decorated with gold and silver strapping, was released by Rama. The horse was allowed to roam all over the country, followed by Lakshmana and the army. If anyone caught and tied the horse, the army would come and fight with the person who had the temerity to challenge the king's steed. If the horse returned unchallenged, the king could declare himself as emperor.

The forest of Naimisha was converted into a veritable paradise, with pavilions and music halls and gardens and *yajnashalas* (ceremonial locations). All the kings of the realm were invited and came to pay homage to Rama and accepted him as their suzerain. Not only were kings invited but also the hermits and sages who lived in the forests. Invitations were also sent to the *vanaras* at Kishkinda, who came with their leader Sugriva, and to the *rakshasas* at Lanka, who came along with Vibhishana. Food, clothes, jewelery, gems, gold and silver were distributed lavishly. There was nobody who went away empty-handed.

Sage Valmiki came with Lava and Kusha. He told them to go and sing twenty cantos of the beautiful poem called the *Ramayana*, before the huts of the sages who had been invited and also before the king himself. He also told them never to accept any remuneration for their services. If they were asked about their lineage, they were to say that they were the disciples of Sage Valmiki.

The children did as they were told and sang twenty cantos in melodious voices, before the royal audience. People were spellbound by the sight of these two hermit boys who sang so sweetly. They also remarked on their uncanny resemblance to Rama. He had looked exactly like them, so many years ago when he went to the forest, wearing bark, with hair in matted locks. Rama was enchanted with the boys and told Lakshmana to give them twenty thousand gold coins and expensive clothes but the boys refused and said that hermit boys who lived on fruits and roots had no necessity for such things, just as they had been told to do by their Guru.

Rama was astonished and asked them, "Who composed this poem and how many cantos are there in it?"

The boys replied, "The venerable Sage Valmiki is the composer of this wonderful poem, which recounts the doings of your Majesty. It has twenty-four thousand verses and six *kandas*. The seventh, or the Uttara Kanda, is now going on. With your leave, we will recite the whole poem, in its entirety, to you, between the functions of the horse sacrifice."

"So be it," said the king.

For many days, Rama and his brothers, as well as the collection of sages, kings and monkeys, heard the whole story of Rama. All were enthralled by the recital. By the end of it, Rama realized that these boys were his own sons, the children of Sita. All the pent-up emotions which he had contained for so many years now surged forward and his heart was choked with love for his exquisite wife, whom he had abandoned so cruelly twelve years ago. He could no longer suppress his feelings. The day that he banished her, he had enshrined her in his heart and thrown away the key. But these young boys, who looked like him and smiled like her, had broken open the door of his heart and let loose the flood of emotion, which threatened to overwhelm him with its intensity. Their smiles brought to his mind only too vividly Sita's charming face. The desire to see her again was too strong to be subdued. Surely, the fates would not deny him this final bid for happiness. He sent messengers to the hut of the sage with this request.

"Go immediately to the Sage Valmiki and request him to bring the mother of these boys to me, for I feel very sure that she is none other than my wife Sita. If he thinks that she is indeed blameless and that her character is without blemish, ask him to let her come and prove her innocence tomorrow, before this august assembly. Tomorrow at dawn, the princess of Videha is welcome to come and display her virtue."

The next morning, everybody from all over the realm, as well as the guests who had been invited for the sacrifice, assembled in the Naimisha forest to watch the final scene in the drama of the lives of their king and queen. Into that motionless crowd of expectant citizens, Valmiki arrived with Sita. Her head was bent to the ground, her palms were folded together in devotion, her eyes were filled with tears, and her heart, with Rama. At the sight of her, dressed in the clothes of an anchorite, looking so divinely beautiful yet so sad, the fickle crowd set up a spontaneous cheer of welcome. They, who had been so eager to send her away, now appeared equally eager to take her back.

Valmiki led her to Rama and said, "Son of Dasaratha, here is your wife, the ever chaste Sita. Fire itself cools at her approach, for she is purer than Agni. Twelve years ago, you abandoned her in front of my *ashrama* through fear of public censure. But I tell you truly, she is as chaste as Anasuya, the wife of Atri. If Sita is tainted, then let my austerities be in vain. Though you loved her and knew her to be innocent, you repudiated her to satisfy your subjects. Now at your insistence, she is here to prove her innocence for the second time."

"So be it," said Rama. "With the gods as witness, Sita proved her innocence once before in Lanka and I accepted her, but still the people whispered and I was forced to send her away, to uphold my dharma as a king. I hereby acknowledge Lava and Kusha as my own sons and will accept Sita too as my wife, if she proves her innocence once more in front of the people of Ayodhya as she did long ago before the *vanaras* and *rakshasas* at Lanka."

As he said this, Rama allowed himself the pleasure of gazing at his lovely wife once again. Bereft of jewels and adornment, dressed in bark as befitting an anchorite, with matted hair tied in a knot on top of her head, stood his queen—the queen of Ayodhya and the queen of his life. His heart smote him as he looked at her. Involuntarily he stretched out his hands toward her. Without thinking, she put her delicate, pink-tipped palms into his. Despite her lack of adornment, she was still incredibly lovely and he couldn't tear his eyes away from her. Sita gazed back at him and, as their hands and eyes locked in a mutual embrace, they felt as if they were drowning in the ocean of love which was mirrored in their gaze. They held infinity in their hands and eternity in their eyes. A ring of interested spectators had formed around them but Sita and Rama stood alone within the circle, gazing at each other as if they could not bear to look away. For twelve long years, they had been starved of this pleasure. Time stopped and they beheld heaven in their eyes, and their whole life passed like a dream in front of their interlocked gaze and still they could not bear to look away.

At last, Sita broke the silence and whispered, "My Lord, do I have your permission to make a public avowal of my purity?"

Rama nodded. Wearing the ochre robes of the ascetics, yet looking as beautiful as a bride, Sita, the daughter of the earth, stepped into the center of the circle and with folded palms, she bowed before her mother earth and said, "O Madhavi! Goddess of the earth, beloved mother! If you know that I have never loved any man but Rama and never thought of any man other than my husband, even for a moment, then please open your arms wide and accept your daughter, for I can no longer bear to live in this vale of tears. Grief alone has been my lot in life and now I long for the comfort of your arms. O mother! Take me to your bosom, as you brought me once out of your womb, to the field of my father Janaka."

Hardly had she finished speaking when the earth split open with a shudder, and out of the chasm there arose a beautiful flower throne on which was seated the goddess of the earth in all her bounty, covered with flowers and carrying the nine types of grains in sheaves in her hands.

She opened her arms wide and Sita ran into them and was made to sit beside her on the throne of flowers. In front of the astonished gaze of the spellbound audience, the earth gaped open once more and the throne carrying Sita and her mother slowly descended into the bowels of the earth, as the gods rained flowers from above. As the gap closed over their heads, the earth shuddered and the wind moaned and the crowd came out of their mesmerized state and a great sigh broke from every mouth.

As she disappeared from sight, Rama woke up from the grip of terror which was holding him and started to weep uncontrollably. He ran to the spot where she had disappeared and called to her piteously. Holding a staff picked up from the sacrificial ground, he leaned on it as if his body were too weak to stand alone and bending his head over it, he cried out loud, "O Janaki! O Vaidehi! O Sita! My beloved wife! Why have you deserted me, just when I thought I could have you back? Once you were taken away by the wicked Ravana but I brought you back and then I was forced to send you away again. At that time, I was able to bear the parting only because I knew that you were alive and being looked after somewhere, but now, I cannot bear to live, when I know I cannot see you anymore. I fear I am being punished for my cruel act in having banished you."

Then, in anger, he smote the earth with the staff and said, "O goddess of the earth, return my beloved to me at once! I have suffered enough. I cannot live without her. Or else open your arms once again and accept me also. I would rather live with her in the nether world than here as a king. Remember I am your son-in-law and have pity on me. You know my valor. If you refuse my reasonable request, I will destroy you, burn your forests and crush your mountains, and reduce everything to liquid."

All the worlds trembled with fear at the agony in Rama's voice, which had changed to anger. No one dared to approach him. At last, Brahma, the creator came to him and said, "Rama! Remember who you are. Let me remind you of your divinity. Immaculate Sita will be reunited with you in heaven for she is none other than your consort, Lakshmi. Do not grieve, but take delight in your children and listen to the rest of the tale of your life, which they will recite at dawn tomorrow. It is an exquisitely beautiful poem, of a life which was ruled by dharma alone. You should be the first to hear it, for it is about you. O Rama! You are undoubtedly the foremost of all *rishis*." With these words, Brahma vanished.

Rama led his two sons to the hut of the Sage Valmiki and spent the night there, grieving for Sita. The whole night he kept murmuring, "Why did you leave me? Why did you leave me? Don't you know I cannot live without you? I know you must have felt the same when I deserted you and that is why I have to suffer the pangs of separation now. But, at least, then I had the satisfaction of knowing that you were alive and I could see you any time I wished, but now you have left me to go to the bosom of your mother and my life is a barren desert. O Sita! O Sita! Will you not return to me?"

The boys too were plunged in sorrow at the loss of their mother and Valmiki had the unhappy task of comforting all three of them. It is only to be expected that a poem which began with the bereavement of the female bird should end with the bereavement of the human couple. At that time, when he had watched the male bird shot down by the cruel arrow, Valmiki had felt as if he had been pierced by the same fatal shot. How much more did he feel now, when he saw the tortured king bemoaning his loss over and over again, throughout the long and lonely hours of the endless night?

The next day, in front of the assembled crowd, Rama asked the children to chant the last portion of the epic. He then distributed wealth to all those assembled there, the kings, the *Brahmins*, the citizens, the tree-dwellers, the cave-dwellers and the *rakshasas*. The *yajna* was over, the people had dispersed and the jungle once more crept over the space which had been cleared for the function.

Rama returned to Ayodhya and spent the rest of his life a lonely ascetic. Without Sita, life had no meaning for him. He never married again but kept the golden effigy of his lovely wife beside him and performed ten thousand *ashvamedha yajnas* in order to please his Guru and the people. His rule was noted for its exemplary nature. There were no diseases among the people and no one died prematurely, the kingdom prospered and thrived and the citizens rejoiced. Rama and Sita had paid for this glory with their unceasing tears. They suffered, so that the rest of the country could rejoice, blossom and flourish. Never once did the citizens think that the price of their prosperity was the sacrifice of their queen—their land was watered with her tears, their happiness bought with her sorrow. She was the sacrificial offering, tied to the stake of their malice, banished to the forest of their poisonous tongues and eventually swallowed in the chasm of their doubt! They rejoiced and sported with their wives, while their king retired to his lonely chamber every night, with only his memories for company.

Rama carried on his duties for the rest of his life with his usual charm and adherence to dharma and showed a pleasant and happy face to all. Lakshmana alone knew that this was just a facade and inside he was burning with regret at what he had done to his queen and waiting for the day when he could join her in their celestial abode.

Thus, many years flew by and Kausalya, Sumitra and Kaikeyi passed away. At last, one day, *Kala*—the Time spirit—came to the palace of Ayodhya, in the guise of an old *Brahmin*. Rama was waiting for him. He had been waiting for thousands of years. Lakshmana brought him in and Rama placed him on a golden seat and asked him what he wanted.

He replied, "If you want to honor me and the gods, then promise me that our meeting shall be private. Anyone who dares to interrupt us should be put to instant death."

"So be it," said Rama. "I'll tell Lakshmana to guard the door and no one will interrupt us." He asked Lakshmana to dismiss the doorkeeper and take up his position, for anyone who dared to enter would be put to death. Then he turned to the ascetic and asked him to freely say whatever he wished to say, without fear of interruption.

"Listen, O king!" said the spirit of Time, "I have been sent by Brahma to recall you to your heavenly abode. Your time on this earth is over. You have accomplished all that you have set out to do. You are Vishnu! The Eternal, the Immutable—the all pervading, protector of the universe. Your stay among the mortals is over. It is time for you to return."

Rama smiled and said, "I'm honored by your visit and happy with your message. I will do as you say."

As they were thus talking, the *rishi*, called Durvasa, who was known for his bad temper, came to the door and asked Lakshmana to allow him to enter. Lakshmana politely barred the way and said that no one could enter. Hearing this, the sage lost his temper and shouted, "Announce my presence immediately or else I shall curse you and your brothers and your whole race, as well as the land of Kosala, so that nothing and no one remains to tell the tale!"

Lakshmana thought for a moment and decided that it was far better for him to give up his life rather than make the whole country and his brothers suffer. He went inside and announced the arrival of the sage to Rama. Rama took leave of the ascetic and hurried outside to meet Durvasa and asked him how he could be of service to him. Durvasa said that he had just ended a thousand-year fast and wanted to be fed immediately. Rama plied him with all the choicest delicacies of the realm. Durvasa was immensely pleased and showered his blessings on the land, instead of his curses and went back to his *ashrama*. With the greatest of sorrow, Rama remembered the promise he had made to *Kala* and going inside with bowed head, he stood lost in thought. Was this the last sacrifice? Was he being asked to sacrifice his dear brother, his alter ego, at the altar of dharma?

Lakshmana knew what was passing through his mind and said cheerfully, "Brother, do not hesitate. Kill me this minute. I am prepared for it. I thought it better for me to die, rather than the whole country be cursed by the sage, as he threatened to do. If you wish to abide by dharma, then kill me. O king. one who does not keep his word will go to hell. In order to keep our father's word, you were prepared to forego a kingdom. What am I, compared to that!"

Rama spoke not a word but summoned his priests and

ministers and asked them what he should do, for he had promised the ascetic that anyone who interrupted them would be executed, not knowing that this would be his final test. The priests and ministers were silent, knowing the agony which was passing through the king's mind. At last, Vasistha spoke. "If a king does not keep to his word, dharma will be corrupted and the morals of the country will decline. But banishment can be given in lieu of death, so it is your duty to banish Lakshmana."

Lakshmana stood with his head thrown back, his eyes gazing fearlessly into Rama's. Rama looked into those beloved eyes which had always regarded him with such love, looked at that beloved form, which he had known since childhood and which had followed him faithfully like a shadow from which one can never be parted. He knew that one need not die when separated from a shadow, but what about the shadow? Would it not come to an end when parted from the body? Pain flowed out of his eyes, while love flowed from Lakshmana's eyes.

"It does not matter, brother," he whispered. "Command me to leave, as sternly as you once ordered me to leave Sita in the forest."

Rama was in anguish. Over and over again, he murmured, "Everything passes. Everything perishes. Nothing will remain. Time is all powerful. Everything will be swept away in the powerful river of time. I have to abide by my promise. I have to be true to the only thing to which I have clung all my life—dharma, the cosmic law of righteousness. I have been tested, time and time again, and I have not failed. Let me not fail now."

He was facing Lakshmana but could not look into his eyes. Instead, he fixed his gaze at a spot just above his head and said in an expressionless voice, drained of all emotion. "In honor of truth, in honor of dharma, in honor of the law, which I have always upheld, I banish you, O Lakshmana, forever. You shall never return to this land of Kosala again, on fear of death!"

Lakshmana looked lovingly at his brother whom he had obeyed implicitly all his life and said, "My dearest brother. Do not grieve. I have loved you all my life and obeyed you without a murmur. It shall be as you wish. Farewell! And once again, fare Thee well. We will never meet again in this life. Perhaps we will meet in heaven."

So saying, he went thrice round Rama and prostrated to him, and went without a backward glance to the banks of the swiftly flowing river Sarayu. The thought of a life apart from Rama was unthinkable. Death was preferable to such a life. He did not even consider it. Going to the Sarayu River, he sat in yogic contemplation on the banks. He gathered in his vital breaths and withdrew into his atman, and merged himself into the Brahman—the cosmic whole. Thus, he sat in deep samadhi. Indra, the king of gods sent his chariot and took Lakshmana, the fourth part of Vishnu, to heaven, where he merged into That essence.

Back in Ayodhya, Rama knew that Lakshmana would never be able to live without him and he himself no longer cared to carry on a life which had ceased to have any meaning for him. Firm in his vows of dharmic discipline, he had been forced to part, one by one, from all those whom he held most dear. He had always known that life was only a dream, a drama in which he had been called upon to play a part. He had come to the end of his lines. The curtain was going up for the final scene and he had already been given his cue to depart. He called his priests and ministers and announced his decision to them.

"I hereby appoint Bharata as Lord of Ayodhya. The southern portion of this fair land of Kosala, will be given to Kusha and the northern to Lava. I myself shall follow Lakshmana."

Bharata and Shatrugna refused to live without Rama and decided to follow him. Many of the citizens for whose sake he had sacrificed his all decided that they could not live in a land without their beloved king. Hearing of his terrible decision, the monkeys and the bears and Vibhishana from across the sea arrived and begged to go with him.

Rama said to Vibhishana, "O Lord of *rakshasas*, stay on in Lanka, for that is your duty. Rule with dharma as your guide. So long as I am remembered on earth, so long will your kingdom endure."

Then, turning to Hanuman, he said, "Live long, O noble Hanuman. Wherever my story is told, wherever the name of Rama is mentioned, you will be there to hear it. This story will be told as long as the sun and the moon shine, as long as people remain on this earth and as long as you are there to hear it!"

Then turning to the bear Jambavan, he said, "O wise one! You shall live till my advent as Krishna, scion of the race of Yadu. Until then, you shall suffer no defeat. When you meet one who is able to defeat you, then you will know that I have returned."

To the others, he said, "If you so wish, you may all follow me. This very day will you enter heaven along with me."

All the people of Ayodhya followed Rama with love and devotion. Even the animals followed him—the cows and goats and elephants, not to mention the monkeys and bears. The very stones on the streets of Ayodhya wept, for they could not follow him, and the trees bent low and brushed his head as he passed. Every creature which could walk or roll or dance or totter followed him. Sumantra was waiting at the banks of the river with the four red horses, which he had freed from the chariot. Guha, the hunter king, was also there. The whole party came to the pellucid waters of the river Sarayu, which circled the land of Kosala like a silver girdle. Rama walked into the icy cold waters accompanied by all the rest. The waters closed over their heads like a benediction. The heavens opened and the celestials rained down flowers.

Brahma spoke. "O gracious Vishnu. Be pleased to return to your celestial abode. Thou art the Soul of All—indestructible, immutable and eternal. Be pleased to give up this form of *maya* and resume your *swaroopa*."

Out of the waters rose the incredibly beautiful form of Lord Vishnu, holding the discus, conch, mace and play lotus in His hands. All the others who had decided to join Him also came out of the waters, endowed with celestial forms, and all rose up to the heavens as the music of the spheres floated down in the velvet darkness.

With the ascension of Rama to his heavenly abode, the twenty four thousand verses were complete. Back in the deserted city of Ayodhya, Lava and Kusha sang the final verses of the song to an unseen audience—the song known as the *Ramayana*—the Way of Rama, the first poem ever to be composed by the *adi kavi* (first poet) Valmiki.

Thus ends the thirty-second chapter of the glorious Ramayana *of Sage Valmiki called "The Rule of Rama."*

Hari Aum Tat Sat

Vasistha says:
As waves are seen in the tangible ocean,
so in the formless Brahman,
the world exists without form.
From the Infinite, the Infinite emerges,
and exists in it as the Infinite.
Hence, the world has never really been created.
It is the same as that from which it has emerged.

— *THE YOGA VASISTHA*

THE BENEFITS OF READING THIS BOOK

Sri Ramaya Namaha!

Homage to Sri Rama.

WHAT FOLLOWS IS THE *phala shruti*, or the benefits which will accrue to those who read or listen to the *Ramayana*. Before we go into that, let us see what we have gained from reading this inspiring book. The *Ramayana*, as we see, starts and ends in sorrow and bereavement. It is meant to portray the stark reality of life in this world, which is filled with meetings and partings, in which we are continuously faced with problematic situations, in which the average human being flounders and wonders how he or she can extricate themself out. Valmiki has put Rama again and again in such situations. He has never tried to cloak the endearing weaknesses in Rama's character with half truths, which might satisfy the mediocre spiritualist, to whom religion is a panacea.

Valmiki's book is meant for those stalwarts like Rama, who have hearts filled with love for the whole of humanity, yet who have to march bravely forward, using the surgeon's knife, when necessary, to root out the evils which they are confronted with, both in themselves and in society. The knife is not merely used against the demon forces but also turned against oneself, ruthlessly used to dig out weaknesses.

Rama was true to his principle of dharma to the bitter end. He spared neither himself nor anyone else, not even those who were closest to him. He was true to all the four aspects of dharma, which have been extolled in our scriptures. These are *satya, daya, tapas* and *tyaga*—truth, compassion, austerity and sacrifice.

275

Valmiki's poemdemonstrates all these aspects very beautifully. His adherence to truth, his compassion to all who approached him, the steadfast way in which he stuck to his austere life in the forest and after parting from Sita, and his ability for sacrificing his own interests for the sake of others have all been brought out in the epic. Valmiki graphically portrays a mighty human being who turned himself into a god by his strict adherence to this relentless cosmic law of dharma. He was indeed a *dharmatman*—the soul of Dharma.

PHALA SHRUTI
(the Benefits of Listening to the *Ramayana*)

Those who hear or listen to this story of Rama will be saved from all misfortune. It grants longevity, victory and power. Those without children will get children and those who want fame will get fame. Those who read it with faith will get dharma, *artha*, *kama*, and *moksha* (righteousness, wealth, pleasure and liberation). The blessings of the Lord Vishnu will always be upon them for Rama is that Narayana, the all-pervading Being, without beginning and without end, who resides in the milky ocean—the ancient divinity. Sita is his eternal consort, Mahalakshmi, mother of the universe, granter of all auspiciousness and prosperity.

May all those who recite this epic with faith and love be blessed with health, wealth and wisdom.

To Thee, O Vanamali! I offer this garland of unfading flowers, called the *Ramayana*.

May all be healthy
May all be at peace with each other.
May all be fulfilled
May all be auspicious.
Let all be happy,
Let all be free from pain.
Let all see reality everywhere
Let none have sorrow.

Thus ends the complete *Ramayana* of Sage Valmiki.

Aum Peace, Peace, Peace.
Aum Shanti! Shanti! Shanti!

Hari Aum Tat Sat

ॐ GLOSSARY

abhijit–constellation which rises at noon

abhisheka–ceremonial bath of a king during the coronation

adharma–unrighteousness

adharmic–that which is not in accordance with dharma

adi-kavi–the first poet

adi-kavya–the first poem

amavasya–day of the new moon

antaryami–the indweller

apsara–heavenly nymph

artha–wealth; material goods

ashoka–type of flowering tree

ashrama–hermitage

ashramites–those who live in an *ashrama*

astra–weapon

asura–demon

ashvamedha yajna–horse sacrifice

atma–soul

atmic–pertaining to soul

avatara–incarnation of the supreme

bhakta–devotee

bhakti–devotion

Bharatavarsha–ancient name for India

biksham dehi–call for alms by a *sannyasi*

boon–in this work, it usually refers to a favor or benefit granted by a deity or saint, often as a result of practicing penance or austerities

brahmachari–one who practices continence

Brahman–the formless Supreme

Brahmarishi–sage who has attained the Supreme

Brahmastra–deadly weapon

brahmic–pertaining to Brahman

Brahmin–one belonging to the priest class

chaitra–name of the month in which Rama was born
    (March/April)
champaka–name of a flowering tree; flower
chowrie–yak tail

daitya–*rakshasa*; demon
danava–rakshasa; demon
darbha–type of grass
daya–compassion
dharma–righteousness; morality; virtue
dharmanuchara–one who practises dharma
dharmatma–the soul of dharma
dharmic–pertaining to righteousness

gandharva–celestial singer
guna–one of the modes of nature
guru–preceptor
gurukula–ancient type of school conducted at the home of the
    teacher

kadamba–type of flowering tree; flower of the same
kama–love; lust
karma–action
kartika–name of month (October/November)
Kshatriya–member of the ruling or warrior caste
kusha–a type of grass

lila–play
linga–stone signifying Shiva

mantra–incantation
mara–tree
maryada purusha–the perfect human being
maya–illusion
moksha–liberation
mridanga–percussion instrument

mritasanjivi--name of magic herb which brings the dead to life

naga(s)–serpent(s)
nagapasa–noose of serpents; a celestial *astra*

palmyra–a type of palm tree
parijata–name of tree; flower of the same
phala-shruti–list of benefits
prayaga–confluence
puja–ritual
punarvasu–name of star under which Rama was born
poornavatara–supreme incarnation
purusha–person; man
pushpa–flower
pushya–constellation under which Bharata was born
putrakameshti yajna–ritual for begetting a son

rajas–quality of action; passion
rakshas–demon
rakshasi–demoness
Ramarajya–rule of Rama
rishi–sage
rita–cosmic order.

sama–one of the vedas
samadhi–superconscious state
samsara–the transmigratory existence
samskaras–character traits carried from a previous life
sanjeevakarani–magic herb which brings the dead back
    to life
sannyasa–life of renunciation
sannyasi(ns)–renunciate(s)
satsang–company of the holy
sattva–quality of goodness; nobility.
satya–truth.
shakti–power; name of weapon
shastra(s)–scripture(s)

shoka–sorrow
shravana–month (July/August)
shudra–the fourth caste
siddhi(s)–supernormal power(s)
sloka–verse
sthithaprajna–person of steady intellect; enlightened person
swadharma–one's personal duty
swarupa–original form
swayamvara–marriage by choice

tamas–quality of inertia, sloth, laziness
tapas–austerity, severe spiritual penance
tampura–stringed instrument; lute
tyaga–renunciation

uttama–highest
uttama Purusha–perfect person

vaishya–the third caste; merchant caste
valmikam–anthill
vanaras–monkeys
Veda(s)–most ancient spiritual books of the Hindu philosophy
vedic–pertaining to the Veda
veena–lute
vijaya–victory; auspicious hour
vishalyakarini–a magic herb which can bring a person back to
    consciousness

yajna–fire ceremony; sacrifice
yajnashala–place where this ceremony is performed
yoga–spiritual practice
yogi–an ascetic engaged in spiritual practices
yogic–pertaining to yoga
yuvaraja–heir apparent; crown prince

ॐ LIST OF CHARACTERS

Agastya–a great sage who had many divine powers

Agni–god of fire

Ahalya–wife of the Sage Gautama who was famous
    for her beauty

Akampana–name of a rakshasa

Aksha Kumara–Ravana's youngest son

Anasuya–wife of Sage Atri, famous for her piety and
    chastity

Angada–son of the monkey king Vali

Anjana–Hanuman's mother

Arjuna–the middle Pandava, to whom Lord Krishna
    gave the advice of the *Bhagavad Gita*

Atri–great sage; husband of Anasuya

Ayodhya–capital city of Rama

Ayomukhi–a *rakshasi* who propositioned Lakshmana

Bhadra–friend of Rama's

Bharadwaja–great sage who lived at the confluence
    of the three rivers, Ganga, Yamuna and Saraswati

Bharata–Rama's brother; son of Kaikeyi

Brahma–the creator; grandsire of the gods

Chitrakuta–name of hill where Rama lived at the
    commencement of his exile

Dandaka–forest where Rama spent his exile

Dasaratha–Rama's father

Dhumraksha–one of Ravana's generals

Dhushana–one of Ravana's generals

Dundubhi–a demon in the form of a buffalo.

Durvasa–sage noted for his bad temper

Dwapara yuga–third age of the Hindu calendar

Ganesha–son of Shiva; the elephant-faced god
Ganga–the holy river
Garuda–the eagle vehicle of Lord Vishnu
Gautama–a great sage; husband of Ahalya
Godavari–river by which was situated Rama's hermitage during the
    last year of his exile
Gokarna–place where Maricha had his *ashrama*
Gomati–a river near Ayodhya
Guha–chieftain of a tribe who helped Rama to cross the Ganga

Hanuman–minister of Sugriva; one of greatest devotees of Rama
Himavan–Lord of the great mountain, the Himalayas; father of the
    goddess Parvati

Ikshvaku–son of Manu and the progenitor of the solar race
Ilwala–name of a demon
Indra–king of gods
Indrajit–Ravana's eldest son

Jambavan–king of the bears
Jambumali–son of Ravana's general, Prahasta
Janaka–king of Mithila; Sita's father
Janaki–another name for Sita, meaning daughter of Janaka
Janasthana–part of the forest of Dandaka where Ravana's garrison
    was stationed
Jatayu–an eagle who tried to help Sita
Jayanta–son of Indra who came in the form of a crow

Kabandha–a demon without a head
Kaikeyi–mother of Bharata; youngest wife of Dasaratha
Kailasa–peak in the Himalayas; dwelling place of Shiva
Kala–the Spirit of Time
Kausalya–mother of Rama, eldest wife of Dasaratha
Kekaya–the name of the country from which Kaikeyi came
Kesari–Hanuman's foster father
Khara–a demon; brother of Dhushana
Kishkinda–name of Sugriva's city
Kodanda–name of Rama's bow

Kosala–name of Rama's country

Krishna–the supreme incarnation of Vishnu

Kubera–god of wealth; Ravana's stepbrother

Kumbha–Kumbhakarna's son

Kumbhakarna–Ravana's younger brother, noted for his outrageous eating and sleeping habits

Kurukshetra–battlefield of the Kurus, where the Mahabharatha war was fought

Kusa–one of the twin sons of Rama

Lakshmana–one of the twin sons of Sumitra; Rama's close companion

Lakshmi–consort of Narayana

Lanka–Ravana's city

Lankini–goddess of Lanka

Lava–twin son of Rama

Madhavi–goddess of the earth

Madhuvana–wine garden of Sugriva

Mahabharatha–the great epic composed by Vyasa

Mahalakshmi–goddess of wealth; wife of Lord Vishnu

Mahaparashva–one of Ravana's trusted generals

Mahendra–mountain on which Parashurama meditates

Maheswara–another name for Shiva

Mahodara–another of Ravana's best generals

Mainaka–a mountain under the sea

Maithili–another name of Sita; princess of Mithila

Malaya–name of a mountain

Mandavi–Bharata's wife

Mandodari–chief consort of Ravana; daughter of Mayan

Manthara–hunchback maidservant of Kaikeyi

Maricha–rakshasa who took the form of the golden deer

Matali–the charioteer of Indra

Matanga–a great sage

Mayan–father of Mandodari; architect of the demons

Mayavi–a demon who fought with Vali
Meghanatha–eldest son of Ravana; known later as Indrajit
Mithila–capital city of Videha; Sita's city

Naimisha–forest where Rama conducted the *aswamedha yaga*
Nala–architect of the *vanaras*, who built Rama's bridge
Nalakubera–one of the sons of Kubera
Nandana–a park
Nandi–the bull vehicle of Lord Shiva
Nandigrama–name of village where Bharata stayed for fourteen
    years
Narada–celestial sage
Narayana–one of the many names of Lord Vishnu
Neela–one of the monkey generals
Nikumbha–one of the sons of Kumbhakarna

Pamba–name of a lake
Panchavati–grove of five trees in which Rama built an *ashrama*
Parashurama–the sixth incarnation of Vishnu
Parvati–wife of Lord Shiva; daughter of Himavan
Prahastha–commander-in-chief of Ravana's army
Prashravana–hill where Rama spent the four months of the rainy
    season
Punchikasthla–name of a celestial nymph
Pushpaka–Ravana's aerial flower chariot

Raghava–name of Rama
Raghu–one of the famous kings of the solar race; great-
    grandfather of Rama
Raghunandana– dear to the race of the Raghus
Raghuvamsa–race of Raghu
Rahu–one of the nine planets which cause the eclipse of the sun
    and moon
(Sri) Rama–the seventh incarnation of Vishnu
Ramabhadra–another name for Rama
Ramachandra–another name of Rama
Ramayana–the way of Rama; the first poem to be composed in
    the world

Rambha–one of the divine nymphs

Rameswaram–name of the temple to Shiva which Rama
founded

Ramphal–the ox-heart fruit

Ravana–demon king of Lanka

Rishyamukha–the hill on which Sugriva took refuge

Rishyasringa–famous sage who conducted the *yaga* for
Dasaratha

Ruma–wife of Sugriva

Sachi–wife of Indra

Sagara–name of the ocean; one of the kings of the solar
race

Sampati–eagle; brother of Jatayu

Samudra–the ocean

Sarama–wife of Vibhishana

Sarasa–mother of the serpents

Saraswathi–name of a mythical river

Sarayu–river which encircles Ayodhya

Satya yuga–golden age

Shabari–very old female ascetic

Shambuka–the *shudra* who was practicing austerities

Sharabhanga–a great sage

Shatrugna–brother of Rama; Lakshmana's twin

Shiva–one of the trinity; also known as Maheswara

Shudra–the fourth caste

Surpanekha–demoness; sister of Ravana

Sita–wife of Rama; princess of Videha

Sitaphal–custard apple

Srutakirti–wife of Shatrugna

Subahu–demon; brother of Maricha

Sudheekshna–sage

Sugriva–monkey king who helped Rama to rescue Sita

Sumantra–charioteer and minister of Dasaratha

Sumitra–second wife of Dasaratha; mother of
Lakshmana and Shatrugna

Surya–the sun god

Suyajna–son of Vasistha

Swayamprabha–a beautiful woman who was guarding the cave to which the monkeys went

Tamasa–name of a river near Valmiki's *ashrama*
Tara–wife of Vali
Tataka–demoness
Thrishiras–one of the demons guarding Ravana's garrison at Janasthana
Treta yuga–period that follows golden age
Trijata–a demoness who was very helpful to Sita
Tulsidas–famous poet who composed the Hindi version of the *Ramayana*

Urmila–wife of Lakshmana; Sita's sister

Vaidehi–another name of Sita; princess of Videha
Vaishravas–father of Ravana
Vaivaswatha Manu–progenitor of human kind
Vajradamstra–demon warrior
Vali–king of Kishkinda; brother of Sugriva
Valmiki–sage; author of the *Ramayana*; the first poet
Vanamali–name of Lord Vishnu; Krishna; one who wears the garland of wildflowers
Vanara–monkey
Varuna–god of the waters
Vasistha–great sage; preceptor of the family of Ikshvaku
Vatapi–demon; brother of Ilwala
Vayu–the wind god
Vibhishana–half-brother of Ravana; a noble demon
Vidyudjihva–magician in the court of Ravana
Vinata–Sugriva's general; mother of Garuda
Viradha–demon
Virupaksha–Ravana's general
Vishnu–the preserver in the trinity of Brahma-Vishnu-Shiva
Vishvakarma–architect of the gods
Vishvamitra–great sage who was born a *kshatriya*
Vyasa–great sage who wrote the *Mahabharata*

Yadu–progenitor of the Yadava race
Yama–god of death
Yamuna–river; tributary of Ganga
Yogavasistha–the advice of Vasistha to Rama
Yudhistira–eldest of the Pandavas; noted for his
    adherence to dharma

Inspiring Books from Blue Dove Press

The Play of God
Visions of the Life of Krishna
by Devi Vanamali, author of *Song of Rama*
Softcover   416 pp. $19.95   ISBN: 1-884997-07-4

"Krishna's biography is an exceptional introduction to the Indian worldview. This is going to become a classic text which opens many doors —doors historical, cultural and spiritual."
— Publishers Weekly

"Highly recommended as a fresh and readable presentation, in English, of the life and meaning of Krishna."
— Library Journal

"This is a valuable treasure to be cherished."
— Swami Chidananda,
Divine Life Society

The Play of God is the account of a spiritual phenomenon. It describes the extraordinary manifestation of the Eternal in the realm of time that occurred in Krishna, the playful and enchantingly beautiful Deity who embodies the highest truths of India's spiritual vision. Readers will find here powerful visions of God as child, playmate, friend, and teacher. What is evoked here is not a religion of moral law and stern obligation, but a spirituality of joy and true desire, love and beauty, contemplation and inner awakening.

Never before has the complete life of Krishna been told in a way that is so engaging and understandable, yet so faithful to the ancient epics of India. The life of Krishna stretches our conception of Divinity and lifts our minds to a higher spiritual plane as we contemplate the unlimited joy of the Eternal appearing to us in a form combining beauty, strength, and astounding playfulness. Spiritual seekers of all traditions will find faith in these pages.

Dancing with the Void

The Innerstandings of a Rare-Born Mystic

by Sunyata

Softcover   330pp. $19.95   ISBN: 1-884997-19-8

Dancing with the Void is the unique story of an unconventional man whose existence was "mind-free, ego-free, form-free, effort-free, time-free and age-free." In his own joyful prose; Sunyata chronicles his life journey from contemplative farm boy and gardener, Emmanual Sorensen, to humble Himalayan cave dweller, "Mr. Nobody."

Born in Denmark, in 1890, Sunyata was from birth, utterly without desire, ambition, or ego. Thus, the name "Sunyata"—and description of "rare-born mystic"—was given to him years later in India by the Sage of Arunachala, Ramana Maharshi.

A lover of silence and solitude, Sunyata remained untouched by the common wordly conditioning that entraps so many. His fateful journeys, inspiring friendships, and the spiritual wisdom shared in these collected writings, all reflect the soul of an authentic seer.

Sunyata's experiences and musing are ever relevant, for they concern something that is of value to all; the illumination and liberation of the human spirit.

EXCERPT FROM THE BOOK:

"In this life play I have not been in quest of Guru, God, Truth, Grace, Salvation, nirvana, or power lust, nor had I any guilt complex. I had no ambition to be different from what I am. Blessedly, I had escaped headucation, and I was free of any imposed knowledge. I had no property. I did not marry. I did not belong to any cliques or creed. I was not attracted by their magnetism. I felt all is within our Self. I had nothing to assert or resent. Nor had I anything to boast about or regret. I was fully contented. I had joy in 'that which is.'"

—Sunyata

Mother of All
A Revelation of the Motherhood of God in the Life
and Teachings of the Jillellamudi Mother
by Richard Schiffman
Softcover   400 pp. $19.95   ISBN: 1-884997-28-7

*"Mother Anasuya Devi (1923-1985) of Jillellamudi was a
beloved spiritual leader in southern India. Here, NPR
commentator Schiffman takes us to the village of the Mother (as
she is affectionately known by her devotees) and acquaints us
with her life and teachings...."*

—Publishers Weekly

*"A magnificent portrayal of a very great human, contemporary
and timeless, a uniquely unusual expression of God's being in
the world."*

**—Joseph Chilton Pearce
Author of The Soul**

"Reading this book is a divine experience—truly inspirational."

**— Dr. Wayne Dyer
Author of Wisdom of the Ages**

The compelling story of one the great spiritual figures of
our time. Mother Anasuya Devi was revered by millions for her
homespun wisdom, motherly love, and extraordinary spiritual
powers. Her profound yet enigmatic teachings powerfully
challenged traditional patriarchal views and rejected the common
Hindu belief that life is an illusion. Married, and the mother of
three children, she was a living witness to her own core teachings
that the earth is sacred and spirituality comes from embracing life
in full. In this personal and moving account, Schiffman tells us of
his several years at the "House of All," Amma's spiritual center,
where every visitor was fed and made welcome. Amma was
considered by many of those around her, including the author, to
be an avatar, an incarnation of the Divine Mother herself. Neither
a preacher nor a proselytizer, she taught through her quiet,
compassionate presence, encouraging all who remained a while
with her to step out of time into the gradual, peaceful
understanding of a deliberate and conscious way of living.

The Wisdom of Sri Chinmoy

Compiled by Andy Zubko, compiler of
Treasury of Spiritual Wisdom
Softcover   410 pp. $19.95   ISBN: 1-884997-23-6

"Chinmoy, the Bengali lecturer and author of Wings of Joy who now lives in New York City and conducts twice-weekly peace meditations at the United Nations, teaches a Hindu method of meditation he calls the 'path of the heart.' This book is a compilation of excerpts from Chinmoy's writings and teachings, grouped thematically and in alphabetical order from 'Advice' to 'Yoga.' ..."   **—Publishers Weekly**

"Sri Chinmoy's glance expresses more than all the words in the world. Following the Indian tradition, he is one who ever revitalizes. The mutual friendship that unites us is proof of the deep resonance that can exist between initiates devoted to the cause of spirituality on earth."

—Pir Vilayat Khan,
Head of the Sufi Order in the West

"Sri Chinmoy listens from the heart, writes with the head, and journeys with the soul. People of all religions will get closer to God from meditating on these universal and soul-searching truths."

—Monsignor Thomas Hartman,
Diocese of Rockville Center, NY

Drawn from more than 1000 books written by Sri Chinmoy in over 30 years of teaching spirituality and meditation, this book provides a new and definitive collection of the writings of this beloved spiritual teacher and peace advocate. These selections, grouped thematically in over 80 subject areas, convey the ancient spiritual traditions of India, while transcending religious dogma and shedding light on all paths to God. Sri Chinmoy emphasizes the necessity of learning, understanding, and listening to the dictates of a higher inner call. Readers interested in the universal ideal of self-transformation will find this guide unlocks the secrets to a life of modern dynamism infused with ancient wisdom.

The Swami Ramdas Trilogy from Blue Dove Press

In Quest of God
The Saga of an Extraordinary Pilgrimage
by Swami Ramdas
Preface by Eknath Easwaran.
Foreword by Ram Dass (Richard Alpert)
Softcover   190 pp. $14   ISBN: 1-884997-01-5

This is the tale of a remarkable pilgrimage. Walking in a God-intoxicated state of total surrender to the divine will, Swami Ramdas traveled the dusty roads of India as a penniless monk. This narrative, told with a keen wit, contains many inspiring accounts of how his pure love transformed many he encountered who at first behaved harshly toward him.

In the Vision of God Volume 1
The Continuing Saga of an Extraordinary Pilgrimage
by Swami Ramdas
Softcover   288 pp. $14.95 ISBN: 1-884997-03-1

Beginning where *In Quest of God* leaves off, this chronicle of Swami Ramdas' pilgrimage is comparable to such famous classics as *The Way of the Pilgrim* and Brother Lawrence's *The Practice of the Presence of God*.

In the Vision of God Volume 2
The Conclusion to the Saga of an Extraordinary Pilgrimage
by Swami Ramdas
Softcover   280 pp. $14.95 ISBN: 1-884997-05-8

In this final volume the story of Swami Ramdas' pilgrimage concludes with the end of his wanderings and relates how he settled down in an ashram created for him by his many devotees. This became more than a center for spiritual aspirants, but also a vehicle to help the needs of the local people.

From the Robert Powell Advaita Library:

Beyond Religion
Meditations on Our True Nature
by Robert Powell, Ph.D.
Softcover   221 pp. $15.95   ISBN: 1-884997-31-7

In this collection of selected essays, reflections, and public talks, Dr. Robert Powell—one of the foremost contemporary writers of *Advaita* philosophy—addresses such topics as Consciousness, Meditation, Existence, World Peace, and the Arrival of the Third Millennium, and addresses their relation to spiritual awakening and "human consciousness transformation".

EXCERPT FROM THE BOOK:
What is the need for religion, for a so-called spiritual orientation in life, at all? If living is a natural function, like breathing, then why interfere? Why can we not continue in our naturally more or less hedonistic way? This would be true if our minds were still functioning in their natural ways, free of complexity, flowing with life. This assumption, as we all know, is no longer valid—if it ever was. Our minds are heavily conditioned, fragmented and deep in contradiction. This conflict in the mind leads inevitably to conflict in society, and thus to chaos. So even if we opted for a simple hedonistic way of life, sooner or later this would be compromised by the ways of the mind.

True religion or spirituality is nothing other than the reversal of this whole process of chaos, conflict, to a state of simplicity, naturalness, and therefore order...

Coming in 2001

The Essence of Sri Nisargadatta Maharaj
Edited by Robert Powell, Ph.D.
ISBN: 1-884997-15-5

Return to Meaningfulness
by Robert Powell, Ph.D.
ISBN: 1-884997-30-9

Robert Powell's Nisargadatta Maharaj Trilogy

The Ultimate Medicine
As Prescribed by Sri Nisargadatta Maharaj
Edited by Robert Powell, Ph.D.
Softcover   240 pp. $14.95   ISBN: 1-884997-09-0

The Nectar of Immortality
Sri Nisargadatta Maharaj's Discourses on the Eternal
Edited by Robert Powell, Ph.D.
Softcover   208 pp. $14.95   ISBN: 1-884997-13-9

The Experience of Nothingness
Sri Nisargadatta Maharaj's Talks
on Realizing the Infinite
Edited by Robert Powell, Ph.D.
Softcover   166 pp. $14.95   ISBN: 1-884997-14-7

"...Sri Nisargadatta Maharaj is my greatest teacher. His words guide my writing, speaking, and all my relationships..."
— **Dr. Wayne Dyer,**
Author of *Your Sacred Self*

"Sri Nisargadatta Maharaj hardly needs an introduction any longer to lovers of the highest wisdom. Known as a maverick Hindu sage, Nisargadatta is now generally acknowledged to rank with the great masters of advaita teachings, such as Sri Ramana Maharshi...,Sri Atmananda...,and the more recently known disciple of the Maharshi, Poonjaji..."
— **Robert Powell, Ph.D.**

Sri Nisargadatta Maharaj (1897-1981), one of the most important spiritual preceptors of the twentieth century, lived and taught in a small apartment in the slums of Bombay, India. A realized master of the Tantric Nath lineage, Maharaj had a wife and four children whom he supported for many years by selling inexpensive goods in a small booth on the streets outside his tenement. In the tradition of Ramana Maharshi, he shared the highest Truth of nonduality, in his own unique way, from the depths of his own realization.

Three Additional Titles from Robert Powell

Dialogues on Reality
An Exploration into the Nature
of Our Ultimate Identity
by Robert Powell, Ph.D.
Softcover   236 pp. $14   ISBN: 1-884997-16-3

Discovering the Realm
Beyond Appearance
Pointers to the Inexpressible
by Robert Powell, Ph.D.
Softcover   200 pp. $14   ISBN: 1-884997-17-1

Path Without Form
A Journey into the Realm Beyond Thought
by Robert Powell, Ph.D.
Softcover   242 pp. $14.95   ISBN: 1-884997-21-X

"Dr. Powell is one of the best known Western writers on
Advaita *philosophy. He comments elegantly on the insights of*
Krishnamurti and Sri Nisargadatta Maharaj, and explains his
own insights on the nature of the unified state. You will find
great gems in his books."
– Deepak Chopra
Author of *The Seven Spiritual Laws of Success*

Dr. Powell is widely recognized as one of the most inspired writers on the subject of *Advaita*, the teaching of non-duality. In each of his books, he takes us on a journey beyond the realm of the ego, beyond the subject and object, good and bad, high and low, to the ground on which the manifest universe rests. This is where the mind and intellect cannot reach and which is beyond words. Yet in these books, Dr. Powell does a masterful job clearly indicating the path to where we ever have been.

Collision with the Infinite
A Life Beyond the Personal Self
by Suzanne Segal
Softcover   170pp. $14.00   ISBN: 1-884997-27-9

"...Segal describes the profound spiritual experience of the egoless state...Many have tried to do what Segal does, but none have achieved such clarity in the task."
—Publishers Weekly

"This is an extraordinary account of the experience of selflessness..."
—Joseph Goldstein
Author of *The Experience of Insight*

"...an amazingly honest, fascinating, and vivid account of one woman's awakening to her essential emptiness—and her eventual discovery, through much pain and fear, that as emptiness-fullness it is freedom from pain and fear...this awakening is available, right now and just as one is, to all who dare to look in at the infinite."
—Douglas Harding,
Author of *On Having No Head*

"...To anyone interested in the subject, I would say , 'Read this book!'"
—Ramesh S. Balsekar
Author of *Consciousness Speaks*

One day, in the early 1980's, a young American woman, Suzanne Segal, stepped onto a bus in Paris. Suddenly and unexpectedly, she found herself egoless, stripped of any sense of personal self. Struggling for years to make sense of her mental state, she consulted therapist after therapist. Eventually, she turned to spiritual teachers, coming at last to understand that this was the egoless state, that elusive consciousness to which so many aspire— the Holy Grail of so many spiritual traditions.

Written in a spare, unpretentious style, this book is Suzanne Segal's own account of what such a terrifying event meant to her when it crashed into her everyday life.

Treasury of Spiritual Wisdom
A Collection of 10,000 Inspirational Quotations
Compiled by Andy Zubko
Softcover   528 pp. $19.95   ISBN: 1-884997-10-4

"...a compendium of over 10,000 sagely chosen short sayings by an 'eclectic array of spiritual teachers and thinkers. Organized under 142 alphabetical headings like 'Choice,' 'Growth,' 'Death,' etc., these pithy bits make good reading."
— Publishers Weekly

"This 'Bartlett's Quotations for the Soul' is a massive collection of inspirational quotations from sources as diverse as Joan Rivers, Jesus, and the Upanishads, covering topics ranging from abundance and desire to self-esteem and work. Because it will be appropriate for use by students, teachers, and speakers, this handy reference will be a strong addition to all collections. Recommended."
— Library Journal

Have you ever been baffled by an intractable challenge that seemed to defy solution? Are you the type of person who savors inspiring words? If you are a thoughtful, spiritually conscious person who would like to apply the wisdom of the ages in a practical way to the problems in your life, this handy reference volume will become an indispensable companion.

In this book you'll find the inspiring words of saints, the vision of shamans, the insights of the enlightened, the teachings of prophets, as well as the cutting insights of both the well-known and not-so-well-known from both East and West. Organized into 142 categories such as Love, Power, Self-Esteem, Adversity, Habits, Grace, Relationships, Health, Abundance, and Death, Treasury provides a valuable resource for speakers searching for the seed of a speech, teachers seeking inspiration, or for the reader who simply needs a few words of guidance and comfort. Whatever your need, you'll find yourself turning to Treasury again and again.

EXCERPT FROM BOOK:

"The poor man's charity is to wish the rich man well...."
—Anonymous (from "Charity")

Wisdom of James Allen
5 Classic Works Combined into One
by James Allen   Edited by Andy Zubko
Softcover   384 pp. $9.95   ISBN: 1-889606-00-6

Little is known of James Allen, the mysterious contemplative Englishman who chose a quiet life of voluntary poverty, spiritual self-discipline, and simplicity during the 19th and early 20th centuries. Influenced by the writings of Leo Tolstoy, Allen came to realize that devoting one's life to making money and engaging in frivolous activities is a meaningless way to live. At age 38, he retired with his wife, to a small cottage in southwestern England to devote the remainder of his life to quiet, thoughtful writing.

Allen's best-known book, the spiritual classic *As a Man Thinketh*, has sold steadily over the decades inspiring thousands and thousands of readers to a life of quiet dignity, self-discipline, and contemplation. This valuable little volume combines four more James Allen books into one exquisite, gift-sized edition. In addition to *As a Man Thinketh*, are: *The Path to Prosperity*, *The Mastery of Destiny*, *The Way of Peace*, and *Entering the Kingdom*.

EXCERPT FROM *AS A MAN THINKETH*:
"The greatest achievement was at first and for a time a dream. The oak sleeps in the acorn; the bird sleeps in the egg; and in the highest vision of the soul a waking angel stirs. Dreams are the seedlings of realities."

"Your circumstances may be uncongenial, but they shall not long remain so if you but perceive an Ideal and strive to reach it. You cannot travel within and stand still without... Whatever your present environment may be, you will fall, remain, or rise with your thoughts, your Vision, your Ideal. You will become as small as your controlling desire; as great as your dominant aspiration."

The Wisdom of James Allen II
4 More Classic Works Combined into One
by James Allen   Edited by Andy Zubko
Softcover   384 pp. $9.95   ISBN: 1-889606-07-3
Four more classics from the author of *As a Man Thinketh*. Includes: *Light on Life's Difficulties*, *Above Life's Turmoil*, *From Passion to Peace*, *The Life Triumphant*

Peace Pilgrim's Wisdom
A Very Simple Guide
Compiled by Cheryl Canfield
Softcover   224 pp. $14   ISBN: 1-884997-11-2

"It is considered the highest level of enlightenment to simply 'walk as you talk.' Peace Pilgrim lived out this message. Indeed, she is my hero." **— Dr. Wayne Dyer,**
Author of *Your Erroneous Zones*

"There is no doubt that she was letting God write the script of her life, every moment of the day." **—Gerald Jampolsky,**
Author of *Love is Letting Go of Fear*

"I am one of many who have admired and emulated the life and wisdom of Peace Pilgrim. Here is an American saint who transcended all national, religious, or sectarian bonds to communicate love, understanding and integrity. Her life was her teaching."
—Dan Millman,
Author of *Way of the Peaceful Warrior*

Peace Pilgrim was an American sage who for 28 years, from 1953 to 1981, walked in faith across North America. Her vow was "to remain a wanderer until mankind learned the way of peace. Walking until given shelter and fasting until given food." Penniless, she owned only what she carried, little more than the clothes on her back, a comb and a toothbrush. She walked many thousands of miles as a witness for both inner and outer peace, inspiring people to work for peace in their own lives. Many lives were transformed by her compelling example.

Designed as a study guide, *Peace Pilgrim's Wisdom*, divides her words into 19 sections to help us assimilate these powerful truths into our own lives.

Cheryl Canfield spent much time with Peace Pilgrim and is one of the five compilers of *Peace Pilgrim—Her Life and Work in Her Own Words*, which currently has over 400,000 copies in print.

Never to Return

A Modern Quest for Eternal Truth

by Sharon Janis, author of *Spirituality for Dummies*
Softcover   330pp. $16.95   ISBN: 1-884997-29-5

"...In a larger sense, this memoir is a dialogue between Indian spirituality and Western psychology. The question that Janis answers in her memoir is: 'Can a westerner come to know Indian spirituality and flourish in its depths, even when it is alien to western ways of knowing?' She answers with a resounding 'Yes.'"   **—Publishers Weekly**

"...Never to Return is a beautiful and poignant spiritual odyssey that is equally provocative and touching, informative and enlightening, humorous and heartbreaking. Sharon Janis writes with an admirable clarity, and her lightness of spirit in the face of adversity is exemplary for us all."

—Joseph Chilton Pierce,
Author of *Crack in the Cosmic Egg*

This highly acclaimed memoir is both a real-life spiritual adventure and a rare and intimate glimpse into a modern-day search for eternal truth.

Raised an atheist, author Sharon Janis survived a painful and dysfunctional childhood with a strength, independence, and curiosity that awakened in her a voracious spiritual hunger. Eventually, her search would take her to an Indian monastery, where she lived for ten years.

Janis has a natural gift for story-telling. Her engagingly humorous and touching personal anecdotes address some of the most delicate topics of human existence: the power and vulnerability of the mind, devotion, death, humility, justice, grace and ultimately, the intimacy between the individual and his or her God.

Lights of Grace
Catalog
from
The Blue Dove Foundation

The Blue Dove Foundation is a non-profit, tax-exempt organization and not affiliated with any particular path, tradition, or religion. Our mission is to deepen the spiritual life of all by making available works on the lives, messages, and examples of saints and sages of all religions and traditions, as well as other spiritual titles that provide tools for inner growth.

The Blue Dove Foundation supports the publication of inspirational books and tapes from Blue Dove Press. The foundation also distributes important spiritual works of other publishers, including hundreds of titles from India, through our web site and *Lights of Grace* catalog.

From Saint Teresa of Avila, to Sri Ramana Maharshi, to Milarepa, the Tibetan yogi—from *The Koran*, to *The Zohar* to *The Mahabharata*—we have assembled an inspired collection of spiritual works at its most diverse and best.

For a free Catalog contact:

The Blue Dove Foundation
4204 Sorrento Valley Blvd. Suite K
San Diego, CA 92121

Phone: (858)623-3330
FAX: (858)623-3325
Orders: (800)691-1008
e-mail: bdp@bluedove.org
Web Site: www.bluedove.org